Subcontractor's
Operations
Manual

Subcontractor's Operations Manual

Sidney M. Levy

McGraw-Hill

New York   San Francisco   Washington, D.C.   Auckland   Bogotá
Caracas   Lisbon   London   Madrid   Mexico City   Milan
Montreal   New Delhi   San Juan   Singapore
Sydney   Tokyo   Toronto

McGraw-Hill

A Division of The **McGraw·Hill** *Companies*

Copyright © 1999 by The McGraw-Hill Companies, Inc. Printed in the United States of America. Except as permitted under the United States Copyright Act of 1976, no part of this publication may be reproduced or distributed in any form or by any means, or stored in a data base or retrieval system, without the prior written permission of the publisher.

1 2 3 4 5 6 7 8 9 DOC/DOC 9 0 3 2 1 0 9 8

P/N 038239-5
PART OF
ISBN 0-07-134858-1

The sponsoring editor of this book was Larry Hager. The editing supervisor was Sally Glover, and the production supervisor was Sherri Souffrance. It was set in New Century Schoolbook per the MHC Modified design by Joanne Morbit of McGraw-Hill's Professional Book Group composition unit, Hightstown, New Jersey.

Printed and bound by R. R. Donnelley & Sons Company.

 This book is printed on recycled, acid-free paper containing a minimum of 50% recycled, de-inked fiber.

McGraw-Hill books are available at special quantity discounts to use as premiums and sales promotions, or for use in corporate training programs. For more information, please write to the Director of Special Sales, McGraw-Hill, 11 West 19th Street, New York, NY 10011. Or contact your local bookstore.

Contents

Preface

Author Sidney M. Levy has been associated with the construction industry for more that 40 years, learning the business as a time clerk and retiring from a senior management position with a major Connecticut based general contracting firm to form his own construction consulting business in Maryland.

During all of those years in the business, he had dealings with scores of subcontracting firms—large and small, experienced and inexperienced, and through it all gained respect for their profession and for many of the individuals and their companies.

Having been fortunate to work with general contractors who recognized the value of maintaining harmonious relationships with subcontractors and welcoming them to the team, he also knew of plenty of situations where less-than-honorable general contractors took advantage of their position in the construction "food chain" and resorted to less-than-honorable relationships with their subcontractors.

And that was one of the reasons for writing this book—to bring a general contractor's perspective into focus and pass onto the reader those facets of the industry that may allow subcontractors to gain from the writer's experience.

Subcontractors, more formally referred to as specialty contractors, form the backbone of the construction industry, providing experience in their chosen field of endeavor and the skilled workers necessary to build America's housing, office buildings, and factories.

There are a handful of subcontractors with annual sales volume in the $100 million plus range and very sophisticated in their business approach, but the overwhelming majority of subcontractors are small-to-midsize companies, many of whom have been family owned and operated for several generations.

The nature of the subcontracting industry is such that it affords those skilled workers with an entreprenuerial spirit the opportunity to start a business of their own. Often lacking sufficient experience in the managerial disciplines that is a requirement of any successful business, they endeavor to learn by trial and error—or they fail completely, pick up their tools once more, or seek employment in another industry.

Even those experienced subcontractors cannot afford to rest on their laurels but must continually hone their skills to keep pace with an ever-changing industry.

According to Mr. Norbert Young, Senior Vice President of McGraw-Hill's Construction Information Group, the average lifespan of a subcontracting firm is 2.8 years.

Construction by its very nature is a risky business, compared by some to an open-air manufacturing plant where every product is completely different from the next one. And add to this risky business those inevitable business cycles and the constant change in government funding of public works projects.

Skill in one's trade is not enough for those subcontractors determined to beat Mr. Young's odds; they must constantly add to their business and management acumen.

But for those subcontractors with business savvy—or at least the willingness to acquire it or hire it—the future can be very bright indeed.

The construction industry has changed quite a bit over the last 40 or 50 years. Handshake deals have become fewer and fewer and structures have become more complex.

And the industry is still changing. It has become more competitive and more demanding of its managers.

Technology is slowly but surely creeping into the construction industry and changing the way in which we work. The widespread use of the personal computer loaded with sophisticated estimating, scheduling, and project management software is becoming commonplace.

Read-only compact discs containing design documents pass from the architect to the general contractor to the subcontractor electronically without generating a trace of paper. The flat files and plan racks of yesterday are giving way to CD and diskette cabinets.

The fax machine, "E" mail and electronically transmitted shop drawings have catapulted the industry forward at warp speed. Fast track is now flash track. Today's manager must have computer skills in their bag of tricks.

Coupled with the shortage of skilled workers and experienced mid-level managers, the new millenium certainly presents some unique challenges and opportunities to those subcontractors willing to stay the course.

The *Subcontractor's Operations Manual* was written to assist subcontractors in solving many of their day-to-day business and operational concerns, which can often spell the difference between longevity or that 2.8-year survival rate.

Subcontractor's Operations Manual

Overview of the Construction Industry in the United States

Let's take a closer look at the industry that we are all a part of, and what an industry it is!

Construction in the United States is one of the most important sectors of the economy—employing about 5 million people annually and generating per-annum gross sales in excess of $400–$500 billion for the past several years. Additionally, $400 to $500 billion is spent yearly on construction material, component, and related industrial manufacturing. Construction contributes 12% to the entire country's gross domestic product (GDP).

There are, at last count by the U.S. Census Bureau, more than 2 million business establishments operating in the construction industry, and they accounted for $582 billion in sales in 1997. About 650,000 of these businesses had less than 5 employees; another 650,000 were single-employee companies. Only 214,000 establishments had more than five people, but these firms accounted for 80% of that $582 billion total. So the construction industry, while dominated by a few giant firms, remains largely an industry of small to midsized companies operating in a rather limited geographic area.

In the residential sector of the construction industry, when home building is booming so are sales at furniture, carpet, and floor-covering establishments and appliance stores. And the industries that manufacture these consumer products will most likely have good years.

Approximately 1.4 million of those 2 million contracting companies are classified as "specialty contractors"—subcontractors. Plumbing and HVAC establishments lead the way with slightly more than

75,000 companies, followed in number by electricians (54,000 businesses), carpentry firms (38,000), then painters (32,000), roofers (27,500), and concrete subcontractors (26,000).

Although the picture may appear to be rosy, we are an industry in trouble. Over the past several decades, production rates have fallen, job-site-related accidents have been on the increase, and shortages of skilled labor are becoming more acute.

And we are industry in transition. The master builder concept of the early twentieth century has vanished. At one time a contractor employed many of the specialty trades required to construct a building—laborers, masons, hod carriers and plasterers, electricians, and plumbers. Oftentimes these master builders maintained staffs of an architect and engineers to provide the prospective client with one-stop shopping.

An Industry in Transition

All things change with time, and as the industry became more competitive the greater majority of general contractors determined that unless they were able to ensure a steady backlog of work, it could be very expensive to retain a large staff of skilled workers in various trades on their payroll. Approaching the midcentury mark, design and construction techniques were becoming more sophisticated and complex.

The field of specialty contractors (subcontractors) expanded, and more and more general contractors began to rely on more and more specialty contractors to perform more and more of their work.

The term "broker" entered the vocabulary of the construction industry at about this time and was meant to denote those contractors who subcontracted all of their work. Some old-line, full-service general contractors who continued to maintain teams of laborers, masons, and carpenters on their payroll and owned substantial amounts of heavy construction equipment viewed these "brokers" as "businessmen" but not true builders. But after all, isn't construction a business?

In 1999 it is difficult to find any significant number of contractors who employ teams of skilled workers on their payrolls year round; specialty contractors are more skilled, more efficient, more flexible, and more competitive in their chosen field of work.

The Construction Manager (CM)

The appearance of the construction manager (CM) represented another change in the way America builds its buildings. The CM became the owner's agent, quite different from the arms-length relationship between owner and contractor bound by the terms of a fixed-price contract.

This CM method of contracting theoretically placed a team of construction specialists under the owner's control who provided construction related management services for a fee based upon a percentage of actual construction costs. The CM would provide specialists in construction scheduling, estimating, purchasing, project administration, and management to guide the owner's project through the construction process just as though they were actually employed by that owner.

As the concept of construction management matured, some owners demanded that the CM, along with providing management specialists, guarantee the maximum price of the construction contract instead of earning a fee based upon the final cost of the project. Two types of CMs emerged: the CM "for fee," one that assumed no responsibility for the project's maximum price but collected a fee for services rendered; and the CM "at risk," who would provide similar services but guaranteed that the project would not exceed a predetermined maximum price, and by assuming this risk, was able to charge higher fees.

Mergers, Acquisitions, and Global Contractors

The 1970s brought with it a new phenomenon—an influx of foreign construction companies establishing operations in the United States or, in some cases, gaining access to this market by acquiring American contractors through outright purchase.

As early as 1960, one of Japan's largest construction companies, Takenaka Komuten, (founded in Nagoya in 1610 and one of the world's oldest continuously operating construction companies) established an office in California. Over the next 20 years, they were followed by more than a dozen other Japanese contractors who opened offices throughout the United States, ostensibly to service their long-term clients such as Sharp, Nissan, NEC, and Toyota, who were planning to build manufacturing or distribution plants in this country. But long after these plants were built, many of these Asian contractors remained and today have expanded their operations in the United States, becoming "Americanized" in the process.

German construction companies were also attracted by the sizable and stable market in this country. Philip Holzman elected to purchase St. Louis contractor Fru-Con rather than setting up its own shop in America. Several years later they added to their U.S. presence by purchasing Charlotte, North Carolina, based J.A. Jones and Lockwood Greene Engineering, headquartered in South Carolina. At about the same time, Great Britain's Woodward, Clyde bought a local New York construction firm and the England constructor Bovis purchased Lehr McGovern, changing its name at first to Lehr, McGovern, Bovis—only to drop the first two names in 1997 to become simply Bovis. England's staid Trafalgar House, with operations in Europe and Asia, owner of the Cunard Shipping Line and John Brown Engineers also came to America to join a select group of foreign builders—only to be purchased by Norway's Kvaerner Group in 1997.

The Swedes, represented by the Scandinavian contractor Skanska, purchased New Jersey's Sordoni Construction and within the past several years has bought up the old-line New York construction company W.J. Barney and moved into the New England area after buying Boston-based Beacon Construction. As of 1998, Skanska (U.S.A.) ranks ninth among the top 400 contractors.

The latest trend appears to be an acceleration in consolidation—larger firms absorbing smaller ones to gain access to either new geographic areas, new markets, or new clients.

Consolidation has been taking place in both the general contracting and subcontracting industry. Fishbach-Moore, after acquiring several local electrical subcontracting firms around the country, reported a consolidated annual volume of $139 million in 1997. Emcor, a giant in the mechanical subcontracting field, reported year-end sales of $1.6 billion in 1997. Most recently, in 1998, Consolidated Capital Corporation, another large electrical contractor, announced that it would purchase seven related companies in the Midwest and Far West for $138 million, adding $277 million to their annual revenue.

Houston based Quanta Services has been acquiring electrical and telecommunication subcontractors to go along with their maintenance business and attained a combined revenue of $152.3 as of December 1997.

In the residential construction industry, Service Experts, Inc. merged with Contract Success Group, Inc. in 1996 and in the process acquired 41 HVAC firms valued at approximately $29 million.

Many experts agree that this trend will continue and this acquisition route presents an opportunity for small, profitable, family-owned construction companies to "cash out" if the current or next generation expresses no interest in continuing to own and operate the family business.

The Importance of the Specialty Contractor

The specialty contractor, more commonly referred to as subcontractor, is a bulwark of the construction industry in the United States. Without the expertise and efficiencies displayed by the subcontracting industry, construction would undoubtedly be less productive and more expensive. General contractors, and the industry at large, recognized this fact decades ago as the "full-service contractor" gave way to the broker, who relied on the subcontracting trades to meet the demands of owners for the most competitively priced project, high quality levels, and on-time completion schedules.

Each year the accounting firm of Deloitte Touche Tohmatsu International publishes a booklet entitled "Insights in Construction." The 1997 edition indicates the following:

The number of subcontractors has risen approximately 10% for the period 1994 to 1996.

These subcontractors, according to the survey, rely more heavily on the private business sector (41%) than the public business sector (25%) for their primary source of work, in contrast with the general contractor's source of work, which is divided almost equally between the public and private sector.

Approximately 81% of the subcontractors responding to the Deloitte Touche survey stated that their average project size was $500,000, and most of this work was in new construction. Fewer renovation and maintenance-type projects were under contract between the years 1994–1996.

The ownership composition of subcontracting firms has changed over the past four years.

Number of owners	1992	1994	1996
1	22%	22%	26%
2 to 4	54%	53%	61%
5 to 9	18%	16%	9%
10 TO 29	6%	8%	3%
30 OR MORE	2%	1%	1%

Union versus nonunion

More subcontracting firms than general contracting firms are unionized, according to the Deloitte Touche survey; however, the decline in union membership has been accelerating more in the subcontracting industry. Between 1994 and 1996, 21% of previously unionized subcontractors had elected not to renew their collective bargaining agreements.

This trend mirrors the gradual decline in A.F.L.-C.I.O. membership in general from its high point after World War II. In 1977, 28% of the total workforce was covered by collective bargaining agreements. By last count in 1995, union membership had declined to less than 15%.

The shift to one-stop shopping

Owners are increasingly seeking a single source for their construction needs—a more cost-effective way to purchase a quality product, avoiding as much risk as possible while achieving rapid delivery of the project.

This desire for single source responsibility has been the accelerator behind renewed interest in the design-build concept, one that appears to have become a more popular project delivery system these days in the private sector as well as the public sector.

And project completion schedules continue to compress. No longer do we speak of "fast track." "Flash track" has become the buzzword of the last decade of the twentieth century and there is no looking back.

Subcontractor Benchmarking

Each year the Construction Financial Management Association (CFMA), a Princeton, New Jersey, association dedicated to the financial management of the general contracting, subcontracting, and real estate development industries, publishes the results of their annual financial survey. This survey provides benchmarking information for various segments of the construction industry in areas such as accounting, management, human resources, corporate policies, risk management, and bonds.

Subcontractors responding to the survey revealed that they are considering implementing the following strategies in order to improve profitability:

- Do what we do—but do it better.
- Improve safety and risk management operations.
- Provide more employee training.
- Pursue design-build projects.
- Reduce overhead.
- Offer related services.

The respondents to the survey stated that the most significant challenges facing their industry over the next five years is the growing shortage of trained field personnel.

How does your company stack up?

CFMA's financial profiles are shown in Figure 1-1—a benchmark balance sheet for subcontractors in the $10 to $25 million annual sales volume category. Figure 1-2 is a composite balance sheet containing "average" financial information compiled from the 336 respondent subcontractors with yearly sales volumes ranging from less than $5 million to more than $50 million.

Figure 1-3 is a breakdown of selected financial data from responding subcontractors with annual sales revenues of less than $5 million, $5–$10 million, $10–$25 million, $25–$50 million, and in excess of $50 million.

Other charts in this survey prepared by CFMA pertain to business practices and human resources policies and provide additional insight into what other subcontracting firms are doing.

- Figure 1-4—Longevity in business.
- Figure 1-5a–1-5e—Companies entering new geographic regions, areas of regional growth, sources of increased competition, source of work, and location of work by region.
- Figure 1-6a and b—Backlog at year end (1997) and comparison of previous year.
- Figure 1-7—Strategies to improve profitability.
- Figure 1-8—Quality programs in effect.
- Figure 1-9—Top five challenges in next five years.
- Figure 1-10a,b,c—Insurance limits, experience modification rates, and claims.
- Figure 1-11a–1-11e—Human Resources practices and employee benefits.

The Coming Millennium

The next century will be one in which communication and information transfer reach higher levels and project management and field productivity yields in the construction industry will come under more intense scrutiny. Coupled with technological advances in products, equipment, and information analysis and transfer, those firms that can effectively utilize these tools will attain and retain the competitive advantage.

Focusing on more effective management techniques

The strength of the construction market in 1997 and 1998 provided impetus to the need to seek out capable, competent employees, and the

Specialty Trades Contractors
$10 to $25 Million Revenue

BALANCE SHEET

	1997 Participants		1996 Participants	
	Amount	Percent	Amount	Percent
Current assets:				
Cash and cash equivalents	$ 494,539	7.6 %	$ 550,552	9.1 %
Marketable securities and short-term investments	115,342	1.8	49,053	0.8
Receivables:				
Contract receivables currently due	3,088,705	47.5	2,843,423	47.0
Retainages on contracts	665,079	10.2	726,166	12.0
Unbilled work	57,943	0.9	45,055	0.7
Other receivables	117,097	1.8	57,340	0.9
Less allowance for doubtful accounts	(33,249)	0.5	(28,804)	0.5
Total receivables, net	3,895,575	59.9	3,643,180	60.3
Inventories	207,120	3.2	267,555	4.4
Costs and recognized earnings in excess of billings on uncompleted contracts	677,364	10.4	404,552	6.7
Investments in and advances to construction joint ventures	7,868	0.1	1,482	0.0
Income taxes:				
Current/refundable	18,990	0.3		
Deferred	6,505	0.1		
Other current assets	95,573	1.5	119,653	2.0
Total current assets	5,518,876	84.8	5,036,027	83.3
Property, plant and equipment	2,044,931	31.4	1,999,173	33.1
Less accumulated depreciation	(1,298,197)	20.0	(1,200,453)	19.9
Property, plant and equipment, net	746,734	11.5	798,720	13.2
Noncurrent assets:				
Long-term investments	95,265	1.5	199,397	3.3
Deferred income taxes	3,395	0.1		
Other assets	140,387	2.2	10,923	0.2
Intangible assets				
Total noncurrent assets	239,047	3.7	210,320	3.5
Total assets	$ 6,504,657	100.0 %	$ 6,045,067	100.0 %

	1997 Participants		1996 Participants	
	Amount	Percent	Amount	Percent
Current liabilities:				
Current maturity on long-term debt	$ 110,402	1.7 %	$ 134,573	2.2 %
Notes payable and lines of credit	398,596	6.1	367,869	6.1
Accounts payable:				
Trade, including currently due to subcontractors	1,548,293	23.8	1,261,614	20.9
Subcontractor retainages	73,219	1.1	230,668	3.8
Other	66,879	1.0	10,377	0.2
Total accounts payable	1,688,391	26.0	1,502,659	24.9
Accrued expenses	507,639	7.8	479,547	7.9
Billings in excess of costs and recognized earnings on uncompleted contracts	704,695	10.8	508,188	8.4
Income taxes:				
Current	38,039	0.6	56,285	0.9
Deferred	46,825	0.7	31,521	0.5
Total income taxes	84,864	1.3	87,806	1.5
Other current liabilities	109,547	1.7	65,599	1.1
Total current liabilities	3,604,134	55.4	3,146,241	52.0
Long-term debt, excluding current maturities	429,610	6.6	412,222	6.8
Deferred income taxes	23,112	0.4	26,248	0.4
Minority interests	104,297	1.6	113,465	1.9
Other	392	0.0	376	0.0
Total liabilities	4,161,545	64.0	3,698,552	61.2
Net worth:				
Common stock, par value	89,174	1.4	161,555	2.7
Preferred stock, stated value	30,597	0.5		
Additional paid-in capital	287,430	4.4	137,944	2.3
Retained earnings	2,085,952	32.1	2,214,843	36.6
Treasury stock	(165,183)	2.5	(167,827)	2.8
Excess value of marketable securities	3,886	0.1		
Other equity	11,256	0.2		
Total net worth	2,343,112	36.0	2,346,515	38.8
Total liabilities and net worth	$ 6,504,657	100.0 %	$ 6,045,067	100.0 %

Figure 1-1a

FINANCIAL RATIOS

	1997 Participants	1996 Participants
Liquidity Ratios		
Current Ratio	1.5	1.6
Quick Ratio	1.3	1.3
Days of Cash	10.4	11.8
Working Capital Turnover	8.9	8.9
Profitability Ratios		
Return on Assets	6.8 %	7.1 %
Return on Equity	18.8 %	18.3 %
Times Interest Earned	7.3	8.6
Leverage Ratios		
Debt to Equity	1.8	1.6
Revenue to Equity	7.3	7.1
Asset Turnover	2.6	2.8
Fixed Asset Ratio	31.9 %	34.0 %
Equity to G & A Expenses	1.1	1.1
Underbillings to Equity	31.4 %	19.2 %
Average Backlog to Equity	2.8	3.9
Average Backlog to Work. Cap.	3.4	4.8
Average Months in Backlog	4.6	6.6
Efficiency Ratios		
Days in Accounts Receivable	67.0	61.7
Days in Inventory	5.2	6.8
Days in Accounts Payable	40.7	32.5
Operating Cycle	41.9	47.9

STATEMENT OF EARNINGS

	1997 Participants		1996 Participants	
	Amount	Percent	Amount	Percent
Contract revenue	$ 16,680,409	97.8 %	$ 16,594,058	99.1 %
Other revenue	373,837	2.2	150,652	0.9
Total revenue	17,054,246	100.0	16,744,710	100.0
Contract cost	(13,735,182)	80.5	(13,919,567)	83.1
Other cost	(554,308)	3.3	(186,405)	1.1
Total cost	(14,289,490)	83.8	(14,105,972)	84.2
Gross profit	2,764,756	16.2	2,638,738	15.8
Selling, general and admin. expenses	(2,180,922)	12.8	(2,088,953)	12.5
Income from operations	583,834	3.4	549,785	3.3
Interest income	29,627	0.2	19,269	0.1
Interest expense	(87,875)	0.5	(71,151)	0.4
Other income (expense), net	31,011	0.2	40,815	0.2
Net earnings (loss) before income taxes	556,597	3.3	538,718	3.2
Income tax (expense) benefit	(116,955)	0.7	(109,122)	0.7
Net earnings	$ 439,642	2.6 %	$ 429,591	2.6 %

NUMBER OF PARTICIPANTS

Survey Year	Number
1997	94
1996	111

Figure 1-1b

Specialty Trades Contractors
Composite

BALANCE SHEET

	1997 Participants		1996 Participants	
	Amount	Percent	Amount	Percent
Current assets:				
Cash and cash equivalents	$1,217,532	9.4 %	$931,055	7.8 %
Marketable securities and short-term investments	161,970	1.3	155,312	1.3
Receivables:				
Contract receivables currently due	5,488,476	42.4	5,360,713	45.1
Retainages on contracts	1,192,353	9.2	1,374,233	11.6
Unbilled work	126,159	1.0	102,320	0.9
Other receivables	320,169	2.5	168,535	1.4
Less allowance for doubtful accounts	(50,596)	0.4	(57,668)	0.5
Total receivables, net	7,076,561	54.7	6,948,133	58.4
Inventories	520,395	4.0	517,064	4.3
Costs and recognized earnings in excess of billings on uncompleted contracts	1,051,851	8.1	1,029,659	8.7
Investments in and advances to construction joint ventures	111,292	0.9	31,708	0.3
Income taxes:				
Current/refundable	23,175	0.2		
Deferred	92,924	0.7		
Other current assets	228,339	1.8	258,198	2.2
Total current assets	10,484,039	81.0	9,871,129	83.0
Property, plant and equipment	3,598,796	27.8	3,521,988	29.6
Less accumulated depreciation	(2,118,300)	16.4	(2,077,973)	17.5
Property, plant and equipment, net	1,480,496	11.4	1,444,015	12.1
Noncurrent assets:				
Long-term investments	190,359	1.5	412,864	3.5
Deferred income taxes	38,801	0.3		
Other assets	747,860	5.8	160,164	1.3
Intangible assets				
Total noncurrent assets	977,020	7.5	573,028	4.8
Total assets	$12,941,555	100.0 %	$11,888,172	100.0 %

	1997 Participants		1996 Participants	
	Amount	Percent	Amount	Percent
Current liabilities:				
Current maturity on long-term debt	$243,603	1.9 %	$186,332	1.6 %
Notes payable and lines of credit	713,182	5.5	598,760	5.0
Accounts payable:				
Trade, including currently due to subcontractors	2,807,515	21.7	2,374,775	20.0
Subcontractor retainages	303,763	2.3	420,335	3.5
Other	141,299	1.1	55,035	0.5
Total accounts payable	3,252,577	25.1	2,850,165	24.0
Accrued expenses	1,206,076	9.3	1,223,479	10.3
Billings in excess of costs and recognized earnings on uncompleted contracts	1,509,019	11.7	1,305,113	11.0
Income taxes:				
Current	71,968	0.6	89,730	0.8
Deferred	38,680	0.3	32,543	0.3
Total income taxes	110,648	0.9	122,273	1.0
Other current liabilities	251,936	1.9	149,011	1.3
Total current liabilities	7,287,041	56.3	6,335,134	54.1
Long-term debt, excluding current maturities	882,785	6.8	1,023,503	8.6
Deferred income taxes	51,003	0.4	57,186	0.5
Other	217,699	1.7	180,862	1.5
Minority interests	29,398	0.2	21,548	0.2
Total liabilities	8,467,926	65.4	7,718,232	64.9
Net worth:				
Common stock, par value	247,383	1.9	424,711	3.6
Preferred stock, stated value	75,756	0.6		
Additional paid-in capital	602,596	4.7	838,943	7.1
Retained earnings	3,648,668	28.2	3,153,218	26.5
Treasury stock	(273,960)	2.1	(246,932)	2.1
Excess value of marketable securities	119,899	0.9		
Other equity	53,287	0.4		
Total net worth	4,473,629	34.6	4,169,940	35.1
Total liabilities and net worth	$12,941,555	100.0 %	$11,888,172	100.0 %

Figure 1-2a

STATEMENT OF EARNINGS

	1997 Participants		1996 Participants	
	Amount	Percent	Amount	Percent
Contract revenue	$36,878,744	95.9 %	$32,229,162	96.8 %
Other revenue	1,577,500	4.1	1,072,682	3.2
Total revenue	38,456,244	100.0	33,301,844	100.0
Contract cost	(32,623,752)	84.8	(27,590,604)	82.9
Other cost	(722,007)	1.9	(1,036,044)	3.1
Total cost	(33,345,759)	86.7	(28,626,648)	86.0
Gross profit	5,110,485	13.3	4,675,196	14.0
Selling, general and admin. expenses	(3,698,199)	9.6	(3,724,400)	11.2
Income from operations	1,412,286	3.7	950,796	2.9
Interest income	73,170	0.2	49,004	0.1
Interest expense	(146,379)	0.4	(160,142)	0.5
Other income (expense), net	(5,314)	0.0	49,567	0.1
Net earnings (loss) before income taxes	1,333,763	3.5	889,225	2.7
Income tax (expense) benefit	(264,091)	0.7	(210,702)	0.6
Net earnings	$1,069,672	2.8 %	$678,523	2.0 %

FINANCIAL RATIOS

	1997 Participants	1996 Participants
Liquidity Ratios		
Current Ratio	1.4	1.5
Quick Ratio	1.2	1.2
Days of Cash	11.4	10.1
Working Capital Turnover	12.0	9.7
Profitability Ratios		
Return on Assets	8.3 %	5.7 %
Return on Equity	23.9 %	16.3 %
Times Interest Earned	10.1	6.6
Leverage Ratios		
Debt to Equity	1.9	1.9
Revenue to Equity	8.6	8.0
Asset Turnover	3.0	2.8
Fixed Asset Ratio	33.1 %	34.6 %
Equity to G & A Expenses	1.2	1.1
Underbillings to Equity	26.3 %	27.1 %
Average Backlog to Equity	4.4	5.2
Average Backlog to Work. Cap.	5.9	6.3
Average Months in Backlog	6.6	7.6
Efficiency Ratios		
Days in Accounts Receivable	53.9	59.1
Days in Inventory	5.6	6.5
Days in Accounts Payable	31.8	30.6
Operating Cycle	39.1	45.2

NUMBER OF PARTICIPANTS

Survey Year	Number
1997	336
1996	307

Figure 1-2b

Selected Financial Data by Annual Volume

SPECIALTY TRADES CONTRACTORS

	All ST Contractors	ANNUAL VOLUME				
		Less than $5 Million	$5–10 Million	$10–25 Million	$25–50 Million	Over $50 Million
Number of Companies	336	43	54	94	75	70
Assets	$12,942	$1,954	$2,970	$6,505	$13,214	$36,484
Liabilities	$8,468	$1,117	$1,838	$4,162	$7,794	$25,052
Net Worth	$4,474	$837	$1,131	$2,343	$5,420	$11,433
% Net Worth to Assets	34.6%	42.9%	38.1%	36.0%	41.0%	31.3%
Revenues	$38,456	$2,173	$7,552	$16,680	$35,037	$113,410
Gross Profit	$5,111	$594	$1,453	$2,765	$5,259	$13,270
% Gross Profit	13.3%	27.3%	19.2%	16.2%	15.0%	11.7%
SG&A Expense	$3,698	$521	$1,195	$2,181	$3,474	$9,542
% to Revenue	9.6%	24.0%	15.8%	12.8%	9.9%	8.4%
Net Income	$1,070	$53	$205	$440	$1,446	$2,725
% Net Income	2.8%	2.4%	2.7%	2.6%	4.1%	2.4%
Current Ratio	1.4	1.8	1.6	1.5	1.5	1.4
Return on Assets	8.3%	2.7%	6.9%	6.8%	10.9%	7.5%
Return on Equity	23.9%	6.4%	18.1%	18.8%	26.7%	23.8%

Note: All $ amounts are in thousands.

Total assets of Specialty Trades respondents increased in all categories, except the Over $50 Million category, where asset size decreased by 4%. Total assets for respondents in the Less than $5 Million category increased 63%. Overall, net worth as a percentage of assets declined to 34.6% in 1997 from 35.1% in 1996. The $5-10 Million and the $25-50 Million categories both reported increases in the net worth to assets percentage of approximately 3.6 percentage points, while the $10-25 Million category reported a decrease of 2.8 percentage points.

Gross profit percentages ranged from 11.7% for companies Over $50 Million to 27.3% for those companies in the Less than $5 Million category. Specialty Trades SG&A expense as a percentage of revenue dropped to 9.6%, from 11.2% in 1996. SG&A expense as a percentage of revenue was significantly higher for the Less than $5 Million category (24% in 1997 compared to 19.3% in 1996).

Net income percentages range from 2.4% for companies in the Less than $5 Million and Over $50 Million categories to 4.1% for those companies in the $25-50 Million category. The greatest increase in the net income percentage came from companies with revenue $25-50 Million (the ratio increased to 4.1% in 1997, from 2.4% in 1996) and from companies $5-10 Million (the ratio increased to 2.7% from 1.1%).

Overall, the return on assets increased 2.6 percentage points in 1997 to 8.3%, and return on equity increased 7.6 percentage points to 23.9%. The highest return on assets ratio was reported by the $25-50 Million category (10.9%). The highest return on equity ratio was reported by companies in the $25-50 Million category (26.7%). Current ratios for all categories in 1997 were consistent with those reported in 1996.

Figure 1-3

shortage of those experienced project managers and skilled workers is becoming more evident every day. Although advance warning of such shortages appeared in articles in numerous trade magazines as early as 1994 they went largely unheeded by contractors.

Skilled tradespeople and trained, experienced managers are not created overnight, and today's construction company executives must begin to invest more resources in systems technology focusing on controlled growth and increased profits while searching for top-quality people for field and office operations.

LONGEVITY OF BUSINESS

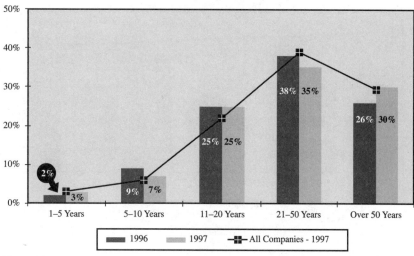

Figure 1-4

COMPANIES ENTERING NEW GEOGRAPHIC REGIONS

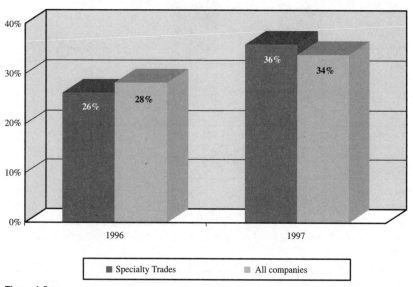

Figure 1-5a

AREAS OF REGIONAL GROWTH

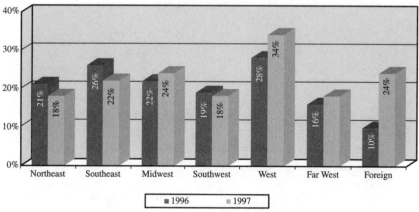

Figure 1-5b

SOURCES OF INCREASED COMPETITION

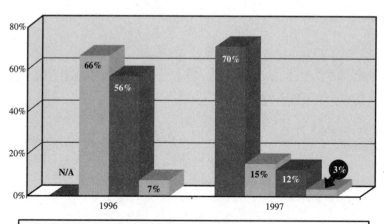

Figure 1-5c

The construction industry is an industry that has not focused much attention on improving either technology or management skills in recent years.

Several years ago, Robert W. Page, an Assistant Secretary of the Army, addressed the Center for Construction Research and Technology at the Massachusetts Institute of Technology (MIT). He said, "Every time this

SOURCE OF WORK

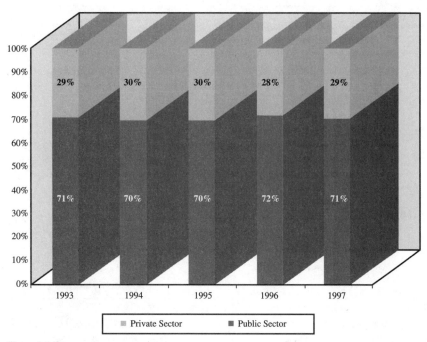

Figure 1-5d

LOCATION OF WORK BY REGION

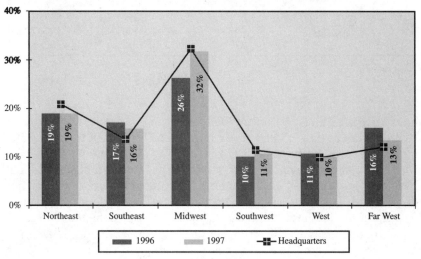

Figure 1-5e

BACKLOG AT YEAR-END

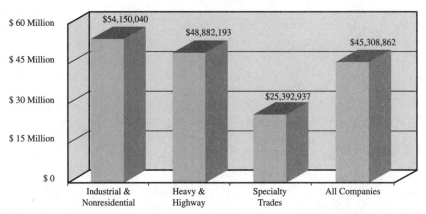

Figure 1-6a

SIZE OF BACKLOG COMPARED TO LAST YEAR

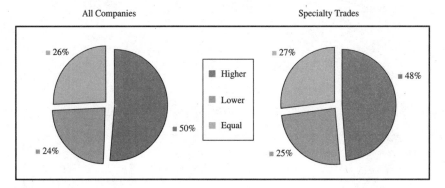

Figure 1-6b

industry has failed, it's because of bad management. I don't know why we don't emphasize that it's extremely important. You've got to start training people in college to at least begin thinking about management. And when they get out they have to understand that there's a bigger deal out there than just engineering or building. They must understand that they are going into business. They will be part of the largest damn private sector business in the United States. Somebody has to manage it."

The companies with the strongest project managers and field superintendents will be positioned to take advantage of the continual push

STRATEGIES TO IMPROVE FUTURE PROFITABILITY

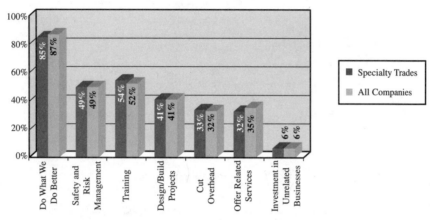

Figure 1-7

COMPANIES WITH QUALITY PROGRAMS

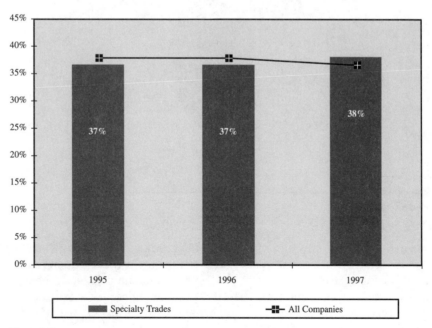

Figure 1-8

TOP FIVE CHALLENGES IN THE NEXT FIVE YEARS

	% Selected as Top Five	% Ranked as #1 Challenge
Shortage of Trained Field Help	67%	36%
Sources of Future Work	52%	22%
Litigation	40%	9%
Workers' Compensation Insurance Costs	35%	5%
Changing Technology	31%	2%

Figure 1-9

UMBRELLA LIABILITY LIMITS

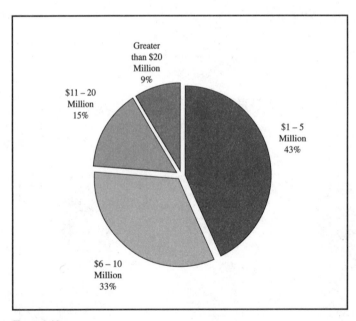

Figure 1-10a

toward greater productivity and benchmarked quality levels. Approximately 85%–95% of all construction dollars are expended in field operations. Productivity at the job site and the utilization of top-quality managers employing the latest technological tools will determine the winners in the next millennium. "Winging it" will not be enough. Utilizing "good people" will not be enough.

EXPERIENCE MODIFICATION RATE

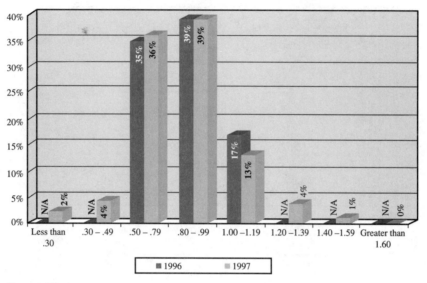

Figure 1-10b

AVERAGE NUMBER OF WORKERS' COMPENSATION CLAIMS FILED IN THE PAST YEAR

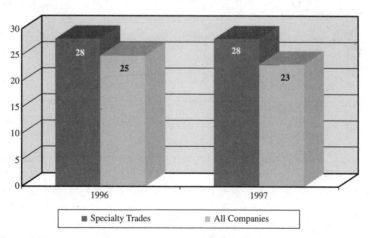

Figure 1-10c

SUBSTANCE ABUSE TESTING PARAMETERS

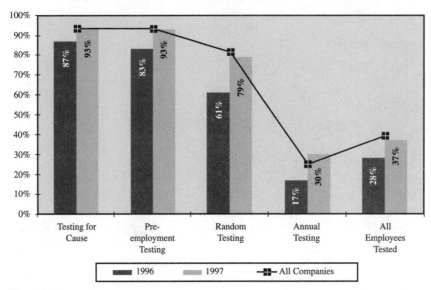

Figure 1-11a

UNION/OPEN SHOP CONTRACTORS

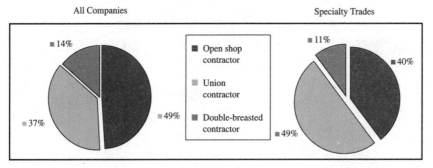

Figure 1-11b

The successful company of the twenty-first century must confront and control a number of key issues:

The Workforce—The demographics of an aging workforce will continue to contribute to labor shortages and, coupled with a shrinking labor pool resulting from lower unemployment, further innovative measures will be required to ensure that the right people are hired, motivated, and retained.

BENEFITS OFFERED TO EMPLOYEES

Benefit	Offered to All Employees	Section 125 Cafeteria Plan	Percent Paid by Company
Health Care - Employee	81%	38%	79%
Health Care - Family	76%	37%	51%
Dental Care - Employee	55%	24%	45%
Dental Care - Family	53%	24%	33%
Prescription Drugs	66%	22%	53%
Vision Care	25%	11%	21%
Group Term Life Insurance	67%	13%	64%
Accidental Death & Dismemberment Ins.	47%	9%	43%
Short-term Disability Insurance	33%	6%	28%
Long-term Disability Insurance	37%	6%	30%
Long-term Care	3%	1%	2%
Cancer Insurance	3%	1%	2%
Child Care	2%	11%	0%
Education	18%	2%	17%

Figure 1-11c

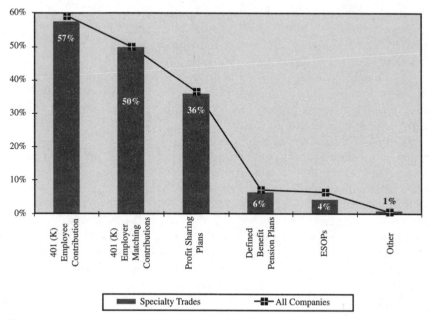

BENEFIT PLANS OFFERED TO SALARIED EMPLOYEES

Figure 1-11d

BENEFIT PLANS OFFERED TO ONLY KEY EMPLOYEES

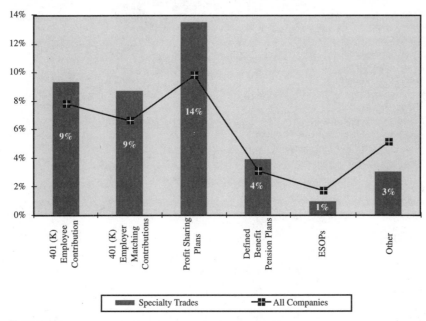

Figure 1-11e

Project Delivery Systems—The shift to design-build and trends toward "flash tracking" will exert more pressure on management to not only keep up with the pack, but also move ahead.

The Quest for Quality—TQM is alive and well, and contractors not actively pursuing quality assurance/quality control activities will find that more and more owners are demanding that contractors "do it right and do it right the first time."

Safety—Government and industry efforts to provide a safer work place is increasing, and contractors now realize that it makes good "cents" to keep accidents to a minimum.

Field Productivity Improvement—Since field operations are where profits are made or lost, it makes sense to institute measures to increase productivity and provide highly trained and motivated field supervisors to oversee those programs.

The challenges facing management in the subcontracting industry will be daunting but not insurmountable. For those companies willing to rise to the challenge, the future looks bright indeed.

Contracts

The construction industry is an industry of contracts—contracts between owners and architects and engineers, contracts between owners and general contractors, contracts between contractors and subcontractors and subcontractors and their suppliers—and so on down the line. Add to this list labor union agreements (contracts), purchase order agreements (contracts), insurance policies and bonds (contracts). Maybe this is why we are known as "contractors."

In the midst of an ocean of contracts, rarely does the recipient of a contract read it through thoroughly and understand all of the provisions contained therein. However, if one is to be bound by the terms and conditions of a contract, shouldn't that person have an understanding of those terms and conditions?

The complex nature of our industry has spawned more and more contracts, and the days of the "handshake agreement," except in rare cases, died decades ago.

Litigation is a major industry in this country, although the trend in construction in recent years seems to have veered away from legal action and toward alternate dispute resolution methods such as mediation and arbitration.

But the contract remains the backbone of our industry's relationships, and too often, parties sign their names to a contract without realizing the consequences of that act.

A wise client once told the writer, "You know, I used to award a construction project on a handshake, but many of the people I dealt with are no longer in the business and I am working with contractors with whom I have little or no experience, so my lawyers insist on preparing a contract for every project we award. And I guess they are right; you definitely need a contract if you are dealing with bad guys, but it is not so important when you are dealing with good guys. However, until you know who the bad guys are, you'd better have a contract."

Standard Construction Contracts

There are standard forms of contracts such as those prepared by the American Institute of Architects (A.I.A.) and the Associated General Contractors of America (AGC). Owners and general contractors often modify these standard contracts by changing several of the provisions in a standard contract or adding other documents as exhibits.

One of the most commonly used standard documents is the A.I.A. General Conditions of the Contract for Construction, identified as A.I.A. Document 201. This contract establishes the relationship of the owner, architect/engineer, general contractor, and subcontractor.

All A.I.A. contracts, including their general conditions contract, contain a warning on the cover sheet:

THIS DOCUMENT HAS IMPORTANT LEGAL CONSEQUENCES; CONSULTATION WITH AN ATTORNEY IS ENCOURAGED WITH RESPECT TO ITS COMPLETION OR MODIFICATION.

This is sound advice. Although most of the A.I.A. or A.G.C. contracts will be awarded to general contractors who will, in turn, prepare their own form of subcontract agreement, an understanding of these contracts by the subcontractor is essential since their provisions are usually included in the GC-subcontractor contract. And there will be times when the subcontractor, dealing directly with an owner, will be issued a standard or modified A.I.A or A.G.C. contract when an award has been made.

Most Frequently Used Construction Contracts

The lump sum or stipulated sum contract

What should be a relatively simple form of contract may not be what it appears. This lump sum or stipulated sum contract is most often used in public works projects or when private construction projects are being competitively bid. An essential ingredient when considering a lump sum contract award is a complete set of plans and specifications. Each bidder for the project will be assembling a lump sum or stipulated sum bid based on the work included in those plans and specifications, no more—no less. And that is where trouble begins.

A perfect set of plans and specifications is rarely, if ever, produced by design consultants, and even if that were to be the case, one subcontractor's interpretation of these plans and specifications may vary from that of another subcontractor.

If evidence of any errors or omissions in the bid documents is uncovered by bidders, they may not alert the architect but might exclude costs that are obviously required to rectify these errors/omissions. The general contractor or subcontractor that does include costs to cover such contingencies may discover that their bid is no longer competitive.

Of course, the proper way to deal with these types of situations is to advise the architect of any errors and/or omissions and request that written clarification be distributed to all bidders as quickly as possible.

The hectic activity that occurs in the general contractor's office when competitive bids are being assembled may result in some of these discrepancies going unnoticed—not being discovered until an award is made or even after construction is underway.

As the project progresses, there may be further disagreements over what was actually required or contained in the bid documents—the contractor having one interpretation, having assembled his or her bid accordingly, and the architect—the interpreter of the plans and specifications—having another understanding.

When the differences in contract interpretation result in additional costs, guess who usually gets caught in the crossfire? The subcontractor, since these problems may not have surfaced during the general contractor/subcontractor negotiating session—and, there again, because both general contractor and subcontractor have differing interpretations about what the plans and specifications may require. There are ways to deal with these kinds of issues, which are addressed in subsequent chapters, but suffice it so say that if the quality of the plans and specifications defining the scope of work in a lump sum contract is poor, both general contractor and subcontractor will undoubtedly become involved in some form of dispute or claim unless these deficiencies are discovered and resolved during contract negotiations.

Pitfalls in lump sum contracts

- Architectural and structural drawings that are not properly coordinated, for example, and floor/wall openings shown on architectural drawings that do not match those on structural or mechanical drawings.

- Overall or partial dimensions for foundations are at variance with superstructure drawings, both structurally and architecturally.

- Elevator shaft size and location shown on architectural drawings are at variance with the opening indicated on structural drawings.

- Mechanical and electrical louver requirements, concrete pads for mechanical/electrical equipment not indicated on architectural drawings nor sized properly, but possibly referenced on some obscure note on a drawing that is likely to be missed by the bidder.

- Partition types in detail drawings that do not coincide with corresponding partition types indicated on architectural floor plans, or as specified in a partition schedule.

- Fire-rated construction details not indicated in areas where required by the local or state building code.

- A finish schedule that does not coincide with other architectural drawings, details, finishes, or notes on the drawings.

- A door schedule and frame schedule that does not coincide with the door/frame size or type indicated on the architectural floor plans, and/or frame throat sizes that do not match corresponding partition and wall thickness.

- Reflected ceiling plans not coordinated with an electrical lighting plan, sprinkler layout, or HVAC diffuser locations.

- Duct work dimensions or location, as indicated on HVAC drawings, that conflict with the space available due to the depth of structural members or structural system.

- Insufficient space above a ceiling(s) to accommodate all of the HVAC, electrical, plumbing, and sprinkler work that is to be installed and still maintain the design ceiling height.

- Wall finishes indicated on floor plans that are contradictory to those in the finish schedule. Wainscot height finishes not properly indicated on Finish Schedule or related wall elevations.

- Notes on one drawing erroneously referring to an unrelated detail on another drawing, or details referring to a drawing that does not exist.

- Invert elevations of site utility conduits/pipes extending from the building on the architectural or mechanical floor plan that are not compatible with the invert elevations on the site utilities drawing.

- Individual room dimensions when added together fail to match the overall floor dimension.

Then occasionally there are problems with the specifications.

- Referencing information provided in another section but not provided in that section.

- Hardware for glass entrance doors included in the glazing section and hardware section. Who is responsible? But you can be sure that the architect will expect a credit from someone!

- Reference to painting of various items of equipment or materials in the mechanical and electrical sections but no mention of this requirement in the painting section of the specifications.

- Ambiguous requirements for responsibility to furnish electrical starters for HVAC equipment. This requirement may be included in both Electrical and Mechanical specification sections or in neither and therefore the responsibility of which contractor is to supply these items may be unclear.

- Failure to include a requirement for temporary light and power in the electrical section, however this requirement is included in the general or supplementary conditions (two sections that most parties just skim through)! The general contractor will expect the electrical subcontractor to furnish this work since electricians are historically assigned this responsibility, but the electrician has not included this work since it was not required in Division 16—Electrical Work.

- Cutting and patching for each trade not specifically assigned, raising the question: Is this the responsibility of the general contractor or subcontractor? (Usually each party assumes the other will perform this work; therefore it is often excluded from both general contractor and subcontractor's estimates.)

- Specification sections obviously used for another project having little applicability to the present project, but the architect will insist it does. (As an example, the writer was involved in five school projects all designed by the same architect. Television and VCR brackets were to have been installed in each classroom and the specified brackets were obviously the wrong type. When this was brought to the architect's attention, he rejected the additional costs to furnish the proper ones—until the writer pointed to a section of the specification which stated that "these brackets shall be able to be rotated so as to be viewed by the patient!")

The cost-plus fee with a guaranteed maximum price contract

This form of contract is referred to as a GMP contract and it finds applicability when an owner seeks to establish a contract sum prior to 100% completion of the design documents. There are several occasions when this type of situation will arise.

Perhaps the owner wishes to employ a GMP in order to obtain a construction loan after interest rates have temporarily dropped, or the owner needs a "not to exceed" contract sum in order to complete a pro forma statement necessary to establish rental rates for a speculative office building project.

But in any case, the general contractor will be required to prepare an estimate based upon less than complete plans and specifications and will include an additional sum, in the form of a built-in contingency, to cover the cost to complete the work in the manner in which the owner, designer, and builder have agreed upon once the drawings have been completed. Oftentimes a GMP contract between the owner and contractor will be based upon plans and specifications that are 60% to 80% complete.

The object of such a contract is to allow the contractor to proceed with that portion of the design (usually the structural system and site work), while the balance of the design is being completed. It becomes important for the contractor, designer, and owner to monitor the completion of the plans and specifications to ensure that they meet the intent and budgetary restrictions of the GMP contract. These contracts generally contain a provision to share any savings if the final cost is less than the GMP. Although there is no hard and fast rule, savings of 25% to 50% will usually accrue to the contractor.

GMP pitfalls to avoid. Both general contractor and subcontractor will have problems completing their work at the originally agreed upon price if the general contractor is unaware of certain dangers to avoid as plans and specifications are being completed in this GMP process.

One of the pitfalls that less-than-experienced contractors will encounter is failure to scrutinize the completion of the remaining 20% to 40% portion of the plans. It is during this time, either inadvertently or through noncommunication, that additional scope may be added to the project as the design consultants refine or modify their original design. If the final design increases the scope of the work significantly, it may also increase costs, costs that the general contractor had not anticipated nor included in the GMP estimate and contract sum. And if this should happen somewhere along the way, there will be a series of disputes between owner, architect, and general contractor concerning each party's understanding of what should have been included in the costs in anticipation of completing the final design.

Now how does something like this affect the subcontractor? When a GMP contract is being negotiated, the general contractors will refer to their own database of costs and will often select certain subcontractors to participate in the process of establishing the project estimate. The general contractor, in inviting the subcontractor's assistance in providing estimating and even design information, will usually announce his or her intention to negotiate a subcontract agreement with all participating subcontractors when the GMP contract has been executed. Or, if the owner requires competitive bidding for all work, subcontractors assisting the contractor in the compilation of the GMP will be given some form of preferred treatment when those competitive bids are received and analyzed.

But unless the general contractor has reviewed and approved the design development drawings as they are prepared to ensure that the scope of work included in the completed contract drawings corresponds with their estimate, both general contractor and subcontractor may have disagreements as to responsibility for absorbing the additional costs when this unanticipated work appears in the completed contract documents.

The general contractor can avoid, or at least mitigate, these problems by requesting design development drawings as the GMP set of plans is being completed, distributing these plans to all subcontractors participating in the program, and requesting that they review and verify scope of work and corresponding costs. If the design is being completed in such a manner that it exceeds the original intent and/or estimate included in the GMP contract, the subcontractors must notify the general contractor, who in turn must advise the owner and the designers before the design has been completed.

If there is one major drawback to a GMP contract format, it is the failure to obtain, review, and analyze the series of design development documents as they are being produced by the architect and engineer to ensure compliance with the contractor's intent and estimate.

The cost plus a fee contract

This form of contract is, as the name implies, based upon cost of the work plus the contractor's fee, generally expressed as a percentage of total cost. Oftentimes, an owner will use a cost-plus contract when an emergency has occurred such as a fire, flood, wind, or other catastrophic events which cause unexpected damage to their building or property. Construction in some cases may commence based upon verbal instructions by the architect or engineer, followed by sketches or possibly complete drawings as the project progresses.

At other times a cost-plus contract may be awarded by the owner of an undeveloped piece of property or a vacant office building when a tenant or potential owner suddenly appears but requires occupancy within a short time frame that does not allow for the time required to develop plans and specifications immediately. This is often the case in tenant fit-up work that can commence with simple partition layout drawings.

In situations such as these where there is insufficient time to assemble a budget, the owner may elect to award the work on a cost-plus basis after negotiating a fee with the contractor. These types of contracts are often awarded to a contractor and subcontractor with whom the owner has successfully worked with in the past.

Pitfalls for the subcontractor to avoid: In the rush to commence "time and material cost-plus" work, a definition of what each party considers to be "cost" may not always be understood. The cost of labor is not just the dollar amount of the worker's hourly or weekly wages, but also includes the cost of social security, unemployment insurance, union fringe benefits, workman's compensation insurance, general liability insurance costs, and, of course, corporate overhead and profit. What an owner perceives as a "reasonable" hourly rate for, say, a carpenter at $18.50 per hour, may not be considered reasonable when this suddenly balloons to $45.00 per hour after all benefits, overhead, and profit have been applied to that base rate.

So it is important prior to starting a cost-plus fee project to be explicit as to what constitutes "cost." This applies not only to direct labor, but also to the cost of project management, project superintendent, if required, other office personnel such as estimators, purchasing agents, and other support staff, unless these costs are understood to be included in the percentage of overhead applied to the "cost of work."

And what about materials? Not only should a reasonable markup be allowed on all materials and equipment purchased, but waste factors have to be included and explained to the owner, who may scrutinize all invoices and wonder why 3,000 square feet of gypsum drywall was purchased to install 2,500 square feet of wall surface.

A good source of what constitutes "cost" can be found in Article 7 of A.I.A. document A-111—Standard Form of Agreement Between Owner and Contractor, where the basis for payment is the cost of the work plus a fee.

- Labor cost.

- Wages or salaries of the contractor's supervisory and administrative personnel when stationed at the site with the owner's approval.

- Taxes, insurance, contributions, assessments, and benefits required by the collective bargaining process, sick leave, medical and health benefits, holidays, vacations. (In the case of salaried employees, remember that they are paid for 52 weeks, but if they take two weeks' vacation, they only work 50 weeks!)

- Subcontract costs.
- Cost of materials and equipment incorporated into the work.
- Cost of other materials and equipment, temporary facilities, and related items.
- Rental charges for facilities, machinery, and equipment.
- Cost of removal of debris from the site.
- Miscellaneous costs—refer to A.I.A. A111 for a complete list of these acceptable costs.

Documentation of cost-plus work.   If a cost plus project is underway for any considerable amount of time, it is very important to keep the client apprised of all costs to date on a regular basis. This will prevent the client from "sticker shock" once the total project is complete and final costs are assembled and presented.

Not only should accurate daily labor cost records be maintained along with a brief description of their activities, but all material receiving tickets should be marked by the job superintendent indicating what the materials were used for and exactly where they were used. If both labor and material costs are accounted for on a daily basis, it will be much easier to reconcile accounts once the project has been completed.

It is important to impress upon the owner the need to have his or her representative sign daily work tickets attesting to the total workforce on the job that day (by trade), any material and equipment deliveries, and a brief summary of that day's activities.

Many contractors and subcontractors will not engage in a cost-plus project unless the owner (or the general contractor's) representative agrees to sign daily work tickets. Even this procedure may not eliminate all disagreements over final project cost, but if a dispute escalates to a claim, the signed daily ticket will be the subcontractor's life preserver.

The construction management (CM) contract

At one point, a construction management contract was a rather simple affair. The CM, acting as the owner's agent, would assist the designers in preconstruction activities such as the preparation of estimates, schedules, and bid packages as the plans and specifications were being completed. Activities prior to the start of construction would consist of reviewing and analyzing bids from contractors and recommending to the owner those contractors to whom contracts should be awarded. During construction the CM will then proceed to administer and manage these contracts on behalf of the owner.

The CM would also monitor the construction schedule, quality levels, and contract compliance and review and approve contractor/subcontractor requisitions and pass them on to the owner for payment, since all such contracts would be in the owner's name. For these services the CM receives a fee based upon the cost of construction.

Some CM contracts permit them to hire a general contractor who will, in turn, contract with subcontractors and vendors. The CM would be responsible for overall supervision of the project. Other CM contracts stipulate that several "prime" contractors—such as excavation contractors, structural steel contractors, mechanical, electrical, and plumbing contractors (MEP)—are to be hired by the owner and managed by the CM. These prime contractors will, if the project requires, hire subcontractors to perform specific portions of their prime contract work. An HVAC prime contractor may hire a ductwork subcontractor, an insulation subcontractor, and an air and water balancing subcontractor, for example.

The CM concept has gone through a number of mutations since its initial implementation. There are two now basic types of construction managers—"for fee" and "at risk."

The construction manager (CM) "for fee."   Although the original concept of the CM's responsibilities has not changed appreciably, the CM "for fee" acts as the owner's agent and extracts a fee for the services the CM provides based upon the final cost of construction; there is no "cap" or upper limit on the total project costs. They are what they are.

Basically the owner is hiring a construction professional to act as his agent and advocate and represent him throughout the entire construction process.

The construction manager (CM) "at risk."   The CM "at risk" will guarantee a maximum project sum and receive a fee based upon providing services similar to that of the CM "for fee." However, if the completed project exceeds the guaranteed maximum price, any cost overruns are absorbed by the CM, thereby reducing the CM's profit.

It would appear that the CM "at risk" has a somewhat vested interest in insuring that costs remain less than the maximum price and some critics claim that this limits their objectivity. The "at risk" CMs may view a contractor or subcontractor's claim for extra work differently because of this vested interest in the CM's own bottom line.

Concerns when working with a CM as a prime contractor.   One of the CM's principal responsibilities is the coordination and scheduling of trades, each under separate contract with the owner; therefore the quality of the CM's staff on the job site is crucial to a smooth and efficiently running project. When the CM staff is inexperienced, additional burdens will be placed on the prime contractors and their subcontractors.

A case in point is the writer's experience working as a "prime contractor" for the general construction portion of work on a five-school CM project with other "primes:" excavating and site contractors, HVAC contractors, electrical contractors, and plumbing contractors.

The CM had five project managers, one assigned to each school. Overall responsibility for all five projects was to have been placed in the hands of an experienced manager stationed at one school, but this manager's background was purchasing, not project management. The remainder of his staff varied from one experienced field supervisor to a business development trainee assigned to the field to get a little mud on his shoes. A diverse lot to say the least.

This lack of an experienced CM management team manifested itself in a number of ways and created significant problems among the other prime contractors and their subcontractors.

The CM's coordination between trades was less than adequate, and when the prime mechanical contractor received approval to install roof drains, the writer's company performing general construction work—including installation of the structural steel system, metal floor, and roof deck—did not receive a copy of the approved roof drain drawings.

The metal deck drawings, according to the contract documents, required frame reinforcement when any opening exceeded 100 square inches, and since these same contract drawings indicated a roof drain that required an 8-inch (50-square-inch) opening in the deck, there was no apparent need for frame reinforcement.

After the roof drains were installed and after the acoustical ceilings had been installed as all five projects were nearing completion, the CM announced that roof deck reinforcement was required since the actual roof drain openings exceeded 100 square inches.

The writer estimated that the cost to retrofit all of these openings would be approximately $75,000, and the CM insisted it was the writer's company's responsibility to install these frames at no cost. A paper blizzard of claims and counterclaims ensued over the next several months occupying much of the writer's time. All of this could have been avoided if the CM had acted responsibly and distributed the approved roof drain shop drawings while the roof deck was being installed. Final payment was withheld, but the golden rule was in effect: "He who has the gold—rules!"

An inspection by a professional engineer, whose services were paid for by the writer's company, indicated that all roof deck openings were adequately supported and finally resolved the issue, avoiding an expensive claim.

So there are roadblocks for subcontractors in the successful completion of CM projects just as there are in many other forms of construction contracts.

Design-build contracts

These types of contracts involve assembling a team consisting of design consultants—architectural, structural, civil, mechanical, electrical, and a general contractor—who act as one entity in dealing with a project owner. This design-build team will assess the owner's construction program and provide both design and construction services. The owner, instead of contracting separately with a design firm and a construction firm, contracts with one firm for both activities. Usually the general contractor is the lead partner in a design-build venture and engages the services of an architectural and engineering firm that has had experience in the type of project under consideration. However many architectural firms are the lead partners in the team and invite a general contractor to join with them.

Although the design-build concept has been around for years, its popularity has increased recently among both private and public project owners. Several federal and local public works agencies have begun using the design-build approach instead of the conventional design-bid process. The U.S. Postal Service has been a leader in implementing the design-build concept.

The design-build concept offers some attractive opportunities for subcontractors and is discussed in more detail in a chapter devoted entirely to the subject.

Turnkey contracts

An owner may find it advantageous to not only pursue a design-build concept, but also to carry it several steps further and enter into a turnkey project. In a typical turnkey contract, the designer/contractor will provide the design and construction and will usually provide construction financing for the project. When the project has been completed and the "key has been turned over" to the owner, full payment is made.

In some cases the turnkey contract requires the builder/designer/developer to equip the project so that it is ready for use the moment it is completed. For example, if the turnkey project is a hotel, all furnishings and equipment required for full operation may be required and provided for in the turnkey contract.

General, Special, and Supplementary
Conditions to the Contract

Attached to any of the standard contracts referred to above, additional contract requirements are often included in the contract specifications or issued as a separate bid document. All too often, these documents are considered "boilerplate," but to do so is a big mistake. These general, special, or supplementary additions to the basic contract may include some significant restrictions on work procedures, but several of these "boilerplate" statements may actually be used to protect the subcontractor.

Wise subcontractors read each of these documents from beginning to end at least once to familiarize themselves with the general and specific nature of their provisions.

The most commonly used supplementary contract document is the A.I.A. Document A201—General Conditions to the Contract for Construction, prepared by the American Institute of Architects.

The A201 document. Although this document is prepared by the architect and is meant to be a companion to the basic construction contract, there are many provisions in A201 that are important to subcontractors and should be thoroughly understood.

The "flow through" provisions in most general contractor/subcontractor agreements are such that the provisions of A201 will also apply to the subcontractor.

All subcontractors should read this document thoroughly from cover to cover at least once and note those provisions that affect them. From time to time the A.I.A. revises A201 at which point another complete reading should be undertaken. Although the most current edition of A201 is copyrighted 1997, many contracts currently in force or in the pipeline may reference the older, 1987 version.

Some key provisions of both versions are discussed here—the first being the 1987 edition.

Throughout the A201 document, the term "contractor" is used, but because of the pass-through arrangement in most general-contractor/subcontractor agreements, these references would apply to the subcontractor as well.

- Article 2—Owner. This article states that the contractor shall be furnished, free of charge, such copies of the plans and project manuals as are reasonably necessary to do the job. (Does this mean that the general contractor is to provide sufficient drawings for subcontractors' use at no cost? It would appear so since the GC can, in turn, request them of the owner.)

Another provision in this article stipulates that the owner may carry out the work himself or herself if the contractor defaults or neglects to do so. (That is why most contracts require general contractors to assign subcontract agreements to the owner in case of default by the contractor.)

- Article 3—Contractor. This article relieves the contractor of liability to the owner or architect for damage caused by errors, inconsistencies, or omissions in the contract documents, unless the contractor realized these errors and failed to report them to the architect. (Therefore the contractor should not require the subcontractor to be responsible for damages caused by these same errors and/or omissions.) The contractor is responsible for taking field measurements and verifying field conditions. (However, general contractor/subcontractor agreement may transfer this responsibility to the subcontractor.)

  Article 3 also states that it is not the contractor's responsibility to ascertain that the plans and specifications are in compliance with local building codes, except if the contractor performs work knowing that it is contrary to building codes. (This should relieve subcontractors from some of the "you should have known" remarks when building officials during site inspections require additional work to be performed that is not included in the contract drawings.)

  Paragraphs 3.10.2, 3.12.4, and 3.12.8 of this article deal with construction schedules and shop drawings and are required reading. For example, approval of a shop drawing that may be at variance with the contract documents does not relieve a subcontractor from complying with those contract documents.

- Article 4—Administration of the Contract. This is another "must read" section. This article appoints the architect as the authority for interpretation of the drawings with respect to their "intent." (This is similar to having the fox watch the chicken coop!)

  Claims and disputes are dealt with in this section and the method by which claims are identified, filed, and resolved makes this section of A201 an important one to read.

- Article 5—Subcontractors. Subcontractors need to read this article since it was written to define what subcontractors are, their duties, responsibilities, and rights. The subcontractor is bound to the contractor by the same provisions of the general contractor's contract with the owner. (Shouldn't the subcontractor want to take a look at that owner contract?) In fact, Paragraph 5.3.1. states that the "Contractor shall make available to each proposed Subcontractor, prior to the execution of the subcontract agreement, copies of the Contract Documents to which the subcontractor will be bound."

- Article 6—Construction by Owner or by Separate Contractors. The owner has the right to issue or award separate contracts in connection with other portions of the project. (But suppose this is a union job, the owner elects to hire nonunion workers, and a job action occurs that delays the project. Who is accountable for those delays, especially if they affect your work?)

- Article 7—Changes in the Work. Work change orders are often disputed, and this article of A201 should be read carefully. The concept of a construction change directive is thoroughly discussed, and a portion of this article deals with situations when contractor and owner, or contractor and subcontractor, cannot agree on the cost of the proposed extra work. Work must proceed, according to this article, and the contractor is obliged to maintain records of the actual cost of the work, to include the following:
  - Costs of labor, fringe benefits, workmen's compensation insurance.
  - Costs of materials, supplies, and equipment, including cost of transportation.
  - Rental costs of machinery and equipment, exclusive of hand tools, whether rented from the contractor or others.
  - Cost of premiums for all bonds and insurance, permit fees, and sales and use taxes.
  - Additional costs of supervision and field office personnel directly attributable to the change.
  - Allowance for overhead and profit.

- Article 8—Time. When signing a contract with a stipulated number of days allotted for construction, according to Article 8, and if not changed by another contract, the term "day" refers to calendar day as opposed to "work" day.

- Article 9—Payments and Completion. This section defines, among other topics, "substantial completion," which is important to subcontractors since many contracts include a provision for a reduction in retention once substantial completion has been reached. The article also discusses partial occupancy and the relief this brings to both contractor and subcontractor once the owner occupies a certain portion of the building under construction.

Review of the 1997 edition of A201.   There are some substantial changes to the latest edition of the general conditions document, and although several significant changes are listed below, a complete review of this contract should be made.

Article 2 requires the owner to designate, in writing, a representative who shall have express authority to bind the owner requiring matters involving the owner's contractual approval or responsibility. This should enhance and speed up the decision-making process when authorization is required to proceed with field changes or other owner approval requests.

Article 3.2.1 requires the contractor to verify field dimensions of any existing condition and report any errors, omissions, or inconsistencies to the architect.

Article 3.2.2 includes a very important change. It stipulates that the contractor is not required to ascertain that the contract documents are in compliance with applicable laws, ordinances, or building codes. This takes some of the steam out of an architect's contention that the contractor is responsible to provide additional items of work during construction when directed to do so by the local building inspector in order to comply with their interpretation of the building code.

Article 3.12.10 states that the contractor shall not be responsible for the adequacy of performance or design criteria as set forth in the contract documents.

Article 4.3.10 denies the contractor the ability to include consequential damages as a cost when submitting a claim. These types of damages that are not acceptable when filing a claim are clearly defined in this article.

Article 4.4.1 and 4.5 requires the contractor to first submit to mediation before notifying the architect of their intent to file for arbitration in the case of contract disputes.

Article 5.2.3 states that upon receipt of an owner's objection to a general contractor's selection of a subcontractor, the general contractor is obliged to replace that subcontractor. However, if the rejected subcontractor was reasonably able to perform the work, the contract time/sum may be increased/decreased as required to accommodate this change.

(It would appear that the rejected subcontractor might be able to recover some costs from the general contractor if disqualified by the owner in a situation such as this.)

Article 7.3.6 deals with construction change directives (CCD) and allows the contractor to requisition for work performed if the costs are not disputed. In other words, general contractors and their subcontractors do not have to wait until a formal change order is issued before presenting an invoice for extra work performed as a CCD.

Article 9.3.1.2 stipulates that a general contractor cannot requisition for those portions of the work for which they do not intend to pay to a subcontractor or vendor. By inference, this means that a general contractor cannot requisition an amount submitted by a subcontractor and upon receipt of payment from the owner, decide not to pay the subcontractor/vendor or otherwise withhold payment.

Article 9.8.5 deals with substantial completion and allows the contractor to apply for retention once written acceptance of substantial completion is received. The owner may, however, withhold sums for incomplete work or work installed but not in accordance with the contract documents.

Article 12.2.2.1 is concerned with corrective work after substantial completion has been reached. The owner must notify the contractor of any corrective work required during the one-year warranty period. If the owner fails to afford the contractor an opportunity to correct the work, the owner waives all rights to require the contractor to do so.

Beware of onerous provisions of the contractor-subcontractor agreement

Although the subcontractor should be aware of the contents of the contract between the owner and the general contractor, including the general conditions provisions, the subcontract agreement with the general contractor has an immediate and direct impact on that subcontractor. Too many subcontractors treat these subcontract agreements as "boilerplate" and, anxious to get on with the work, give the contract a "once over lightly," sign it, and return it back to the GC without thoroughly understanding its provisions. The only time it may be read is upon receipt of a threatening letter from the general contractor demanding that the subcontractor comply with specific provisions—or else.

Subcontractors consistently sign contracts anticipating that none of its highly restrictive clauses will ever be invoked. In fact, if they read the subcontract agreement word-by-word in the presence of their lawyer, it is doubtful that many such contracts would ever be signed.

A look at some of the more onerous provisions in the standard general contractor-subcontractor agreement will prove the point and should impress upon the subcontractor the need to read and understand the provisions of their subcontract agreements. If any provisions require modification or should be deleted in their entirety, review them with the general contractor, expressing concerns and requesting that deletions or modifications be made.

In the writer's experience over the years, many subcontractors have resisted signing their subcontract agreements until various changes were made and, in more cases than not, these changes have saved the subcontractors from the need to file a claim or have offered protection against claims directed against them from the general contractor.

Although it may be difficult to raise these objections during negotiations with the general contractor, especially when the particular job is important to the company, raise them! In many cases the general contractor may agree entirely or at least modify some terms—and therefore nothing is lost.

Review of Typical General Contractor-Subcontractor Agreements

The pay when paid clause

Although one paragraph in the subcontract agreement may state that "Payments on account of the subcontract amount, subject to the provisions of Article ____, shall be made as follows: on or about the twentieth (20th) day of each month in the amount of 90% (assuming 10% retention) of the value of the subcontractor's work properly invoiced and satisfactorily completed during the preceding month."

There may be another paragraph hidden somewhere that contradicts this payment schedule and states that "Payment to be made 20 days from receipt of payment from the owner." This is the "pay when paid clause." Many state courts have ruled on the validity of the "pay when paid" clause, and in some cases this practice seems grossly unfair. For example, if the reason for delay of payment from the owner was due to the general contractor's failure to provide some documentation completely unrelated to any subcontractor's performance, the subcontractors are being penalized for something not of their doing, or beyond their control to correct.

Subcontractors should contact the attorney general's office in their respective states to determine whether the "pay when paid" practice has been ruled illegal, since several states have addressed this matter, particularly when it involves public projects.

While most general contractors will be insistent upon including a "pay when paid" clause in the subcontract agreement a subcontractor should attempt to delete this provision.

Binding subcontractors to all contract documents

The provision binding the subcontractor to all of the contract documents may appear as follows: "The subcontractor shall be bound to the contractor by the terms and provisions of all of the contract documents, and assumes toward the contractor, with respect to the subcontractor's work, all of the obligations and responsibilities which the contractor, by the contract documents, has assumed toward the owner."

Unless the subcontractor has actually seen and read all of the contract documents between the owner and the general contractor, how can the subcontractor agree to abide by them?

This provision should be struck from subcontract agreements since the subcontractors ought not to concern themselves with other obligations and responsibilities that the contractor assumed with the owner. When strong objections are raised by the subcontractor, the general contractor will generally agree to delete this provision. (The general contractor might not care to have the subcontractor review this document. It may allow the general contractor to, say, reduce retention to 5% when the project is 50% complete, but their subcontract agreement may not include such a provision!)

Receipt of complete drawings, specifications, addendums, etc.

One of the most common complaints registered by subcontractors after they have signed the subcontract agreement is that they did not receive all of the addenda and updated revisions to the plans and specifications that are included in the contract they executed.

Don't sign an agreement that references specific documents when they were not transmitted to the subcontractor by the general contractor. If presented with a "complete" set of contract drawings by the general contractor, scan each page to ensure that all drawings are acceptable and accurately represent the scope of work negotiated in the subcontract agreement.

Most general-contractor/subcontractor contract disagreements occur because of documents in that agreement which were never received or reviewed by that subcontractor—yet the executed subcontract agreement includes these very same documents!

Time is of the essence

Consultation with a lawyer regarding the meaning of this provision is advisable, but essentially it means that if subcontractors do not "prosecute the work" (perform) as rapidly as possible and delays can be attributed to their not "prosecuting the work" as quickly as possible, the subcontractor judged responsible for the delay(s) will be assessed any and all damages created by the delay(s).

When a "time is of the essence" clause is included in the contract, whenever the subcontractor's work is delayed by others, a letter must be dispatched to the general contractor outlining the nature and extent of the delay. (Refer to the section on sample letters for the format for such a delay letter.)

Articles dealing with "intent" of the contract documents

A typical paragraph will read, "The subcontractor shall provide and pay for all labor and materials _____ and shall complete the work in accordance with the contract documents. All work or materials which, in the opinion of the contractor may fairly be inferred from the plans, drawings, specifications, and details as necessary for the satisfactory completion of the subcontractor's work shall be executed and furnished by the subcontractor."

This provision is almost as onerous as the one in the Article 4, A.I.A. A201 document allowing the architects to be the interpreters of the drawings they prepared.

When competitively bidding a project, subcontractors will be expected to include in their bids the work specifically required by the plans and specifications. They should not be required to include additional costs to incorporate the designer's intent. It is incumbent upon the architect and engineer to prepare the plans and specifications with sufficient clarity to make their "intent" crystal clear. But in the real world this does not often occur.

Although many subcontractors will be persuaded to sign a contract containing a clause such as this, if the question of intent, inference, or interpretation should arise, there are some defenses that can be raised to defuse these kinds of situations, and these matters are discussed in the chapter on disputes and claims. If, in fact, the "intent" is not clear, subcontractors ought to qualify their bids, making note of exactly how they have interpreted the "intent" as it relates to their trade.

Proceeding with extra work without an agreed-upon cost—The directive to work clause

Be alert for the article that states, "Should the contractor and subcontractor be unable to agree as to the amount to be paid or allowed (for change order work), if so ordered in writing by the contractor, the work shall go on under the order or orders of the contractor upon the understanding that the reasonable value of such work shall be paid or allowed, and in the case of the failure of the parties to agree, the determination of the amount to be paid or allowed, as the case may be, shall be referred to arbitration."

NO! If the contractor directs the subcontractor to proceed with extra work on this basis the subcontractor should not proceed until as many mutually acceptable costs as possible are defined. The subcontractor should submit hourly rates for workers and obtain agreement on these rates; obtain written agreement that materials will be paid when documented by actual invoices.

Submit hourly, daily, and weekly rental rates for any equipment or tools that may be required during the course of the work, and get an agreement requiring the general contractor's on-site representative to sign daily tickets verifying actual labor, materials, and equipment utilized that day. If claims arise resulting in arbitration, the subcontractor will have had sufficient documentation accumulated to win the case.

Usually, a general contractor will not issue a formal change order to the subcontractor until the general contractor receives one from the owner, if, in fact, the owner has requested a contract scope change. So unless there is an agreement to pay for extra work prior to the general contractor receiving a corresponding change order from the owner, the subcontractors may find themselves waiting a long time for payment if the general contractor does not aggressively pursue this matter.

And there is another pitfall! Just suppose that the portion of change order work completed by your company totals $75,000 but is only a small portion of a much larger cost proposal being presented to the owner, and suppose a dispute arises over a portion of the proposed change order having nothing to do with your work, but the ensuing dispute takes months to resolve. In the meantime, the $75,000 in acceptable extra work performed by your company remains unpaid.

The company attorney ought to be able to include some language in the subcontract agreement that would prevent something like this from happening. Or better yet, obtain the general contractor's written agreement before starting the work to pay for this extra work within a specified period of time, whether or not payment is received from the owner.

The perform or else article

A typical "perform or else" article will state, "Should the subcontractor fail to prosecute the work or any part thereof with promptness and diligence, or fail to supply a sufficiency of properly skilled workmen or materials of proper quality, or fail in any other respect to comply with the contract documents, the contractor shall be at liberty, after 72 hours [some contracts stipulate 48 hours], to give written notice to the subcontractor to provide such labor or materials as may be necessary to complete the work and to deduct the cost and expense thereof from any money then due or to become due the subcontractor."

This clause can be dealt with by documenting the reasons why work could not proceed. For example, if conditions created by the general contractor or other subcontractors have prevented your firm from "prosecuting" the work diligently, these reasons should be included in a letter responding to the general contractor's demand. Such a letter should be sent certified mail, return receipt required, in order to ensure proof of delivery.

Termination clauses

General contractor/subcontract agreements usually contain a termination clause, one that is triggered if the owner fails to pay an approved requisition or defaults on a significant provision of the contract, or simply goes out of business.

But there is another termination clause that a subcontract agreement may include, one which is referred to as "termination for convenience" allowing the GC to terminate a portion or all of the subcontract agreement at any time and for any reason.

The advantages of such a clause, from the general contractor's perspective, is that subcontractors can be relieved of a portion of their work, or all of their work, if it appears that the subcontractor cannot satisfactorily complete the work, but the subcontractor has not violated any provision of the contract that would invoke punitive provisions. For example, to accommodate a general contractor a small HVAC contracting firm may have agreed to incorporate plumbing and fire protection as part of their scope of work. In assuming these added responsibilities, they may not have been prepared to properly staff and manage this additional work, only to find themselves unable to keep up with the general contractor's ambitious schedule, and the work in question falls behind schedule. If the subcontract agreement contains the terminate for convenience clause, the GC can, upon discussion with the HVAC subcontractor, relieve them of these added work tasks after the subcontractor has been properly compensated for all acceptable work put in place at the time of termination. Any such termination will have no effect on the subcontractor's reputation.

Compensation if the termination for convenience clause is enforced

Any such termination clause in the subcontract agreement should be specific as to the method by which the subcontractor will be compensated if the clause is invoked.

These costs would include the following:

1. All direct costs—labor, materials, equipment, field office, and trailer rentals. All such costs documented with invoices and payroll printouts.

2. Overhead and general administrative expenses. To avoid any disputes, a percentage figure for overhead should be included in the termination clause.

3. Profit—Once again, a percentage amount should be included in the appropriate contract clause.

The termination clause should also include any costs that will not be reimbursed:

1. Expenses incurred in preparing the termination costs.
2. Unabsorbed or underabsorbed corporate overhead. (The Eichleay Formula described in the chapter on claims and disputes outlines the method by which unabsorbed or underabsorbed overhead is calculated.)
3. Any other specific costs which may be the source of a potential dispute.

The general contractor must give the subcontractor ample written notice prior to actual termination by including number of days to be included in the termination clause. This notification will take the form of a stop work order requesting the following:

- No additional work is to be performed, or if some additional work is required it should be very clear as to the extent of the added work.
- No further orders for materials or equipment are to be placed.
- All subcontractor agreements (second, third, fourth tier) are to be canceled.
- An order to sell all fabricated materials, after offering them to the general contractor first.
- An order to sell any excess materials, after offering them to the general contractor first.

The subcontractor will prepare and send a written "termination claim" to the general contractor within 60 days after termination has occurred, setting forth all monies owed as a result of the termination, with sufficient documentation to support the "claim."

Termination for convenience clauses should be warily viewed by the subcontractor and may be evidence of similar past practices of a particular general contractor.

The arbitration clause

Most contracts now include an arbitration clause. Without such a clause, any claims would have to be litigated—an expensive and time-consuming process. Costs to arbitrate can be considerably less than the cost to litigate, and the local office of the American Arbitration

Association (AAA) can provide a complete listing of all associated costs which are based, among other criteria, on the dollar value of the proposed claim. There are many private alternate dispute resolution companies that can be contacted to provide mediation and arbitration services.

One of the advantages of arbitration is the length of time required to commence and conclude arbitration, which is usually considerably less than the time required to obtain a court date and complete all legal proceedings.

Arbitration clauses, if deleted from a subcontract agreement, force the parties involved in a dispute to litigate. And since litigation costs are so expensive, a claim of moderate value may not be pursued since the legal fees may well exceed the value of the claim. This places the claimant at a distinct disadvantage, and deletion of an arbitration clause should be strongly resisted.

The 1997 edition of A.I.A. A201 document requires mediation as a first step in the dispute resolution process, which, if unsuccessful, is to be followed by arbitration.

Mediation, a nonbinding dispute resolution process, involves the appointment of a professional mediator. By allowing each party to present its case in an open forum, the mediator will then assign each party to a separate room. By using shuttle diplomacy, pointing out the weak and strong points of each party to the dispute, the mediator will attempt to effect a compromise solution.

Parties to the mediation process may call an end to proceedings whenever they wish, at which point filing for an arbitration hearing will be scheduled.

Read the warning label!

Recall that warning on the cover of the American Institute of Architects document:

This document (or contract, as the case may be) has important legal consequences.

A contract is a legal, binding agreement obligating all parties to that contract to certain rights, obligations, and responsibilities. Doesn't it make good business practice to thoroughly understand these rights, obligations, and responsibilities?

3

An Introduction to Bonds and Achieving Bondability

Bonds are a requirement for bidders on public works projects, either as a general contractor or a prime subcontractor. And more and more private project owners are requiring bonds from either their general contractor and/or major subcontractors.

Although many bonding agencies also sell insurance, there is a distinct difference between a bond and an insurance policy. An insurance policy is a loss-funding instrument, and it forecasts the possibility and probability of a loss occurrence by consulting actuarial tables and the insurance company's prior experience in a particular risk. Insurance policies determine the cost of periodic payments (premiums) based upon the amount required to cover any anticipated losses.

A bond, on the other hand, is a loss-avoidance instrument, and its cost is determined by prequalifying the credit strength of a company requesting the bond. A surety bond is an agreement under which the bonding company guarantees to an owner that the contractor or subcontractor will perform the work in accordance with the terms of the contract.

Some Significant Bond Statistics

Between 1994 and 1995, according to figures published by Dun & Bradstreet in mid-1997, there was a 9.8% increase in construction company failures: 9,158 firms failed in 1995, including 3,680 general contractors, 299 heavy construction firms, and 5,179 subcontractors. Liabilities of these failed firms exceeded $1.8 billion. Forty-two percent of the firms that failed in 1995 had been in business for more than 10 years; 28.6% were in business from six to ten years, and 29.4% were in business five years or less.

Bonding companies collected premiums worth $1.208 billion in 1995 but incurred direct losses of $393,587,000 during that period.

If 1996 and 1997 follow the same scenarios, bonding companies will become more selective in their issuance of bonds, and increased rates will also be likely.

In fact, 1997 saw its share of failed construction firms. In mid-1997 one of the country's largest construction companies, San Francisco based F. Guy Atkinson, experienced serious financial difficulties that required their bonding company to step in and insure completion of at least a dozen major projects.

Bond Terminology

Understanding various terms used in the bond community will make it somewhat easier to read and understand these instruments.

Calling the bond—notification to the bonding company that the contractor/subcontractor has failed to live up to its commitment as stated in its bond, and the surety is being requested to provide sufficient funds to cover those unfulfilled commitments.

Consent of surety—when a construction project has been successfully completed and all bills paid, the project owner will be requested by the principal (the contractor) to "sign-off" so that the surety can be notified and the bond can be terminated.

Dual obligee—where two parties have a financial interest in the project such as an owner and a lender.

Guarantor—the underwriter or surety company.

Obligee—the project owner.

Penal sum—the amount of the bond (generally the amount of the contract).

Premium—the cost of the bond.

Principal—the contractor.

Surety—the bonding company (not the insurance agency transmitting the bond).

Various Types of Construction-Related Bonds

Bid bond

By underwriting a bid bond, the bonding company assures the owner of a project that the low bidder, when selected, will be able to fulfill all terms and conditions of the bid and enter into a contract with the owner.

If for some reason the apparent low bidder declines or is otherwise unable to accept the construction contract being offered by the owner, and the second lowest bidder is selected, the bid bond of the low bidder will be forfeited, except in unusual instances.

The funds available from the defaulted contractor's bid bond will be used to compensate the owner for any losses incurred in the award of a contract to the next highest bidder.

For example, assume that several contractors had submitted bids and corresponding bid bonds in the penal sum of 5% of their bid:

Bidder #1–Bid $1,200,000.00	Bid bond required–$60,000.00
Bidder #2–Bid $1,260,000.00	Bid bond required–$63,000.00

For some unjustifiable reason, Bidder #1 declines to accept the contract award when notified that they are the low bidder and the owner awards the contract to Bidder #2 whose price was $60,000.00 higher than Bidder #1. Bidder #1 will forfeit their $60,000.00 bid bond and the surety will be obliged to pay the owner for any damages up to but not exceeding the "penal" sum of the bid bond, i.e., $60,000.00.

In this case, since Bidder #2's price was $60,000.00 higher than Bidder #1, the forfeiture of Bidder #1's bid bond will cover all owner's costs for the award to the second bidder.

But if Bidder #2's quote had been, say, $1,265,000.00, requiring a bid bond of $63,250.00 and the spread between Bidder #1 and #2 was actually $65,000.00, the owner would not be able to recoup all costs, being short by $1,750.00 ($65,000 – $63,250).

If a 10% bid bond had been required, all costs would have been covered under the same scenario—default by Bidder #1—award to Bidder #2.

How a bid bond may possibly be withdrawn with no penalty.   There are some extenuating circumstances whereby a low bidder on a project may be able to decline to accept a contract and not forfeit their bid bond.

Reluctance to accept a bid by the apparent low bidder most frequently occurs when all bids are announced at a public bid opening and the low bid is significantly lower than the next bid, and, in fact, substantially lower than all other bids, which appear to fall within a somewhat narrow range.

The low bidder's first reaction would be that some portion of the work was omitted from their estimate or an arithmetical mistake has been made in extending or totaling items within the estimate.

If the contractor has irrefutable evidence that a mistake had been made during the preparation of its bid, in many cases the public agency may allow the contractor to withdraw its bid and not forfeit its bid bond.

The withdrawal of a bid bond in the face of overwhelming evidence of a serious error in the bid preparation is not automatic, and in many cases, the low bidder may have only two choices: accept the contract and hope for the best or forfeit the bid bond.

It is therefore extremely important for a subcontractor posting a bid bond to keep every scrap of paper, every adding machine tape, and every quote received and incorporated in its bid. Nothing should be discarded until the selection of the bidder has been made and not challenged.

The withdrawal of a bid and accompanying bid bond, with no penalty can also be arranged if the owner changes the conditions of the bid documents after all bids have been received. The low bidder, if so inclined, may decide not to accept a contract based upon these changed bid documents and can request that its bid bond be returned.

The performance bond

The purpose of the performance bond is to protect the owner from the consequences of a contractor or subcontractor's inability to complete the project or their portion of the project as required by the terms of the contract.

If the contractor or subcontractor fails to complete the project in accordance with the terms and conditions of its contract, the owner of the project may invoke the provisions of the performance bond to cover the defaulting contractor's obligations. The owner "calls" the bond.

This performance bond in some instances may be used to satisfy liens placed against the owner's property by various subcontractors or material suppliers that have not been paid by the general contractor, however these unpaid obligations are generally covered by the payment bond.

The payment bond

Under the terms of the payment bond, the underwriter guarantees that the contractor will honor all legitimate invoices relating to work incorporated into the construction project. This includes payment to subcontractors—either prime, second, or third tier—and all other labor, materials, and equipment provided for the project.

What Else Is Available to the Owner to Ensure That All Bills Are Paid?

Retainage, the device by which an owner pays only 90% to 95% of each progress payment, allows the owner to withhold either 10% or 5% of the total project's cost until the owner is satisfied that all work is satisfactorily completed and all bills are paid.

Partial lien waivers indicating that the general contractor has used funds received from a progress payment to pay all subcontractors and suppliers for labor and material incorporated into the project during the previous pay period also assures an owner that money is being dispensed properly.

A final lien waiver submitted by all subcontractors and suppliers and generally augmented by the general contractor's Final Lien waiver also assures the project owner that all payments have been made to all trades working on the job.

It is not unheard of for either a general contractor or a subcontractor to falsify a lien waiver, either an interim or final one because of serious financial problems and the need to take funds from one project to pay vendors on another project.

Needless to say this is a serious matter that may qualify as fraud or false certification of an official document and can lead to criminal prosecution.

The threat of "calling a bond" and, more importantly, the act of carrying out this threat call spell disaster for contractors or subcontractors who, with this blight on their record, will have a difficult time maintaining or increasing their bonding capacity.

Other Types of Bonds

The maintenance bond provides the owner of a project with assurance that the contractor will fulfill his or her obligations to provide maintenance or corrective warranty work during a prescribed period of time. These types of bonds may be required to ensure that the contractor responsible to maintain or repair mechanical or complex electrical systems will be available to do so, or in their absence make provisions for another company to provide these services, especially if either the general contractor or subcontractor is not local to the area of the project.

The supply bond is generally issued to ensure delivery and payment of certain types of materials and equipment that are critical to the completion of the project. A supply bond might be required if a specialized piece of equipment, possibly custom made, is being fabricated in a foreign country where any number of factors could disrupt on-time delivery, including a storm at sea preventing the ship carrying the equipment from delivering it on time; or worse yet, the sinking of the ship or derailment of a train carrying the materials or equipment from the port to the job site. This type of bond is similar to an insurance policy.

License or permit bonds may be required by a government agency prior to the issuance of a license to do business. Many public agencies require that contractors post a bond in order to receive a license to engage in business in a state or municipality. Certain contractors such as road contractors or excavating contractors are often required to post a bond if they plan to work in a public highway. The bond assures the agency that all work will be performed in accordance with its specifications, and if failures occur, the bond is available in case the contractor fails to correct the work as directed by the public agency.

The lien bond indemnifies the project owner against the potential of having liens filed against his or her property. This provision is similar to one in a standard performance bond, but in some states where "no lien" laws are in effect, the lien bond provides the owner with an added measure of security.

Roofing bonds are furnished by the manufacturer of the roofing components or materials and take effect once that manufacturer has inspected the completed roof to ensure that it meets the manufacturer's installation requirements and warranty criteria.

Why Are Bonds So Important?

Mere acknowledgment that a contractor or subcontractor can furnish a bond sets them apart from the field. It establishes a degree of financial strength.

In order to be "bondable," a subcontractor or contractor must have exhibited a series of financial and management strengths.

But there are more tangible reasons for obtaining bonding ability:

1. Required by many general contractors and/or owners as a requisite for being placed on a bidder's list.

2. When bidding public works projects as a prime contractor.

3. Contracting with a construction manager, when bonding is a requirement.

4. Using one's bonding ability to negotiate projects with a general contractor to the exclusion of other subcontractors who are not bondable.

Required by many general contractors

Since the ability to obtain a bond requires a certain degree of financial and managerial expertise, some general contractors require their subcontractors to provide proof of bonding capability. This may take the form of obtaining a letter from the bonding company stipulating that if a bond in the amount of "X" is required for this project, subcontractor "Y" has the ability to provide such a bond.

In many cases the general contractor may only require proof of bondability and not the bond itself.

Subcontractors unable to provide such proof may be excluded from a selected bidder's list. This may be particularly true if the subcontractor is working outside of his or her normal geographic area, or a general contractor from another part of the country comes into the subcontractor's primary working area but is not familiar with that subcontractor's ability to perform the project in question. Some project owners require a general contractor to bond all subcontractors whose contract amount exceeds a certain sum, and many general contractors maintain a similar policy whereby they require any subcontractor whose contract exceeds a predetermined amount to obtain a bond.

An owner acting as his or her own general contractor on a specific project may also require bonds from each subcontractor as added insurance.

Bidding Public Works Projects

Public works agencies require the prime contractor, whether a general contractor or subcontractor, to provide a bid bond, performance, and payment bonds, and, in some cases, maintenance bonds.

Due to the enactment of several laws these requirements are statutory. Various state and federal laws come into play as far as bonding requirements for public works projects.

The Heard Act of 1893 was the first such act legislated by Congress requiring contractors to post bonds when working on federal projects. This act was superceded by the Miller Act, placed into law in 1935 and remaining in effect today.

The Miller Act required a contractor engaged in work involving federal funds to provide a payment and performance bond on all contract work exceeding $25,000.00.

Most states have followed suit and have enacted "Little Miller" laws requiring contractors to provide payment and performance bonds for various types and sizes of state or municipal-funded construction projects.

There are intricacies involved in invoking the Miller Act or "calling" the bond that are best discussed with the company attorney. For example, claimants, such as a subcontractor, having a direct relationship with the general contractor can merely notify the public agency of their desire to "call" the general contractor's bond, but subcontractors or suppliers having no direct relationship with the general contractor must give written notice to the prime contractor within 90 days from the date when the claimant furnished its last item of work in place, whether it be for labor or materials.

New York's Wicks Law

Along with state-enacted "Little Miller" laws, there may be other bits of legislation—either state or municipal—that may require a prime contractor to be bondable in order to bid on public works projects in that state at that time.

In New York, the Wicks Law, enacted in 1921, was done so in an attempt to curb corruption in the construction industry in that state.

This law mandated that for every contract exceeding $50,000.00, there must be several "primes," depending on the nature of the project. One prime was required for the electrical portion of the work, another prime was required for the plumbing work, a third prime was required for the HVAC work, and a fourth prime was required for the general construction work. Some credit this law for the creation of the construction manager inasmuch as these four primes, working without the direction of a general contractor, required some sort of coordinating manager.

Negotiating with a General Contractor in Need of a Bondable Subcontractor

There may be times when a qualified, bondable general contractor is at the upper limits of his or her bonding capacity but wishes to submit a proposal on a project requiring a bid and performance and payment bond.

They may be faced with a dilemma—having a marginal amount of bonding capacity available but not enough to meet the needs of the project at hand.

The general contractor may be able to augment their own bonding capacity by engaging a subcontractor(s) who has the ability to bond portions of their work.

For example, a general contractor may have only $10 million bonding capacity available at the moment but wishes to submit a proposal on a $15 million project requiring a bond. If the mechanical and electrical portions of the work exceed $5 million and the general contractor can contract with subcontractors who can provide bonds for that $5 million portion, then the GC theoretically requires only $10 million of bonding to meet the owner's requirements.

A subcontractor in this position has several advantages: its bid to the GC may be accepted even if it is higher than the competitors, because this subcontractor has something additional to offer—bondability.

This is not to say that the subcontractor should take unfair advantage of its position, but it may offer the subcontractor an opportunity to work with a general contractor that the subcontractor has not been able to work with on several other occasions—for any number of reasons.

Achieving Bondability and Increasing Bonding Limits

The criteria for obtaining bonding capability or increasing bonding capacity rests with the three "C"s—Character—Capital—Capacity. Some bonding companies add another "C"—Continuity (of business).

Character

There are a number of ways in which a bonding company views a company's character.

- Has the company been involved in any litigation defending itself against questionable business practices?

- Has the company been "blackballed" from bidding on any public works projects?

- Has the company failed to complete a project for reasons other than the owner deciding to cancel the work for legitimate reasons?

- Does the company enjoy a good reputation in the industry in the area in which it conducts business?

The bonding company looks for signs that the company is viewed favorably in the contracting and business community in which it operates and is recognized as a company that meets its obligations within a reasonable period of time.

In order to check on character, the bonding company is likely to contact suppliers and other construction companies with whom the company has had business dealings over the years.

Capital

Capital equates to financial stability and depth of financial resources. Bonding companies will generally require contractors to furnish them with financial statements for their last three years of operations. Although they prefer certified, audited statements prepared by Certified Public Accountants (CPAs), if bonding is requested during the current year where a complete, audited year-end statement is not available for that year, an interim statement accompanied by the CPA's opinion letter will often suffice.

In the case of audited statements, the bonding company will also require an accompanying letter from the CPA following the guidelines established by the American Institute of Certified Public Accountants. This letter can take one of four forms:

1. An unqualified opinion—The CPA states that the audited statements comply fully with all generally accepted accounting procedures.

2. A qualified opinion—This type of opinion states that accepted accounting and auditing procedures have been followed in all cases except one, two, or possibly more exceptions, and each exception is spelled out in the letter.

3. Disclaimers—When the auditor cannot vouch for certain data or information upon which to base a conclusion, the accountant will state that examination of the client's financial statement was limited based upon these uncertainties.

4. An adverse opinion—When the CPA is of the opinion that the contractor has not properly presented his or her financial position correctly, this will be so stated in a cover letter.

Obviously the contractor or subcontractor should not attempt to pursue bonding based upon their accountant's intention to write an adverse opinion.

Types of accounting methods used in the construction industry. There are several different accounting methods used by contractors, and bonding companies will scrutinize each method when reviewing a financial statement.

Cash basis—This method of accounting establishes income when it is received and costs and expenses when they are paid.

Accrual basis—Using this method of accounting, income is entered when it is earned with no regard for when expenses or costs are paid.

Percentage of completion—Income is booked by estimating the percentage of completion of a specific construction contract or contracts when work is in progress.

Completed contract approach—Income is reported in the year in which the construction contract work was totally complete or substantially complete and accepted by the client. Using this form of accounting, all costs associated with the project(s) are accumulated, and when compared with the revenue from the project, creates either a profit or loss for that year.

This form of accounting allows the contractor to defer tax consequences, either profit or loss, until the end of the project and not the end of a calendar year.

Bonding companies prefer the percentage of completion or completed contract approach and generally shy away from accepting financial statements based upon the cash or accrual method.

Capacity

The bonding company's investigation of capacity is really a look at the company's human resources, management approach, planning procedures, marketing techniques, and general performance.

The bonding company will request a resume of each key person in the company in order to gain more insight into the technical and managerial experience of these top people. A bonding company will want to review all project manager's resumes and estimator's resumes and learn more about the experience of the personnel in the Accounting Department.

Other factors that will come under scrutiny in evaluating the company's capacity will be:

Estimating procedures—Along with evaluation of the estimators, they will consider the manner in which the estimate is prepared. Do the estimators use customized or standard estimating software, or are estimates prepared manually? How is the company's database of costs assembled? How is it updated? How successful has the company been in obtaining awards? Were their estimates substantially lower than their competitors, or were they within a reasonable range of the other bidder's prices?

Or, if any awards were significantly lower than their competitors', were there justifiable reasons for being substantially lower?

The bonding company will want to know how overhead and profit percentages are established for each particular bid and whether the estimate is reviewed by upper management or a department head before it is released.

All of these questions, and possibly more, will be asked by the bonding company.

The management of the company, on a day-to-day basis, will be another area of investigation, and the bonding company will want to know how daily operations are handled. If top management is involved in every little detail on a daily basis, the bonding company may consider this as a negative factor. Managers must manage—but should avoid micromanaging—lest they miss the "big picture."

The bonding company will want to know who the other key players in the daily operation of the company are, how they interface with each other, how they communicate with each other, and how they appear to get along with each other.

Since costs are of major concern to a construction company, the bonding people will want to see how costs are controlled—how costs are accumulated in the accounting department, to whom they are distributed, how they are reviewed, and what action is taken if these costs appear to be excessive.

Business planning is another key element in the Capacity equation. All businesses need a plan—both short term and long term. The obvious question of succession of both management and ownership in any company is a critical issue; in a small company it is crucial. What happens if the present owner dies or is unable to run the company? Who will assume command?

But beyond the obvious, the bonding company would like to ascertain that some plan has been established for future growth of the company—in either volume or profit or both.

An organizational chart of the present management structure will be required and this chart can be used to incorporate potential additions to the staff as anticipated growth occurs.

For example, if one of the current owners is listed as Estimator/Purchasing Agent and another chart includes a blank space identified as "Future Purchasing Agent" or "Future Estimator" at the same time the current owner-estimator-purchasing-agent is listed as "Vice-President—Operations," this clearly shows that the company is prepared to grow in the future.

The underwriter will be very interested in the company's plans for growth and capacity for additional work since the underwriter is basically concerned about increased corporate stability—both from a management and a financial standpoint.

If the company's operations involve ownership and maintenance of expensive equipment, the underwriter will inspect records to determine if this equipment is being utilized effectively and whether it is being maintained properly. Residual value will be of importance since it adds to or subtracts from the asset base.

Since most construction work is labor intensive and future work depends upon availability of labor, whether a subcontractor is union or nonunion may come into play.

The union subcontractors have the ability to expand or contract their forces by relying on the union hiring hall to either send them more workers or act as a sponge to absorb excess workers during slack periods. Nonavailability of skilled workers will limit a subcontractor's ability to acquire more work. The nonunion subcontractor must be prepared to demonstrate an ability to tap a pool of trained craftsmen if their sales volume suddenly increases.

Obtaining That First Bond

Obtaining the assistance of a professional surety producer is the first step, and if the company's in-house financial person is unfamiliar with methods to locate one, a call can be made to:

National Association of Surety Bond Producers
5301 Wisconsin Avenue, N.W., Suite 450
Washington, D.C. 20015-2015
Telephone: 202-686-3700

When the need to become "bondable" is apparent, the time required to actually obtain a bond is a lengthy one. Bondability is often a key factor in any future business plan and should be considered by all established companies.

The type of information that will be required when a bonding agent is contacted and schedules an initial visit to the company is as follows:

1. An organizational chart containing key employees and their responsibilities.

2. Detailed resumes of the company owners and their key personnel.

3. A business plan outlining the type of work the company presently engages in, how work is obtained (via competitive bidding, negotiated work), geographic area in which the company operates, plans for company growth, and profit objectives.

4. List of recently completed projects, largest projects completed to date, as well as current projects. For those projects currently under construction, names and addresses of client contacts, contract sums, anticipated completion dates, and projected gross profit earned will also be required.

5. Ownership succession plan—how the business will continue if the present principal owner(s) die, are disabled, or decide to retire. Insurance policies for key people naming the company as beneficiary may be required.

6. Supplier and other subcontractor references will be necessary, including contacts, addresses, and phone numbers.

7. Evidence of a line of credit with a bank.

8. Letters of recommendation from general contractors, owners, architects, and engineers with whom the company has worked.

The Financial Statement

Depending upon how long the company has been in business, the surety may wish to see fiscal year-end statements for the past three to five years. Each of these statements must include:

- The accountant's opinion page
- A balance sheet listing assets, liabilities, and net worth
- An income statement that includes gross profit, operating profit, and net profit, before and after taxes
- Cash flow statement
- Schedules of contracts in progress and complete contracts. These schedules for each project ought to contain the following:
  Change orders issued and executed
  Amount billed to date on uncompleted projects
  Costs incurred to date on uncompleted projects
  Revised estimate of the cost to complete the project
  Estimated gross profit
  Anticipated date of completion
- Schedule of general and administrative expenses
- Aging schedules of accounts receivable and payable
- Explanatory notes attached by the accountant to more fully explain anything in these statements that may require clarification or amplification.

Indemnity Agreements

Surety bonds guarantee a company's performance and payment of job-related bills and other obligations, and the contractor is expected to fulfill these obligations.

The bond underwriters will require that the company receiving the bond will sign an indemnity agreement that obligates the company to protect the surety from any loss or expense.

This agreement may take the form of a personal indemnification requiring the posting of personal possessions—the owner's house, automobiles, etc.

The purpose of the indemnification agreement is to insure that the company obtaining the bond will stand fast in the face of a problem relating to potential default and make every effort to resolve any difficulties which may cause the bond to be called.

Calling the Bond

If it becomes necessary to make a claim against a general contractor's bond, the first step is obtaining a copy of all such bonds. When a general contractor has been required to provide a payment and performance bond for either private or public works contracts, the subcontractor should request a copy of the bond. Some general contractors are reluctant to provide copies because they are of the opinion that any subcontractor requesting a copy of his or her bond has a concern that there may be future problems in collecting monies owed.

In the private sector, the general, supplemental, or special conditions will usually contain procedures for proper notification to the bonding company in case of default in payment by the general contractor.

A copy of the general contractor's bond will include the name and address of the bonding company, the broker's name and address, the bond number, and also instructions to follow if a claim is going to be filed.

In the public sector, there may be specific federal, state, or local government regulations and procedures for filing a claim against a bond.

A typical provision, oftentimes included in government bid documents, will read as follows:

Enforcement of right to payment on bond: Suit on bond, procedure and judgment. (a) Any person who performed work or supplied materials for which a requisition was submitted to, or for which an estimate was prepared by, the awarding authority and who does not receive full payment for such in accordance with Subsection (XX) within sixty days after the date such materials were supplied or such work was performed, may enforce his right to payment under the bond by serving a notice of claim on the surety that issued the bond and a copy of such notice to the contractor named as principal in the bond within one hundred and eighty days of the applicable payment date provided.

The notice shall contain the following information:

1. The amount claimed.

2. Name of the party for whom the work was performed or to whom the materials were supplied.

3. A detailed description of the bonded project for which the work or materials were provided.

Notification should be by registered or certified mail and addressed to the surety with a copy to the principal or claimant.

The notification and filing dates may vary from state to state and public project to public project but the basic procedures and information required to file the claim will not vary to any great degree.

When anticipating the filing of a claim against the bond, the contract documents should be thoroughly scanned to ensure that the proper procedures are being followed within the prescribed time frame for such filing.

What is the position of the bonding company when a claim is made?

Similar to insurance companies, sureties are regulated and are required by law to investigate any claims made against their bonds.

Most sureties will thoroughly investigate any claim against the bond and have experienced construction experts on their staff who are trained to not only get the facts but attempt to resolve the issues presented in the claim. If the general contractor is in default on the bond and it appears unlikely that it will be unable to meet its financial commitments and complete the project, the bonding company can take several approaches to this problem:

- They can provide financing to the contractor so that the project can be completed.
- They can take over the project with a replacement contractor.
- They can tender the entire penal sum of the bond to the owner.
- They can allow the obligee (owner) to complete the project with the funds available.

Most sureties will attempt to resolve the issues surrounding the claim if the general contractor is not in such total default requiring the radical measures listed above.

Not all sureties take the same approach to claims resolution. Some will conduct meetings where staff lawyers merely ask enough questions to assess their liability and don't really appear to be searching for some common ground upon which a settlement can be made. Others will act as real problem solvers.

In fact, when selecting bonding companies, it is wise to question them about the techniques they use to settle claims if the situation arises. A bonding company with a large staff of construction experts, engineers, and skilled mediators will serve all parties well if a claim is made.

A competent claim staff will attempt to act as a mediator, and after assembling all of the facts surrounding the claim, try to effect a settlement that is fair to all parties.

Helpful Bond-Related Forms

The following forms will assist contractors in preparing for meetings with the bonding company in anticipation of obtaining bondability:

- Figure 3-1. Contractor's Questionnaire
- Figure 3-2. Status of Contracts Report
- Figure 3-3. Contracts Completed Since Last Report (To be used when bonding capacity is being reviewed or updated)
- Figure 3-4. Bank Reference Letter (sample)

NATIONAL ASSOCIATION OF
SURETY BOND PRODUCERS

Prod
Cont
Acct
Bnkr

CONTRACTOR QUESTIONNAIRE

1. Name of Firm: _____

2. Address: _____ 3. Yr. End (Fiscal) _____

_____ _____ _____
(city) (state) (zip)

4. Phone: ( ) _____ 5. Contracting Specialty: _____

6. Contact Person: _____ 7. Title: _____

8. Year Business Started: _____ 9. Type of Business: ☐ Corp. ☐ Part. ☐ Prop. ☐ Sub. S. Corp.

10. State of Incorporation: _____ 11. Area of Operation: _____

12. List the corporate officers, partners or proprietors of your firm:

Name	Yr. of Birth	Position	Percent Owned	Name of Spouse
A.				
B.				
C.				
D.				
E.				

13. Will the above individuals and spouses personally indemnify Surety? ☐ Yes   ☐ No
If no, explain: _____

14. Is there a buy/sell agreement among the owners of the business?   ☐ Yes   ☐ No

15. Is this agreement funded by life insurance?   ☐ Yes   ☐ No

16. Corp. Indemnity? ☐ Yes ☐ No
17. Cross/Corp Indemnity? ☐ Yes ☐ No

18. How many people does your firm employ? _____ 19. How many work crews? _____

20. Has your firm or any of its principals ever petitioned for bankruptcy, failed in business or defaulted so as to cause a loss to a Surety? ☐ Yes ☐ No.

If yes, please explain: _____

_____

_____

21. Is your firm or any of its owners or officers currently involved in any litigation?
☐ Yes ☐ No. If yes, explain _____

_____

22. What percentage of the firm's work is normally for:

Government Agencies _____% Private Owners _____%

23. What percentage of the firm's work is normally subcontracted: _____%

24. Are bonds required of subs?   ☐ Yes   ☐ No.

Figure 3-1

25. What trades do you normally subcontract? _____

26. What is largest amount of uncompleted work on hand at one time in the past?

        Amount: $_____   Year: _____

27. What is the largest job you expect to do during the next year? $_____

28. What is the largest uncompleted work program expected during the next year? $_____

29. What is your expected annual volume next year? $_____

30. What trades do you normally undertake with your own forces? _____
_____ | **31. SIC CODE:** |

32. Do you lease equipment? ☐ Yes ☐ No   33. Type of lease? _____

    34. What are the terms of the lease? _____
_____

35. Name of your CPA: _____

    Address: _____

    Phone: _____   Contact Person: _____

36. On what basis are taxes paid? ☐ Cash ☐ Completed Job ☐ Accrual ☐ % of Completion

37. On what basis are financial statements prepared? ☐ Cash ☐ Completed Job ☐ Accrual
                                      ☐ % of Completion

38. On what level of assurance are financial statements prepared? ☐ CPA Audit ☐ Review ☐ Compilation

39. How often are financial statements prepared? ☐ Annually ☐ Semiannually
                                        ☐ Quarterly ☐ Monthly

40. Do you have a full time accountant on staff? ☐ Yes ☐ No   41. Yrs. experience _____

42. Are job cost records kept? ☐ Yes ☐ No

    43. How often reviewed? _____   44. How often updated? _____

    45. Do they show job detail? ☐ Yes ☐ No   46. Frequency? _____

47. Name of your Bank: _____

    Address: _____

    Phone: _____   Contact Person: _____

48. Amount of line of credit: $_____ 49. Expiration date: _____ 50. What is interest rate? ___%

    51. UCC Filing? ☐ Yes ☐ No   52. How is credit secured? _____

53. Is your firm union? ☐ Yes ☐ No   54. What is firm's Dun & Bradstreet Number? _____

    55. D & B Rating: _____ 56. Pay Record: _____ 57. Date of Rating: _____

    Remarks: _____
_____

58. Previous Bonding Companies:

Name	Reason for Leaving
A.	
B.	
C.	

59. List five of your largest contracts:

Job Name	Contract Price	Gross Profit	Completion Date	Bonded?
A.	$			☐ Yes ☐ No

    Owner: _____ Design Professional: _____

Figure 3-1 *(Continued)*

B. _____ _____ $ _____ _____　☐ Yes ☐ No

Owner: _____ Design Professional: _____

C. _____ _____ $ _____ _____　☐ Yes ☐ No

Owner: _____ Design Professional: _____

D. _____ _____ $ _____ _____　☐ Yes ☐ No

Owner: _____ Design Professional: _____

E. _____ _____ $ _____ _____　☐ Yes ☐ No

Owner: _____ Design Professional: _____

60. List five of your major suppliers:

Name	Address	Telephone	Contact
A.			
B.			
C.			
D.			
E.			

61. List five subcontractors (or contractors if you are a subcontractor) that you do business with:

A. Name: _____

　　Address: _____ Telephone: _____

　　Contact: _____ Job: _____

B. Name: _____

　　Address: _____ Telephone: _____

　　Contact: _____ Job: _____

C. Name: _____

　　Address: _____ Telephone: _____

　　Contact: _____ Job: _____

D. Name: _____

　　Address: _____ Telephone: _____

　　Contact: _____ Job: _____

E. Name: _____

　　Address: _____ Telephone: _____

　　Contact: _____ Job: _____

62. List three Architects you have done business with:

A. Name: _____

　　Address: _____ Telephone: _____

　　Contact: _____ Job: _____

B. Name: _____

　　Address: _____ Telephone: _____

　　Contact: _____ Job: _____

C. Name: _____

　　Address: _____ Telephone: _____

　　Contact: _____ Job: _____

Figure 3-1 *(Continued)*

63. List key personnel, foremen or supervisors:

	Name	Position	Yr. of Birth	Yrs. Exper.	Previous Employer
A.					
B.					
C.					
D.					
E.					

64. List any life insurance in effect on key personnel:

	Name	Beneficiary	Amount	Cash Value
A.			$	$
	Insurance Company:			
B.			$	$
	Insurance Company:			
C.			$	$
	Insurance Company:			

65. List other insurance coverage currently in effect:

	Limits in '000's		Carrier	Expiration Date
	BI	PD		
A. General Liability:	$	$		
B. Auto Liability:	$	$		
C. Umbrella:	$	$		
D. Owner's Protection:	$	$		

66. List any subsidiaries and affiliates of the contracting firm:

	Firm Name	Ownership	Type Business	NANDA Code
A.				
B.				
C.				
D.				
E.				

REMARKS: _____
_____
_____
_____
_____

Completed by: _____

Title: _____

Date: _____

NASBP Contractor Questionnaire, 2/87 Edition

Copyright 1987 by National Association of Surety Bond Producers

Figure 3-1 *(Continued)*

STATUS OF CONTRACTS REPORT

Contractor: _____

Date of Analysis: _____

Nanda Code: _____

UNCOMPLETED CONTRACTS — BONDED AND UNBONDED

Project Number	Description & Location Name of Owner	Contract Price*	Original Estimated Gross Profit	Billings To Date**	Cost To Date*	Cost To Complete*	Expected Date of Completion

*To include all approved change orders. If cost plus, indicate upset price.
If straight cost plus project with no upset price, circle contract price.

**Requisitions including retainage.

Figure 3-2

CONTRACTS COMPLETED SINCE LAST REPORT

Project Number	Description & Location / Name of Owner	Final Contract Price	Final Cost	Final Gross Profit or Loss	Date Contract Completed	REMARKS
						Signed:

NASBP Status of Contracts Report, 1/88 Edition • Copyright 1988 by National Association of Surety Bond Producers

Figure 3-3

(Date)

Mrs. Karen Miller
John T. Ostheimer Agency, Inc.
16 Elm Place, P.O. Box 1001
Rye, New York 10580

   Re: (Principal)

Dear Mrs. Miller:

The above named contractor opened an account with this bank
in **(month/year)**.

The contractor's average account balance is ($).
His/her present account balance is ($). He/she is a
(Borrower/Non-Borrower) account.

This contractor has a line of credit in the amount of ($..).
The line of credit has an expiration date of (month/day/year)
The present amount outstanding on his/her line of credit is
($..). Credit is extended on a secured/unsecured basis.
Security consists of (please list).

The highest credit ever extended to this contractor was ($..)

**In closing please include any general remarks you may wish to
make)**

Sincerely,

(Bank Officer)
(Title)

Figure 3-4

4

Starting the Project Off on the Right Foot

Once the prebid process has been concluded, the general contractor must begin to "buy out" the project, and low bidders and apparent low bidders will be interviewed in an attempt to define and refine their scope of work and enter into negotiations prior to an award being made.

Revisiting the Bid Documents

Quite often the preparation of a bid can become hectic, and with late-breaking instructions from the general contractors, the issuance of numerous addenda, and architect and engineer clarifications, little time remains to look for the fine points in some of the boilerplate that accompanies the specifications and bidding instructions, much less review the estimate to ensure that everything is included.

Before the commencement of negotiations with the general contractor, it is wise to revisit the bid documents and particularly the General, Supplemental, and Special Conditions portion of the specifications. A quick review may highlight some of the other obligations that will be required by the general contractor and their subcontractors.

Specific Points to Remember

1. On public works projects in particular, specific sections of the specifications will deal with payment terms—not only to general

contractors, but also from general contractors to their subcontractors and from subcontractors to their subcontractors. Several states have enacted laws that require the general contractor to pay their subcontractors within 30 days after receiving payment from the public agency. There are also requirements that subcontractors pay their subcontractors within 30 days after receipt of payment from the general contractor.

Many states have enacted laws stipulating that the "pay-if-paid" clause in construction subcontract agreements is nonenforceable. In other words, if payment is withheld from the general contractor for reasons not related to a subcontractor's performance, that subcontractor is entitled to be paid.

2. A review of the specifications should be made to ascertain whether there is or is not a limitation on working hours. When a project is located in an urban area, oftentimes the owner will place restrictions on the hours when work can start and the hours when work must cease, and may include a restriction on Saturday or Sunday work.

3. Again, when urban projects are involved, it is not unusual for various site parking restrictions to apply. Designated areas for subcontractor parking may not be sufficient for the projected manpower requirements for the project and some provisions for carpooling or the use of public transportation may result in unanticipated additional costs. Restrictions on the size and location of material storage areas may also exist.

4. Tucked away in some obscure place within the bid documents or the specifications may be a statement such as "This Contractor/Subcontractor shall be responsible for all information contained in the Construction Drawings and Specifications as related to their work. If the drawings and specifications conflict, then the greater quantity and/or quality shall apply." Knowing beforehand that this type of restrictive statement is in the bid documents, the subcontractor may wish to further review their estimate and/or qualify their bid when discussing the scope of work with the general contractor.

5. Scheduling is becoming more important to owners and general contractors these days, so look for statements such as, "Should this Contractor or any Trade Contractor be found solely responsible for causing a delay to the Construction Schedule, then said Contractor(s) may be liable for all costs and/or damages in order to expedite the work." And this clause may require that contractor to include costs to expedite the work of other trades that were dependent upon your work to start their own tasks.

6. Unit Prices—occasionally general contractors will "Mix and Match"—including in their bid one subcontractor's low bid and another subcontractor's low unit prices. During negotiations not only base bid costs need to be reviewed but unit prices as well. Remember that the unit prices generally include all fees, both general contractor and subcontractor, so an agreement on equitable unit prices is important. Review the potential for application of unit price work during the course of the project. A low unit price may be disastrous, if accepted by the subcontractor only to find out that due to the nature of the job, substantial units of that work must be undertaken.

7. Subcontractors should check daily cleaning and trash removal requirements, which can result in significant costs, if not already included in the estimate. When daily cleaning is required the cost could be as much as $75–$100 per day and if the project life is one year, this seemingly inconsequential cost could balloon to $19,000 to $25,000 (assuming 255 working days per year). And if the subcontractors become lax in their cleaning operations, the general contractor will most certainly threaten back charges and possibly engage a cleaning service to do this work—for which the lax subcontractor will be obliged to pay.

8. Many projects require attendance by the subcontractor's foreman and/or project manager at weekly project meetings and if there are two or three meetings each week, sufficient time will have to be allocated to meet this contract requirement while maintaining adequate job site supervision of the work in progress.

9. Review of the specifications for requirements to file daily reports with the general contractor, maintaining current "as-built" drawings at the job site should also be made.

10. Layout of one's work may be included in the specifications and if such layout requires the services of a licensed surveyor provisions ought to have been included in the budget for this item.

11. Compliance with OSHA regulations is always included in bid documents, but specific monetary fines for violations such as not wearing a hard hat appear in more and more specifications. Fines of $100.00 for each occurrence, if strictly enforced by the general contractor can be another incentive for the subcontractor to abide by all safety regulations.

Does Anyone Really Read the Specifications?

Most general contractors do not thoroughly read the complete set of specifications, and based upon the writer's experience, many subcontractors do not thoroughly read all applicable sections of their specifications—and many general contractors and owners not only know this but exploit this knowledge!

Years ago, the writer negotiated a $34 million project with a national developer of commercial projects who stated over and over "All I'm asking for is compliance with the plans and specifications—nothing more—nothing less." This seemed like a fair approach and work proceeded on their twin midrise office buildings. The suspended concrete slabs placed on the upper floors of the buildings were of high quality and were level to within $\frac{1}{4}$ inch in ten feet, a respectable quality level for an office building. But this degree of levelness did not comply with the specification requirement of $\frac{1}{8}$ inch per ten feet. After most of the slab work had been completed, the writer had been negotiating a $20,000 change order with the owner for additional finish hardware requirements requested by the architect.

The owner's on-site representative was an experienced professional and, as it developed, attempted to use this concrete slab specification deviation as a ploy to cancel the additional costs for the finish hardware changes.

The concrete specifications required that an "as-built" drawing be prepared after the slabs had been poured to assure compliance with the specification. When this "as built" was presented to the owner's representative, he stated, correctly, that it did not meet the specification requirement of a level factor of $\frac{1}{8}$ inch in ten feet—a degree of levelness highly unusual for office construction. He reiterated, "All I'll ever require is for you to meet the plans and specifications—and you apparently have not—so rip out the slabs and replace them according to the specifications." This was his opening negotiating ploy to cancel out the $20,000 hardware change order, because he did state that the $\frac{1}{4}$-inch levelness could be "tolerated"—if_____!

It occurred to the writer at that time that this is a situation in which many contractors find themselves because they don't read the specifications and are not aware of their complete contract obligation to the owner. It certainly sets up a defensive position that is difficult to defend.

By the way, the client's senior vice president visited the site at about the same time and declared the slabs to be some of the finest he had seen in quite a while. When the writer suggested to the on-site rep that he might not want to contradict his boss on this matter, no credit was given and the $20,000 hardware change order was approved!

But the lesson to be learned is that you should read the applicable sections of the specifications, which may not necessarily cause you to change your bid but will at least make you aware of what might be expected in the way of contractual obligations if called upon to comply fully with the contract.

General Contractor Negotiating Techniques

When interviewing subcontractors, a general contractor's negotiating technique can be as varied as there are shades of gray, but may be categorized into one or more of the following methods:

General Contractor No. 1 will perform a complete review of the contract scope to insure compliance with all aspects of the bid documents. Some general contractors may prepare a Subcontractor Interview form (Figure 4-1) for this purpose and upon completion of the interview have the subcontractor acknowledge, by signature, the agreed-upon scope and price. At the conclusion of the interview, the general contractor may announce that upon reviewing and evaluating other bids, the subcontractor will be notified whether or not he or she is the successful bidder. This is a very straightforward approach to a negotiation—selecting a subcontractor on price and scope compliance.

General Contractor No. 2 will perform a detailed review of each subcontractor's bid, during which the subcontractor is expected to provide breakdowns of their bids so that the general contractor may analyze each bidder's proposal to determine if there are substantial discrepancies in each bidder's quantities. The general contractor, at the conclusion of the interview, may advise the subcontractor that certain portions of the subcontractor's bid appear to be significantly higher or lower than competitors and request that the subcontractor review his or her proposal, make any appropriate adjustments, and so advise the general contractor—another straightforward approach.

General Contractor No. 3 will conduct a negotiation session where the general contractor does not analyze the scope of work, but the purpose of the meeting is merely to have the subcontractor reduce its price. This often results in an award where scope of work becomes an issue as construction progresses because there was no meeting of the minds on scope definition at the time that contract negotiations took place. The purpose of the entire interview was to extract a lower price and the potential for future disputes is inevitable.

General Contractor No. 4 will make an offer without regard to review of scope of work, and this offer appears to be below the subcontractor's cost, but the general contractor will indicate with certainty that he or she has received such a low bid and is giving your company an opportunity to match it. Whether or not the apparent "low bid" is legitimate or not, this approach by a general contractor is generally on a "take it or leave it basis."

SUBCONTRACTOR NEGOTIATION FORM			Page 13 of 16

CONCRETE—SCOPE OF WORK (Cont'd) Including but not limited to the following:

ITEM	YES	NO	EXPLANATION AND/OR COMMENTS
19. Percentage for added work			
20. All work in accordance with local, state laws & regulations			
21. Restoration of damage to property			
22. Equal Employment Opportunity provisions			
23. Scaffolding for own work			
24. Personnel hoist for own work			
25. Contract amount shall include a minimum of two (2) moves of shanties field offices, sheds, etc. Hookup of electric services to be at Subcontractor's expense			
26. Working hours			
27. Stand-by requirements			
28. Perimeter rails —provide—maintain			
29. Rails at interior openings— provide—maintain			
30. Kickboards—install - maintain			
31. Conform to all OSHA requirements not elsewhere assigned to others			
32. Remove stripped lumber from floors daily			
33. Off-site disposal of rubbish and firewood			
34. Load rubbish onto containers provided by			
35. Project Work Rules			
36. CGL Insurance to include X, C & U coverage			
CLEANUP & PROTECTION			
1. Broom-clean slabs prior to placing fill and finish			

Figure 4-1a

SUBCONTRACTOR NEGOTIATION FORM			Page 14 of 16
CONCRETE—SCOPE OF WORK (Cont'd) Including but not limited to the following:			
ITEM	YES	NO	EXPLANATION AND/OR COMMENTS
2. Broom-clean slabs after stripping and removing forms			
3. Clean concrete from inserts, slots, reglets etc.			
4. Cut off nails, ties, etc.			
5. Concrete spillage, drippings, etc., to be removed immediately from adjacent surfaces of stairs, walls, bricks, etc.			
6. When floors are being added to existing building, protect existing areas from splashing concrete			
7. Protect stair nosings during concrete placement			
8. Flush form with water or air before placing concrete			
9. Provide protection above & below men working in shafts			
WINTER PROTECTION			
1. Heated concrete			
2. Provide temporary enclosures & heat			
3. Snow removal inside building site			
4. Protect subgrade against freezing			
5. Covering & protecting foundation concrete against freezing			
6. Curing blankets—furnish, place, and remove			

Figure 4-1b

This general contractor is one to be wary of.

- They may be in trouble on this project, having submitted an unrealistically low bid in order to obtain a contract, and are faced with the prospect of enhancing whatever profit, if any, included in their bid—at the expense of any subcontractor willing to work at any price.

- Their purchasing agent is either lazy or inexperienced, or both, probably one who knows little about the project at hand and even less about the technique of negotiations.

- This general contractor may actually have a subcontractor's bid that, when compared to other bids, is unrealistically low, but the general contractor is willing to gamble that somehow this subcontractor will complete his or her work, or at least a major portion of it before going out of business.

Of the four above techniques, only numbers 1 and 2 can be considered professionally conducted interviews where the general contractor was truly concerned about selecting a qualified subcontractor who was fully aware of what is to be expected of him or her prior to the issuance of a subcontract agreement. The other two techniques will, more than likely, only lead to future misunderstandings, disputes and potential claims.

Events That Lead to Potential Disputes

1. The subcontractor did not receive or review any other drawings than those specifically pertaining to their trade. For example, the miscellaneous metal subcontractor did not receive copies of site plans, which may have revealed stair rails or abrasive nosings on exterior stairs. The mechanical subcontractor did not receive electrical drawings that may have contained improper circuiting, voltage, and amperage for the required equipment. Vice versa, the electrical contractor may not have received the mechanical drawings.

2. The subcontractor did not review any General, Supplementary or Special Conditions to the contract and was not aware of other contract responsibilities for which they normally are not responsible. Assuming, for example, while it may have been customary to have the general contractor trench and backfill for a particular trade, the bid documents require the appropriate subcontractors to perform this work with their own forces.

3. The subcontractor did not acknowledge receipt of any addenda or bid clarifications issued during the bid process and therefore has not included costs for same in its bid, but failed to qualify its bid accordingly.

4. Unit prices were not furnished as requested, nor was the subcontractor aware that the general contractor was obliged to include several unit prices related to the subcontractor's trade in his or her bid to the owner. The subcontractor did not understand that each unit price was to include their overhead and profit when this work was required and when unit price work is omitted from the contract, the credit due the contractor is unit price less 10 or 15%.

5. The subcontractor did not fully understand the nature of the Alternates to the Bid and therefore did not either include subcontractor cost, or included incomplete or lower costs than required. The subcontractor failed to indicate that the price for Alternate work would remain valid for only a specific time, say 3–4 months after contract award and failing to do so must honor the price for the entire length of the contract.

6. The subcontractor did not include permit fees as required by the bid documents, or failed to qualify his or her bid accordingly.

7. The subcontractor was unaware of the insurance requirements for the project at hand and these requirements are higher than they normally provide, or these requirements are so excessive that they can only be obtained at a substantial additional cost.

8. The subcontractor was not aware that the project was tax exempt and therefore included sales tax in his or her bid, or, conversely, did not include sales tax, assuming the project was tax exempt.

9. The subcontractor was not aware of retainage requirements that were more stringent or more lax than normal.

10. The subcontractor was unaware of the project's schedule requirements and either included escalation of labor, material and equipment costs, based upon one assumption, or failed to include these costs based upon another project completion date.

11. The subcontractor took exception to certain portions of work, but failed to qualify them in his or her bid or otherwise advise the general contractor.

12. The subcontractor's bid included an assumption that "or equal" products would be acceptable, without providing the general contractor with specific information about what they considered "or equal" products.

13. The subcontractor was not advised by the general contractor that requisitions for materials and equipment stored off-site could not be honored.

14. The subcontractor was not aware of any restrictions on allowable overhead and profit percentages for change orders.

15. The subcontractor was not advised by the general contractor, nor did the bid documents indicate, a billing and payment schedule.

All to often these topics are not addressed by either general contractor or subcontractor during the bid, bid review or negotiation process and represent many of the reasons for disruptive and costly disputes and claims.

It is important that subcontractors are familiar with all of the bid requirements prior to the submission of their bids, and this can only be achieved by a thorough reading and understanding of the bid documents.

Some Pitfalls to Avoid When Negotiating with a General Contractor

- A general contractor may have used one subcontractor's base bid but another subcontractor's unit prices or alternate prices in order to achieve the lowest combination. These situations should be addressed during the bid review process.

- Request, or at least have access to, a complete set of bid documents, plans and specifications, for review prior to the general contractor's bid interview.

- Don't assume that product or equipment substitutions will be acceptable unless specifically discussed with the general contractor at bid time.

- Inquire as to whether one's bid is competitive or not. Often a general contractor will not provide this information unless asked, and even then may be reluctant to discuss other subcontractor bids. But if they do, it may be an indication of an improperly prepared bid (errors when multiplying unit costs, duplication of costs, incorrect interpretation of scope of work, etc.) that can be quickly corrected so that a revised bid can be submitted.

- With respect to alternates, ascertain when the owner must either accept or decline to accept the alternates. Obviously beyond a certain point in time, it becomes more costly to implement an alternate without requiring retrofitting and incurring labor, material and equipment cost increases.

The Preconstruction Conference

Most general contractors will conduct a preconstruction conference prior to the start of construction. This may take the form of Subcontractor Meeting No. 1 or a separate meeting in which the general contractor's game plan is discussed and questions are solicited from all attendees.

A detailed construction schedule is generally presented and reviewed by the general contractor at that time if such a schedule was not furnished as part of the bid documents. All subcontractors attending these meetings should be well prepared, having thoroughly reviewed all of the contract documents and developed a list of questions and/or clarifications with respect to these documents or to the general contractor's method of handling day-to-day issues. This may be the first time that the firm has worked for a particular general contractor, and a professional first impression is in order—one that indicates that your company not only knows its portion of work thoroughly, but also fully understands its obligations under the terms and conditions of its subcontract agreement.

The subcontractor's project manager and supervising foreman should attend these preconstruction meetings to not only meet the general contractor's project team, but to meet their counterparts from other subcontracting firms hired for the project. It is important to keep detailed notes of this meeting and all subsequent meetings.

The topics generally to be reviewed at the preconstruction meeting:

1. All general contractor team members will be identified and introduced and, in turn, each subcontractor will introduce his or her team members and indicate which part they will play in the construction project.

2. The project schedule will be reviewed and the general contractor will usually ask for comments from each subcontractor regarding the time allotted for their various work tasks and confirmation that their work sequencing is proper. The general contractor should review these comments when received and incorporate them into his or her schedule, if they feel it is appropriate, after which the Baseline Schedule will be prepared and formally issued to the architect. The importance of the Baseline Schedule cannot be dismissed and is fully explained in Chapter 8—"Understanding the Construction Scheduling Process."

3. Review of shop-drawing submission procedures, number of copies, stamps required, requirements for substitution/"or equal" requests.

4. Change-order procedures, along with the change-order format, allowable percentages for overhead and profit, and, hopefully, procedures for field changes. If the general contractor does not broach this subject, the subcontractor should. If Field Order forms have been developed by your firm, bring one along for review and acceptance by the general contractor. (See Figure 4-2, Sample Field Order Form.)

Field Instruction

Date:_____   Order Number:_____

Job Name:_____   Job Number:_____

1. This Field Instruction, (F.I.) is issued for the purpose of:

    ___ Requesting an estimate
    ___ Directing work be performed
    ___ Directing work be stopped
    ___ Other_____

A general description of the work situation involved here is as follows:

_____
_____
_____
_____

                Signed:_____

IF IN THE SUBCONTRACTOR'S OPINION THIS F.I. INVOLVES WORK WHICH INCREASES THE CONTRACT AMOUNT, OR TIME OF PERFORMANCE, HE SHALL NOT PROCEED UNTIL SECTION 2 OR 3 IS COMPLETED BELOW.

2. The Contractor and Subcontractor acknowledge this F.I. will result in an increase/decrease/no change to the Subcontractor's Contract Price. The Subcontractor is hereby directed to proceed with the work on the following basis:

    ___ Detailed estimate is accepted in the lump sum amount of $_____
    ___ Time and material plus overhead and profit as called for in the Subcontractor/Contractor Agreement
    ___ Unit Price
    ___ The approximate estimate is accepted with supporting details and exact price to follow within 7 days

            Amount of approximate estimate $_____
    ___ Other

              Signed: _____

         Signed and Accepted: _____
                      Subcontractor Rep.

3. The Contractor hereby directs the Subcontractor to perform the Work described above at no change in Contract Price on the basis that the Work is included in the original Contract.
              Signed: _____

4. The Work will not be performed.

5. The final amount of this F.I. which will be processed as a Change Order is:

     Signed: _____ $_____

Note: Whenever time and material work is to be performed, daily work tickets must be presented to the Project Superintendant for signature. Failure to do so may result in rejection of payment request.

COPY: Office   Subcontractor   Field

Figure 4-2

5. Establish a procedure for submission of Requests for Information (RFIs) and Requests for Clarification (RFC) and how these documents are to be expedited if necessary. Figure 4-3 is a sample Request for Information (RFI) form.

6. If necessary, present a written list of questions/clarifications developed to date having to do with the plans, specifications or subcontract agreement. Request a written response within an appropriate period of time.

7. Review the status of your company's manpower requirements during the length of the project and discuss any material/equipment delivery concerns that may affect the overall construction schedule.

8. If the general contractor has not prepared a site logistics plan, inquire about areas in which field office and material storage trailers can be placed. What site security measures the general contractor plans to employ, if any. Request specific areas for on-site stored materials and inquire about how much space will be allotted for these stored materials. Will adequate provisions be made for site accessibility for trucks, cranes, and other large pieces of equipment?

9. If daily cleaning is required and rubbish is to placed in dumpsters provided by the general contractor, inquire about the location of these dumpsters.

10. Inquire about normal working hours and if work can be performed after or before these normal working hours. (The general contractor may require that their superintendent be present whenever workers are on site and they may be reluctant to have their super work beyond a certain number of hours per week.)

11. Although this meeting occurs prior to start of construction, the general contractor will most likely review project closeout procedures, which may include daily preparation of as-built drawings and submission of various daily reports to be incorporated into the final project documents.

12. The requisitioning process will be explained—when each subcontractor is to submit his or her requisition, the documentation required along with his or her submission, anticipated payment and disbursement dates, and the requirement for lien waivers.

13. The contractor's safety program will be discussed, along with the general contractor's intent to strictly enforce the use of hard hats and personal protective clothing. Attendance at weekly Tool Box Talks and any other key provisions of their program will also be reviewed.

Frank Mercede & Sons, Inc.
700 Canal Street
Stamford, CT 06902
203-967-2000

Request for Information #00001
Dimensional Clarifications

Project: Westover Elementary School   Job: 2125
Fletcher Thompson
Two Lafayette Square   February 28, 1997
Bridgeport, CT 06604

In Reference To RFI/FT/00001

Enclosed are three RFI's regarding dimensional clarifications from our steel subcontractor. Upon our review we need the input from your designer.

Requested by: Frank Mercede & Sons, Inc.

Signed: _____
    By: Ken Friedrichsen
    Date: _____

ANSWER

Answered by: Fletcher Thompson

Signed: _____
    By: Jerry Czubatyz
    Date: _____

Figure 4-3

14. Submission of a detailed Schedule of Values may be required prior to submission of the first application for payment. Determine the format and details required for this submission. (Remember this will be used by the general contractor for approval of all future applications for payment so it should be accurate and reflect the way in which it is expected that work will be reimbursed.)

15. If the contract is for a public works project, review the payroll forms relating to certified payroll reporting. Did the company receive a copy of the Prevailing Wages Schedule according to the provisions of the Davis-Bacon Act? If not request one.

16. Are there specific Equal Opportunity requirements relating to minority hiring practices? If so become familiar with all such requirements.

17. Copies of interim and final lien waiver forms should be distributed by the general contractor and the submission process reviewed.

18. A review of both Allowance and Alternate items in the contract need to be discussed. Will they be accepted/rejected by the owner, and if so, when?

The Letter of Intent in Lieu of a Subcontract Agreement

The general contractor, in an attempt to ensure a rapid start to construction may, on occasion, express a desire to have the subcontractor proceed with the work with either a verbal commitment or by acknowledgment of a Letter of Intent. With tens or even hundreds of subcontract agreements and material and equipment purchase orders to issue, it is often difficult for a general contractor to prepare all of these written agreements in a timely fashion, and the quick preparation of a Letter of Intent may satisfy the general contractor's requirements, but is it a secure instrument for the subcontractor?

Favorable past relationships with a general contractor may have dictated that it is sufficient for a subcontractor to proceed on either a verbal agreement or a terse Letter of Intent. But there is always the possibility that management will change and with it corporate policy— so be aware of what constitutes an acceptable letter of intent and what does not. And to be on the safe side, even though past relationships with a general contractor have been trouble-free, take the added precaution of confirming a verbal agreement in writing; this should not offend the general contractor.

As far as a Letter of Intent is concerned, there is a proper way to prepare one, and there are others that offer the subcontractor little or no protection.

Letters of intent that do not protect the subcontractor

Example 1

Please proceed with the submission of all shop drawings pertaining to the Westfield Hospital Maternity Ward project. A formal contract will be forthcoming within two weeks.

What's wrong with this Letter of Intent?

First of all, in order to obtain shop drawings, firm orders must be placed with suppliers thereby committing your firm to the issuance of your purchase orders without the benefit of corresponding commitments from the general contractor. Secondly, what is the specific scope of work to be undertaken—all shop drawings? What about reimbursement of profit and office overhead if something goes awry and work does not continue?

Example 2

Pursuant to the issuance of a formal contract, you are authorized to proceed with the work contained in the contract documents for the Chestertown Pharmaceutical Corporation project located on High Street, Chestertown, Maryland.

What's wrong with this one?

Are you convinced that you fully understand the scope of work to be included in the contract and have you reviewed all of the contract documents that may be included in the contract when issued? Once again, your firm is being requested to commit certain human resources and dollars to a project without a full understanding of the exact nature of the work being requested and exact terms of compensation for work performed, unless they have been agreed upon. And if that is the case, why not include these terms in the Letter of Intent?

Example 3

This letter represents a Notice to Proceed to allow (Subcontractor) to proceed with all of the work included in Division (X) of the contract documents. A formal subcontract agreement will be prepared and submitted to your office within the next thirty (30) days.

Why is this Notice to Proceed not adequate protection for your firm?

A Notice to Proceed is generally issued after a contract is executed, not before. You may have taken issue with some of the provisions of

Division (X), but once work proceeds based upon this Notice to Proceed, won't your bargaining power be decreased since work started without having taken exception to any of the provisions of Division (X)?

And, of course, in all three examples there is no mention of compensation if a subcontract agreement is not finalized, but some work had already started—i.e., no mention of cancellation and compensation procedures.

A proper Letter of Intent should specify the exact, more or less, tasks that are to be performed by the subcontractor, during a specified length of time, and the compensation that will be made after these tasks have been completed. For example:

October 25, 1998

Subcontractor X is hereby authorized to submit structural steel shop drawings to include joist and metal deck drawings in accordance with Specification Division 0550 and Drawings S-101 through S-123, dated September 25, 1998, prepared by Abbott Engineering, Inc. These drawings are to be submitted not later than November 25, 1998, prior to which time it is anticipated that a formal subcontract agreement shall be issued and fully executed.

The total cost of these drawings, to include the contractor's overhead and profit, shall not exceed $150,000.00 and will be paid by the undersigned upon presentation, review, and acceptance of these shop drawings by the engineer not later than November 25, 1998. Please acknowledge acceptance of this Letter of Intent not later than October 28, 1998.

Charles Jourdan, Vice President

Triple A Construction Company

Dealing with Shop Drawings

One quality in a subcontractor that is of considerable importance to a general contractor is the way in which the subcontractor approaches the task of submitting shop drawings. They must be submitted promptly and in the proper manner.

The first step in the process is to read that section of the specifications pertaining to shop drawing submissions. A Shop Drawing Submission Checklist is helpful in determining what is required for the job at hand, since these requirements can vary considerably from job to job.

Although it may appear to be proper and expedient to accept shop drawings from equipment and material suppliers and merely pass them on to the general contractor for approval, a critical interim step is required—review these drawings for completeness and conformance to the contract requirements.

Any changes required can be determined at this time and if a firm price with the vendor has been negotiated and the equipment or material fails to meet the contract requirements, additional costs may be avoided if this correction is made now not several weeks later.

The shop drawing log

The general contractor may require the submission of a shop drawing log that lists not only the anticipated date of submission of the shop drawing but also the expected delivery of the equipment or material once an approved shop drawing is received from the architect and/or engineer.

Caution: Approach this process promptly and accurately.

The general contractor will undoubtedly incorporate each subcontractor's shop drawing submission dates and subsequent material/equipment delivery dates into its overall project schedule. This schedule will display events that are to occur prior to and subsequent to the delivery of key materials and equipment and the general contractor will rely on accurate information when preparing and transmitting a schedule to the owner, architect and other key subcontractors. If delays in shop drawing submissions occur and material and equipment deliveries are delayed as a result, these delays may affect the performance of other subcontractors and the overall construction schedule. No doubt the general contractor will hold the subcontractor(s) who deviated from the schedule responsible and assess that subcontractor(s) all costs to accelerate their work and the work of other affected subcontractors.

After reviewing the appropriate specification section, some subcontractors find it easier to create a checklist to ensure compliance with the specific requirements of the project at hand. A typical checklist is set forth in Figure 4-4. This form can be customized to fit the subcontractor's individual requirements.

Starting off on the right foot is often as simple as becoming familiar with the current project's contract requirements. By taking the time to gain familiarity with these contract requirements, the subcontractor that does so not only sets off on a path of Total Quality Management but displays the degree of professionalism that is not lost on either the project owner or the general contractor.

Shop Drawing Submittal Check List

Project: _____

Project No.: _____

	Yes	No
1. Review specification section	_____	_____
2. Review submittal specification section	_____	_____
3. Schedule of shop drawing submittals required?	_____	_____
4. Certification stamp required?	_____	_____
5. Number of copies required	_____	_____
Plans _____		
Catalog sheets _____		
6. Procedures for submission of samples?	_____	_____
Number _____		
Size _____		
7. Procedures for submission of "or equals"	_____	_____
8. Material Safety Data Sheets (MSDS) required?	_____	_____
9. Procedures for resubmission of drawings?	_____	_____
10. Requirement that sub. pay A/E for other than 1st review?	_____	_____
11. Does "Revise and Resubmit" allow for release of matls/equip?	_____	_____
12. Will partial submissions be allowed?	_____	_____

Figure 4-4

5

Safety

It Pays

The Safety Record in the
Construction Industry

In the early 1980s, the construction industry in the United States was rife with accidents and injuries. Work-related injuries were 54% higher than other industries, making it one of the most hazardous workplaces in the country.

Direct and indirect costs to the industry were calculated at $8.9 billion dollars (1979 dollars), resulting in reduced productivity, delays in completing projects, increased administrative time, and damage to equipment.

Between 1980 and 1987, workman's compensation costs in the United States doubled, presenting the industry with a $5.26 billion bill (1989 dollars).

Something had to be done, and pressure from clients and scores of contractors and the public at large, brought safety professionals into the forefront of an industry sorely in need of their expertise. Their efforts began to pay off.

Department of Labor studies revealed that 1995 was the second consecutive year in which injuries in the construction industry fell below those in the manufacturing sector. The development and administration of effective contractor organized in-house safety programs, coupled with better worker training programs and federal and state OSHA program enforcement had a dramatic effect on the construction industry.

Although some of the more dramatic decreases in job-related illnesses and injuries may have come about by underreporting in previous years, the improvements in construction safety have been
impressive.

1987	1988	1989	1990	1991	1992	1993	1994	1995
*14.7	14.6	14.3	14.2	13	13.1	12.2	11.8	10.6

*Refers to rate of illnesses/injuries per 100 full-time workers

The U.S. Labor Department's Bureau of Labor Statistics in early
1998 reported that 1996 figures revealed that construction related
illnesses/injuries per 100 full-time workers dropped even further to
9.9 cases.

But construction still retains the dubious honor of having the second
worst safety record of any goods producing sector of the U.S. economy.
Manufacturing continued to rank No. 1 with 10.6 illnesses/injuries per
100 full-time workers.

Worker's age a factor

Worker age, as reported in a June 1997 article in the *Wall Street
Journal*, was seen as a contributory factor in the frequency of accidents. Older workers were found to be five times more likely to have a
fatal transportation related accident and 3.8 times as likely to be
killed by objects and equipment. These death rates existed across all
industry lines.

Age	Fatality Rate
15-19	4.85
20-24	4.9
25-34	4.95
35-44	5.0
45-54	5.1
55-64	7.0
65+	19

Five hundred and thirty six (536) of the 21,000 serious injuries
among older workers in 1994 resulted from climbing ladders and falls
accounted for 13% of older worker deaths as compared with a 10%
fatality rate for all workers. It would therefore appear that older
workers in the workforce need additional training and monitoring in
order to administer an effective safety program.

Why have these accident rates been dropping?

Increase in training—both quality and quantity is the answer.

Some union collective bargaining agreements include provisions for funding their own safety programs. For example, the carpenter's union instituted training safety instruction in 1993 which was designed to familiarize their members with the new OSHA scaffolding standards. And nonunion contractors are spending substantial sums of time and money on safety training, aided by their various trade organizations. Research shows that most injuries occur during the worker's first months on the job, and most accidents occur in firms employing less than 1,000 workers, so particular attention is being paid to these situations.

An awareness of a shortage of skilled construction workers in the workforce has been apparent for years and these shortages are slowly reaching the critical stage. Loss of a skilled worker, either temporary or permanent, resulting from an accident or job-related illness will be sorely felt by those contractors depending upon productive crews to get the job done, and this is adding impetus to the need for effective administration of a safety program.

Contractor and owner awareness of positive effects of a good safety record

A significant side benefit of a good safety record is lower costs—in the field and in the office. Lower costs can be transposed into lower overhead costs and can play a key role in the preparation of a project's estimate. High insurance costs can add several percentage points to a contractor's overhead, or conversely, shave several points off of the corporate overhead; these two or three percentages points, one way or another may be the determining factor in winning a bid.

Research and dissemination of information developed by the insurance industry

Insurance companies have a major stake in the effort to attempt to halt runaway premium costs and they are gathering and passing on to their contractor clients' reams of statistical data regarding the types and occurrence rate of various job-related injuries. Some insurance companies conduct studies on topics as varied as slip resistant materials in order to determine exercise regimens to assist workers in avoiding or lessen the severity of job related injuries.

Better communications between Department of Labor and the industry

OSHA has become more "user-friendly" in recent years, and under the direction of a new deputy director, the word has gone out to not only enforce compliance with OSHA regulations during a field inspection, but also to apply some commonsense standards and attempt to create a less adversarial relationship with the contractor.

Safety on the job site has many facets:

- Humanitarian—prevention of accidents to improve quality of life on the job site.

- It's the Law—OSHA regulations must be enforced to comply with various state and federal laws and programs.

- Retain Productivity—preventing the loss of key personnel or productive work groups resulting from a disabling injury.

- It pays!

Safety Pays?

Beside the obvious answers—desire to reduce pain and suffering of workers on the job site and the avoidance of fines levied by OSHA, there is a definite "bottom line" approach to safety that can affect year-end profit and loss statements—either positively or negatively.

Worker's compensation insurance costs can impact the company's overall profitability by either increasing or decreasing corporate overhead. If a company's desire is to keep corporate overhead to a bare minimum so as to remain competitive in the marketplace—attention must be paid to accident-related insurance costs.

Take a case in point. The writer contracted with a structural steel fabricator and erector in New England that had a rather poor workman's compensation rating of 1.4 which meant that its accident record was 40% higher than the average for their trade. One of their recent projects, however, required them to abide by very strict safety rules included in their subcontract agreement with a safety conscious general contractor. Among many other safety rules and regulations they were required to provide all ironworkers with safety belts when working above 6 feet off the ground. And this regulation was strictly enforced.

Although there was a great deal of opposition from these wild and wooly ironworkers, these safety rules were strictly enforced. The management of the steel subcontracting firm recognized the merit in these regulations and adopted them into their own safety program. Since modification rates are based upon claims over a three-year period it took their firm some time to work off their poor injury record, but they were determined to do so.

By 1966 their ironworkers had worked 225,000 hours without one day lost to injury.

The company's worker's compensation rating dropped from 1.4 to 0.75—and as a result they have saved millions of dollars in insurance premiums and have become more competitive in the process.

Worker's Compensation Insurance

Although worker compensation laws are governed by individual states and their provisions vary from state to state, three factors remain more or less constant in calculating insurance premiums.

Experience Modification Rate (EMR)—a multiplier that is calculated based upon past insurance experience of the individual or company policyholder and is used to forecast future benefit payments to employees who have filed insurance claims.

Manual Rate—the insurance premium rate based upon the type of work performed. Various trades are classified into "families" referred to as classification codes, which are assigned four digit numbers. Each classification code has a corresponding premium rate based upon worker accident claim experience for that trade.

Payroll units—a figure derived by dividing an employer's total annual direct labor costs by 100.

Worker's Compensation Insurance Premiums (WCIP)—obtained by using the following formula:

$$WCIP = EMR \times Manual\ Rate \times Payroll\ Units$$

The following hypothetical spreadsheet vividly displays how a good experience modifier can dramatically reduce insurance costs:

A Typical Insurance Cost Breakdown Reflecting the Effects of Good Safety

Class	Payroll	Dev. Rate	*Safe* Premium	*Normal* Premium
	ABC Construction Company–Insurance Cost Breakdown			
Clerical	$ 100,000	0.38	$ 380	$ 380
Sales	100,000	0.90	900	900
Carpenters	$1,000,000	14.50	145,000	145,000
Executives	200,000	6.80	13,600	13,600
Raw Total			$ 159,880	$ 159,880
Experience modifier			0.77	1.00
			$ 123,107	$ 159,880
State assessment (17.5%)			+ 21,554	+ 27,979

Table (*Continued*)

Premium discount (24.5)	– 30,385	– 0
Premium before dividend	$ 114,367	$ 0
*Premiums derived from good safety experiences		
Divident (30%)	– 34,310	– 0
Total insurance cost	**$ 80,057**	**$ 187,859**

Safety does pay—savings resulting from an effective safety program in this hypothetical illustration amounted to $107,802. Now have your accountant determine how much contract work would have been required to generate this much additional corporate profit.

The Leading Causes of Job-Site Fatalities

OSHA lists the most frequently encountered violations to assist the subcontractor in "zeroing" in on those areas.

- Falls—33%
- Struck by equipment—22%
- Trenching and excavation—18%
- Electrical—17%

The Department of Labor's OSHA Division

Enforcement activity is on the rise in OSHA after a period of budget cuts that severely hampered their operations over the past several years.

In 1997, however, OSHA ratcheted up their inspections in the construction industry and conducted 10,000 more such inspections than the previous year. Of the 34,264 inspections conducted that year, 25,939 were safety inspections, 7675 stemmed from complaints, and 1,201 were accident related.

OSHA reported 83,710 violations, 53,995 of which were classified as "serious."

OSHA fines can be severe and each contractor should periodically review their operations to insure that they have a safe job site and comply with all reporting requirements. Repeated violations of the same nature will result in substantially increased fines.

The following list of the 25 most frequently cited OSHA construction-related violations includes the corresponding paragraph section of the OSHA CFR 1926 manual referencing the subject:

1. Unprotected sides and edges [1926.501(b)(1)]

2. Safety training and education—Employer responsibility [1926.21 (d)(10)]

3. Scaffolding—Tubular welded frame scaffolds [1926.451(d)(10)]

4. Head protection [1926.100(a)]

5. Wiring design and protection—Ground Fault Protection [1926.40 (b)(1)]

6. Requirements for protective systems—protection in excavations [1926.652(a)(1)]

7. Scaffolding—General requirements [1926.451(a)(13)]

8. General health and safety—accident prevention responsibilities [1926.20(b)(2)] (Employer instituted program to provide for frequent job site inspections)

9. Hazard Communication—written hazard communication program [1926.59(e)(1)]

10. General health and safety—accident prevention responsibilities [1926.20(b)(1)] (Employer responsibility to initiate and maintain all OSHA required programs)

11. Wiring methods—temporary wiring [1926.405(a)(2)]

12. Wiring design and protection—grounding [1916.404(f)(6)]

13. Fall protection training program [1926.503(a)(1)]

14. Ladder use [1926.1053(b)(1)]

15. Excavations —General Requirements—Inspections [1926.651(k)(1)]

16. Stairways—Stairrails and handrails [1926.1052(c)(1)]

17. Scaffolding—General Requirements [1926.451(a)(4)]

18. Fall protection—holes [1926.501(b)(4)]

19. Excavations—General Requirements—Access and egress [1926.651 (c)(2)]

20. Housekeeping [1926.25(a)]

21. Excavations—Protection of employees from loose rock or soil [1926.651(j)92]

22. Electrical—Identification, splices, and terminations [1926.405(g)(2)]

23. Roofing work on low slope roofs [1926.501(b)(10)]

24. Residential construction [1926.501(b)(13)]

25. Hazard Communication—employee information and training [1926.59(h)]

Note the general categories of these 25 most frequent violations:

- Electrical—4
- Excavation work—5
- Failure of employer to provide proper training—6
- Scaffolding and ladder work—4

The Focused Inspection

On October 1,1994 OSHA initiated its Focused Inspections Initiative, another attempt by that agency to become more "user-friendly." The purpose of the Focused Inspection is to assist responsible contractors and subcontractors who have implemented effective safety programs. Regular OSHA inspections are in-depth and address all areas and classes of hazards on a construction site. The Focused Inspection places inspection emphasis on the four leading causes of death:

- Falls from elevated areas
- Struck by an object or machine
- Caught in/between
- Electrical hazards

These four categories comprise 90% of all construction fatalities. Figure 5-1 (Construction Focused Inspections Initiative) and Figure 5-2 (Construction Focused Inspection Guideline) include more detail on this comprehensive program and additional information can be obtained by contacting the local OSHA office.

The Five Most Frequently Cited OSHA Reporting and Paperwork Violations

1. Failure to provide the log and summary of occupational injuries and illnesses.
2. Failure to adhere to the general duty clause of the OSHA Act (a citation based upon no specific violation or a citation issued after a previous one had been ignored).
3. Failure to report a fatality or multiple hospitalization incidents.
4. Failure to record occupational injuries and illnesses on the Supplementary Record form.
5. Failure to record and report occupational injuries and illnesses on the required OSHA Log form.

CONSTRUCTION FOCUSED INSPECTIONS INITIATIVE

Handout for Contractors and Employees

The goal of Focused Inspections is to reduce injuries, illness and fatalities by concentrating OSHA enforcement on those projects that do not have effective safety and health programs/plans and limiting OSHA's time spent on projects with effective programs/plans.

To qualify for a Focused Inspection the project safety and health program/plan will be reviewed and a walkaround will be made of the job site to verify that the program/plan is being fully implemented.

During the walkaround the compliance officer will focus on the four leading hazards that cause 90% of deaths and injuries in construction. The leading hazards are:

- Falls (e.g., floors, platforms, roofs).

- Struck by (e.g., falling objects, vehicles).

- Caught in/between (e.g., cave-ins, unguarded machinery, equipment).

- Electrical (e.g., overhead power lines, power tools and cords, outlets, temporary wiring).

The compliance officer will interview employees to determine their knowledge of the safety and health program/plan, their awareness of potential job-site hazards, their training in hazard recognition and their understanding of applicable OSHA standards.

If the project safety and health program/plan is found to be effectively implemented the compliance officer will terminate the inspection.

If the project does not qualify for a Focused Inspection, the compliance officer will conduct a comprehensive inspection of the entire project.

If you have any questions or concerns related to the inspection or conditions on the project you are encouraged to bring them to the immediate attention of the compliance officer or call the area office at:

_____ .

_____ **qualified as a FOCUSED PROJECT.**
(Project/Site)

_____   _____ .
(Date)   (AREA DIRECTOR)

This document should be distributed at the site and given to the Contractor for posting.

Figure 5-1

OSHA's New Scaffolding Standard—What Goes Up Sometimes Comes Down

At least five construction workers die each day in America from falls from elevated surfaces. On February 6, 1995, OSHA enacted a new safety law that applied to all construction operations taking place above six feet (1.8 meters) off the ground. As of November 29, 1996, new requirements for scaffolding became effective as part of revised 29CFR 1926, Subpart L.

CONSTRUCTION FOCUSED INSPECTION GUIDELINE

This guideline is to assist the professional judgment of the compliance officer to determine if there is an effective project plan, to qualify for a Focused Inspection.

YES/NO

PROJECT SAFETY AND HEALTH COORDINATION; are there procedures in place by the general contractor, prime contractor or other such entity to ensure that all employers provide adequate protection for their employees?

Is there a **DESIGNATED COMPETENT PERSON** responsible for the implementation and monitoring of the project safety and health plan who is capable of identifying existing and predictable hazards and has authority to take prompt corrective measures?

PROJECT SAFETY AND HEALTH PROGRAM/PLAN* that complies with 1926 Subpart C and addresses, based upon the size and complexity of the project, the following:

_____ Project Safety Analysis at initiation and at critical stages that describes the sequence, procedures, and responsible individuals for safe construction.

_____ Identification of work/activities requiring planning, design, inspection or supervision by an engineer, competent person or other professional.

_____ Evaluation/monitoring of subcontractors to determine conformance with the Project Plan. (The Project Plan may include, or be utilized by subcontractors.)

_____ Supervisor and employee training according to the Project Plan including recognition, reporting and avoidance of hazards, and applicable standards.

_____ Procedures for controlling hazardous operations such as: cranes, scaffolding, trenches, confined spaces, hot work, explosives, hazardous materials, leading edges, etc.

_____ Documentation of: training, permits, hazard reports, inspections, uncorrected hazards, incidents and near misses.

_____ Employee involvement in hazard: analysis, prevention, avoidance, correction and reporting.

_____ Project emergency response plan.

* FOR EXAMPLES, SEE OWNER AND CONTRACTOR ASSOCIATION MODEL PROGRAMS, ANSI A10.33, A10.38, ETC.

The walkaround and interviews confirmed that the Plan has been implemented, including:

_____ The four leading hazards are addressed: falls, struck by, caught in/between, electrical.

_____ Hazards are identified and corrected with preventative measures instituted in a timely manner.

_____ Employees and supervisors are knowledgeable of the project safety and health plan, avoidance of hazards, applicable standards, and their rights and responsibilities.

THE PROJECT QUALIFIED FOR A FOCUSED INSPECTION

Figure 5-2

The new standard applies to all scaffolding used in construction, repair, and demolition operations. Aerial lifts are also covered by this rule, but crane or derrick suspended personnel platforms are not.

OSHA now requires that all contractors and subcontractors involved in scaffolding work appoint a Competent Person (CP) to ensure that the installation and maintenance of scaffolding erected by their company is safe.

The CP must have had the necessary training and experience to determine that proper fall protection and scaffolding is in place. The CP must be knowledgeable about the requirements of 29 CFR 1926.450(b), that section of the OSHA regulations pertaining to the qualifications of a Competent Person.

Some of the important features of this new scaffolding regulation are:

1. All platforms are to be fully decked so that there is no opening greater than 1 inch (2.54 cm) and all walkways must be a minimum of 18 inches (45.72 cm) wide (except ladder jack scaffolds, top plate bracket scaffolds, roof bracket scaffolds).

2. If the front of the scaffold is more than 14 inches (35.56 cm) away from the face of a structure, either a guardrail system or personal fall arrest system must be in place to protect workers from falling between the scaffold and the structure. The only exception to this rule concerns plastering and lathing operations where the front edge of the scaffold can be no more than 18 inches (45.72 cm) away from the structure if there are no guardrails or any fall protection system in place.

3. Scaffold components manufactured by different manufacturers are not allowed unless the components fit together without the use of force and the scaffolding's structural integrity is not compromised. Scaffold components made of dissimilar metals cannot be assembled unless the Competent Person determines that galvanic action will not reduce the strength of any component.

4. All supported scaffold with a height-to-base ratio of more than 4:1 (including outrigger supports, if any) must be restrained from tipping by guying, bracing or equivalent means. These restraints are to be installed in accordance with the manufacturer's instructions and are to be repeated every 20 feet (6.10 meters) vertically for scaffolding three feet (.91 meters) or less and every 26 feet (7.92 meters) or less for scaffolds greater than 3 feet wide (.91 meters). All supported scaffolding must be secured from movement every 30 feet (9.14 meters) horizontally.

5. Scaffold poles, legs, frames and uprights must bear on baseplates and mudsills or other adequate firm foundations. These foundations must be capable of supporting the scaffolding when fully loaded.

6. Access to and between scaffold platforms more than two feet (60.96cm) above or below the point of access shall be by portable ladders, scaffold stairways, hook-on ladders, ramps, walkways or equivalent means. The use of cross braces as a means of access is strictly prohibited.

7. Fall protection is required for all scaffolding set above 10 feet (3.048 meters). The top edge height of toprails placed in service after January 1, 2000 must be between 38 and 45 inches (96.5 cm and 114.3 cm). Toprail heights for scaffolding placed into service prior to January 1, 2000 must be between 36 and 45 inches (91.44 and 114.3 cm). Steel or plastic banding cannot be used as a toprail or midrail. Plastic, manila and synthetic ropes can be used as guardrails if they are inspected as often as necessary to insure their integrity. Cross bracing is an acceptable substitute for midrails if the cross-bracing point is between 20–30 inches (50.8–76.2 cm) above the work surface.

8. Employees working on scaffolding must wear hard hats, but they must also be protected against falling objects such as hand tools and construction debris.

9. Employee training is necessary when workers are required to use scaffolding, and CFR 1926.454, Paragraphs (a)(1) through (a)(5) are to be consulted for further elaboration on the following five areas.
   a. The nature of electrical hazards, fall hazards, and falling object hazards.
   b. Correct procedures for protection against electrical hazards, erection and maintenance and disassembling of fall protection and falling object protection systems.
   c. Proper use of the scaffold and handling of materials on a scaffold.
   d. Maximum intended load on the scaffold and load-carrying capacities of the scaffolding being used.
   e. All pertinent requirements of Subpart L of the OSHA regulations.

What to Do When an OSHA Inspector Appears at the Job Site

1. The general contractor's superintendent will meet the inspector, verify credentials, and determine the nature of the inspection—whether routine, initiated by receipt of a complaint and whether the inspector wishes to tour the entire site.

2. A call will be placed to the general contractor's office requesting that either the director of safety or their project manager come to the site to accompany the inspector.

3. The general contractor's site superintendent will generally request that all major trade subcontractor foremen assemble and accompany him on the inspection tour. Each trade foreman should bring with him or her a pad and pencil to make notes of any applicable inspector concerns or violations. If a camera is available, bring one along in case a photo is needed to dispute a citation.

4. If any OSHA related documents are requested of any subcontractor's foreman, bring them along, but no more than specifically requested.

5. Do not volunteer information, but if a violation is discovered and the inspector inquires about the time necessary to correct the violation, respond but without acknowledging responsibility for the violation.

6. Avoid making any statements that may be construed as admission of a violation of any OSHA rule or regulation.

7. Citations will be issued by OSHA's area director and when received are to be posted on the job site for three days. Any corrective work must be completed within the time frame indicated in the citation.

8. If any subcontractor disputes the violation assessed against its company, don't voice the objection at the time of the inspection. Consult the documents accompanying the violation to determine how the violation can be disputed.

9. A closing conference with the OSHA inspector should be requested to insure that everyone understands the findings of the inspection.

Developing the Company Safety Program

The structure of a company safety plan should encompass the following components:

- Statement of company policy
- Objective of the Accident Prevention Program
- Appointment, duties, and responsibilities of a Safety Director or Safety Coordinator
- Responsibilities of field supervisors and relationship to Safety Director
- Procedures for reporting job related injuries and illnesses
- Working rules and regulations of the safety program
- A Hazard Communication (Hazcom) program
- Procedures for dealing with safety violators

Statement of company policy

The statement of company policy simply states the reason for the implementation of a safety program, a sample of which is set forth below:

ABC Corporation recognizes that accident prevention is a problem of organization and education, which can and must be administered to avoid pain and suffering to our employees and reduce lost time and operating costs to our company. Pursuant to this, I state and pledge my full support and commitment to the following:

1. That the Company intends to fully comply with ALL safety laws and ordinances.
2. That the safety of our employees and the public is paramount.
3. That safety will take precedence over expediency or short cuts.
4. That every attempt will be made to reduce the possibility of accident occurrence.

> Sincerely,
> John Hancock
> President—Drywall Interiors, Inc.

Objective of the Accident Prevention Program

This is almost a repeat of the statement of company policy, but contains somewhat more detail.

Objective of the Accident Prevention Program

This firm recognizes that accident prevention is a problem requiring both organization and education in order to combat. To be successful, this policy must be administered vigorously and intelligently to accomplish a reduction in lost time, avoidance of much pain and suffering to our employees and last, but not least, a reduction in operating costs due to lower insurance rates.

We rely primarily upon our supervisory personnel both in the field and in the office to furnish the sincere and constant cooperation required to administer this program.

Effectiveness of the Accident Prevention Program will depend upon the participation and cooperation of management, supervision of employees and a coordinated effort in carrying out the following basic procedures:

1. Planning all work to minimize losses due to personnel injury and property damage.
2. Maintaining a system for prompt detection and correction of unsafe practices and conditions.
3. Making available and enforcing the use of personal protective equipment, physical and mechanical guards.
4. Maintaining an effective system of tool and equipment inspection and maintenance.
5. Establishing an educational program to instruct all participants in the basics of accident control and prevention by instituting:
   a. New employee orientation training
   b. Periodic safety meetings
   c. Use and distribution of safety bulletins and similar materials
   d. Instruction in proper and prompt reporting of all accidents and a system for immediate investigation to determine the cause of the accident and take steps to prevent recurrence.

Safety Equipment

The use of personal protective equipment that meets or exceeds minimum OSHA standards and state and local requirements will be mandatory. Such equipment will be furnished by the Company.

Inspection of Tools and Equipment

All equipment and tools must meet or exceed minimum OSHA regulations. Equipment and tool inspection programs must meet or exceed minimum OSHA requirements, including the maintenance of required records or other documentation.

General Safety Reference

The reference material for this Safety Program is contained in Department of Labor, Occupational Safety and Health Administration (OSHA) manual CFR 1926.

Safety Director or Safety Coordinator

The duties of the Safety Director/Coordinator include the following:

1. Responsibility for coordinating and monitoring the Accident Prevention Program
   a. Oversee accident investigations. Accidents resulting in serious injuries or accidents that could have caused serious injury will be investigated by the Safety Director.
   b. Oversee the proper use of safety equipment.
   c. Perform frequent and unannounced job-site inspections.
   d. Attend and participate in regular Safety Meetings.
2. Continual review of job safety reports and preparation and dissemination of monthly summaries of safety violations, field inspections, and general program administration items.
3. Immediate documentation of critical conditions and steps to be taken, and by whom, to correct conditions as necessary.
4. Maintain liaison with insurance carriers regarding accident prevention problems.
5. Review and take action, as required, on all safety program violators.

Responsibilities of field supervisors and their relationship with the Safety Director

The field supervisors, present at the job sites daily, are the first line of defense in any accident prevention program, and the field supervisors need not only have formal training in accident prevention, but also the ability to communicate their knowledge to every tradesman under their supervision. The manual must contain provisions for conducting Weekly Tool Box meetings, and it should also include forms for daily inspections of the work site.

Procedures for reporting job-related injuries and illnesses

This part of the Safety Program must contain clear and concise information for the reporting of all job-site-related accidents or illnesses, whether or not they required time lost from work. There are two types of accident and illness forms required—one required by the company's Safety Director and the other to comply with OSHA reporting requirements. The field supervisor should have received both forms in their safety packet along with all of the other forms required at the beginning of the project.

Working rules and regulations of the safety program

This is the "nuts and bolts" of the program outlining the specific items of protective personal equipment required for general use and for specific operations—i.e., goggles/face shields for all metal cutting tasks, ear protection when operating certain pieces of equipment, and so forth. If powder actuated tools are used, a separate training program in the proper use of these tools will be required.

Details relating to "red tagging" of defective equipment will be included in this section of the program and it is wise to set forth detailed procedures for the proper use of electrical extension cords since this is one of the Top 25 OSHA violations.

A hazard communications (HAZCOM) program

This is another topic on OSHA's Top 25 Hit List and, as such requires not only training, but also coordination between the field and the office.

HazCom was initiated when OSHA became aware of the use of products containing hazardous materials frequently incorporated into, or used in, various tasks on construction projects. The improper handling, storage, and use of some of these dangerous products was responsible for a great deal of injuries and job-related illnesses, hence the creation of the Hazard Communications program.

Prior to the shipment of any hazardous products to the job site, a Material Safety Data Sheet (MSDS) is to be sent by the vendor to the office for dissemination to the field. When the product does arrive at the construction site, the provisions of the corresponding MSDS are to be followed for storage and handling of the product. In case of spillage or contact with the skin or eyes or if the product is ingested or inhaled, the instructions in the MSDS will include first-aid procedures and the type of medical treatment required.

The supervisor must keep an accurate and orderly file of all MSDS and not allow any product to be delivered to the site unless the appropriate MSDS sheet has preceded it.

Disciplinary action for safety rule violators— A model policy

One of the Safety Director's primary responsibilities is the monitoring of safety violations. Each field supervisor must be repeatedly instructed on the prompt and proper reporting of safety violations. A disciplinary process is an integral part of any safety program and this should be reviewed, in detail with all new workers, and from time to time, with long-term workers to refresh their memories. In this era of lawsuits and restraints on unfair firings and dismissals, it is important that employees review the company's disciplinary rules and sign them to acknowledge receipt and complete understanding. If these procedures are not followed and a safety violator is dismissed without proper documentation, a lawsuit may be waiting around the corner.

And, of course, any rules regarding drug use on the site must be approached with extreme care and intimate knowledge. The often-told story about the firing of an employee who appeared to be "spaced out" on drugs, but merely had a reaction to a prescribed medication does not need to be retold. But the poor employer who indiscriminately fired this worker is probably still writing off the cost of the lawsuit.

A typical disciplinary procedure portion of the safety program

"Compliance with OSHA and company safety rules and regulations is a condition of employment at (Company name). All employees working for (Company) will be trained in and must familiarize themselves with both OSHA and company safety rules and procedures before beginning to work on a project. A copy of the company's safe work rules and procedures will be provided by your supervisor.

Management personnel at all levels—including project managers, field supervisors and foremen are responsible for taking action when a violation is observed. If a violation is observed, they must take action immediately to correct the violation and enforce this disciplinary policy.

Employees who fail to follow safety rules and regulations established to protect them and their fellow employees endanger themselves and others.

The following procedure will be followed when a violation is observed:

First warning: The first time an employee is observed violating any safety rule, the employee shall be given a first warning. The first warning will be an oral warning to the employee and so noted in their personnel file.

Second warning: The second time an employee is observed violating any safety rule, the employee shall be given a second warning. The second warning will be an oral warning accompanied by a written safety violation notice. A copy of the written safety violation will be given to the employee, the employee's union steward (if applicable), and the company's safety coordinator. A copy of the notice will be placed in the employee's personnel file. The employee will be required to meet with the safety coordinator for counseling.

Third warning: The third time an employee is observed violating any safety rule, the employee shall be given a third warning. The third warning will be a written safety violation notice. A copy of the written notice will be given to the employee, the employee's union steward (if applicable) and the safety coordinator. A copy of the notice shall be placed in the employee's personnel file. A meeting with the employee, foreman, safety coordinator, and top management will be held to determine why the employee has failed to comply with the company's rules. Top management must determine what action will be taken at this time.

Employees who accumulate three warnings in a 12-month period may be suspended from work without pay for up to one week.

Fourth warning: The fourth time an employee is observed violating any safety rule, the employee shall be given a fourth warning. A fourth warning will be a written safety violation notice. Employees who do not follow safety rules, especially after being warned several times, are a threat to themselves and their co-workers. Therefore employees who receive a fourth warning may, at management's discretion, be terminated from employment or be subject to other disciplinary action deemed appropriate by management.

The actions listed above must be taken whenever a safety violation is observed. If you have any questions concerning this policy or safety procedures, contact the Safety Coordinator."

It is critical that administration of this policy be consistent. Employees will not take this disciplinary policy seriously if they know that safety violations have occurred and no oral or written warnings were issued.

Each project manager and foreman or lead man should have copies of Safety Violation forms either in his or her briefcase or in the job trailer. A typical Safety Violation Form is shown in Figure 5-3 and is also contained on the diskette accompanying this book.

SAFETY VIOLATION NOTICE

Employee's name:_____

Job title:_____

Job site and location:_____

Date and time of occurrence:_____

No. of prior offenses:_____

This is to advise you that you are hereby placed on notice that you were observed violating the following company rule, policy or procedure. *(Describe rule, policy, or procedure that was violated.)*

_____

_____

_____

Supervisor's comments *(Describe action that was taken to prevent violation from happening again.)*

_____

_____

_____

Supervisor's signature:_____   Date:_____

Employee's comments:_____

_____

Employee's signature:_____   Date:_____

Figure 5-3

The carrot and the stick approach to a safety program

Strict and consistent enforcement of a safety program is necessary in order to enforce top management's continued commitment to the program. Some companies supplement their enforcement program by offering incentives to safety conscious employees.

These incentives can be based upon achieving either short-term or long-term goals or a combination of both.

A short-term incentive can take the form of presenting a small gift such as a Swiss Army knife to an employee who exhibited some on-the-spot safety measure. Safety stickers to be worn on one's hard hat are a highly visible short-term safety award.

Long term incentives, for continued safety consciousness or accident-free records can take the form of a cash or merchandise bonus, extended vacation time with pay, or a prepaid weekend for two at a nearby resort hotel.

Fluor Daniel, the Virginia-based subsidiary of international contractor Fluor Corporation developed a Hazard Elimination Program several years ago that was responsible, in large measure for millions of work hours per year without a lost-time accident.

Their Hazard Elimination Program works on a "point" basis. Whenever an employee spots a safety violation, takes corrective action, and reports the violation and action to his or her supervisor, the employee safety committee evaluates the hazard as either Type I, Type II, or Type III. (Type I hazard is a minor one and Type III constitutes a violation that could create imminent danger.)

Based upon the category of the violation, points are awarded to the individual, totaled monthly and entered into the program's tally sheet.

Those Fluor Daniel's employees who achieve high scores receive company recognition and awards ranging from gifts to paid time off.

The program has been highly successful—one project in Mississippi exceeded five million work hours without a disabling injury.

Remember! A solid safety program reduces corporate overhead, increases employee morale, creates positive public relations, and just makes good business sense.

6

Documentation

Documentation, as it relates to the construction industry, can be defined as the creation and maintenance of events as they occur throughout the life of a construction project.

These records are meant to serve multiple purposes:

1. Provide a record of daily project activities for field or office use if personnel changes are required.
2. Provide updated database information.
3. Provide a record of daily events and activities in the event that disputes or claims arise either during construction or after the project has been closed out.

The construction industry is rife with disagreements, disputes, claims, and litigation arising out of disagreements over contractual obligations. The need for effective documentation during the life of a construction project becomes an essential part of the subcontractor's day-to-day activities.

Although owners, architects, engineers, and general contractors have recognized the advantage of resolving disputes by means other than litigation, due to the nature of the industry, disputes will inevitably occur on many projects, and the best means to combat these claims is by developing an effective record of the events that transpire during the project.

As Yogi Berra once said, "It ain't over until it's over." He must have been thinking about the construction industry!

Properly documented project records can be the deciding factor in settling a claim against a defective product or faulty workmanship that may occur years after a project has been completed.

Due to the complexity of the industry these days, verbal instructions without written confirmation may result in misunderstandings or misinterpretations of those verbal commitments leading to future disagreements.

For example, in today's fast-paced construction projects, it is often expedient to proceed with changes to the contract documents based upon verbal agreements between the subcontractor and general contractor or between subcontractor and owner.

As one old saying goes, "The Road to Purgatory is Paved with Good Intentions," and oftentimes verbal commitments, given in good faith, are not met, and in some instances, strongly denied.

So the need to document becomes an integral and important element in the construction process. The real trick is to document that which appears to be essential without adding to the already heavy workload placed upon field supervisors and office personnel.

Documentation commences with the bidding process and will continue through to final payment and project sign-offs—and beyond.

During the Bidding Process

Bid documents can be confusing, misleading, ambiguous and include plans and specifications that are less than perfect. Interpretation and assumptions made by the subcontractor without substantiation and agreement by the general contractor or owner can be dangerous and the source of future disputes unless these interpretations and assumptions can be clarified at bid time or, at latest, prior to final negotiations and contract award. Since the A.I.A General Conditions document specifically designates the architect as the interpreter of the plans and specifications, all such requests for information and clarification must be directed to that source via the general contractor prior to the submission of the bid or, once again, before final negotiations are concluded.

Therefore, the bidding process becomes the first instance of documentation taking place even before a subcontractor award is made.

But there are other forms of documentation that will occur before, during, and after a bid has been prepared and submitted to the general contractor.

The bidding process

1. It is important that the subcontractor receives all of the bid documents and after reviewing them, record exactly what was received. If the bid documents have been received from the general contrac-

tor with an accompanying transmittal, check the contents outlined in the transmittal carefully. If certain documents are listed but not included, notify the general contractor immediately, both verbally and in writing.

Quite often questions will be raised by other bidders, and either addenda or clarification letters will be issued by the architect or engineer and these addenda or clarification letters may inadvertently not have been transmitted to all bidders. Since these documents generally have cost implications, an accurate estimate can only be completed when all such documents have been received and reviewed.

2. If answers to questions posed during the bidding process are not received by the subcontractor, the bid should be qualified. Although general contractors are reluctant to qualify their bid to an owner because any such qualifications, particularly on public works bids can disqualify them, the same rule does not necessarily apply to subcontractors. If in doubt qualify your bid!

3. Even if one's bid contains no qualifications, it is important for subcontractors to include a complete listing of bid documents in their written proposals to the general contractor. List the plans (and their issue/revision dates), specifications, addenda, responses by architect/engineer to clarification issues, and any other documents used in formulating the bid. If a particular document, sent to others, was not included in your bid package, the listing of documents effectively qualifies the bid.

4. Retain every quantity take-off sheet, every estimate sheet, every adding machine tape, every scrap of paper generated during the preparation of the estimate until the general contractor requests an interview prior to awarding a contract. A quick review of these estimate worksheets prior to such a meeting may reveal an error, which if corrected could revise the price upward or downward.

During Construction

1. Maintenance of a Daily Log. There are Daily Log books with preprinted day, date, and year pages, but if none are available, any bound volume will do. Loose-leaf binders should not be used since pages may be inserted or removed and if required as a job record in a legal proceeding they will not be acceptable as such.

These Daily Logs should contain Date, Day, Month, Year and, as a bare minimum:

- Manpower each day, including number of foremen, journeymen, apprentices, or helpers on the job.
- Equipment at the job site, whether idle or working, listed by type, hours operated, and task performed.
- Work tasks performed that day and the location within the building or the site where these tasks took place. The more specific the location and the activity, the better.
- Extra work performed or requested and whether this direction was verbal or written. If verbal, note the person authorizing the work (which should be supplemented by a written authorization form). If a specific sum was agreed upon, it should be so noted. If the work was to be performed on a Time and Material basis, indicate same.
- Any discrepancies in the plans or specifications that were brought to the attention of the general contractor during the day (to include the name and title of that representative).
- Visits to the job site—by building inspectors, your company's personnel, or the general contractor's. Architect, engineer, or owner visits should also be noted.
- Weather conditions, generally recorded at the start of work, midpoint during the workday, and prior to quitting time. Temperature readings are to be included, one for each of the three time frames.
- Materials received at the site, referenced to a specific receiving ticket number and where they were used.
- Materials ordered either from the company's warehouse or from a vendor.
- General notes concerning overall job progress or observations of any unusual occurrences.
- Name and signature of person completing the Daily Log.

2. Issuance of Requests for Information (RFIs) or Requests for Clarification (RFCs). Rarely will a project proceed without the need for clarification of certain portions of the specifications or drawings. On some projects, these requests are minimal, but on others the quality of the plans and specifications is such that RFIs or RFCs are required shortly after work commences and may continue on a daily basis for several weeks or months. If that were the case, a procedure for the issuance and tracking of any response to these queries is important. Although there are software programs for project management that specifically include RFI and RFC forms and tracking devices, it is possible to maintain such a log without sophisticated hardware. Figure 6-1 is a typical RFI tracking log.

- -

The City of Stamford				E X P E D I T I O N				Today's Date 28MAY97
Westover Elementary School								Frank Mercede & Sons, Inc.
ST-RR02				Request for Information				Page 1

- -

TYPE	TO	FROM	CHANGE NUMBER	TITLE	ISSUE	APPROVED DATE	RESPOND DATE	REF	STATUS
RFI	FT	FMS	00001	Dimensional Clarifications		28FEB97		RFI	NEW
				Enclosed are three RFI's regarding dimensional clarifications from our steel subcontractor. Upon our review we need the input from your designer.					
RFI	FT	FMS	00002	Addendum 3 Steel Clarifications		03MAR97		RFI	NEW
				Please clarify the following questions that have arisen from Addendum #3. The enclosed RFI #4 from our steel fabricator outlines two questions that need your input. They refer to drwgs A308 & A312.					
RFI	FT	FMS	00003	Steel Clarification		05MAR97		RFI	NEW
				Enclosed please find drwgs E1 through E5 (PRELIMINARY). They have been provided to facilitate a number of questions from our steel supplier regarding missing dimensions and beam clarifications.					
RFI	FT	FMS	00004	Truss Question		07MAR97		RFI	NEW
				Our steel supplier "General Steel Fabricators" has submitted his RFI #6 in regard to DRWG S201. Please Advise.					
RFI	FT	FMS	00005	Missing Pier Information		10MAR97		RFI	NEW
				1) The pier @ K.8 & 14.3 the size of the pier box is needed.					
				2) The pier @ S & 40 the size of the pier box is needed.					
RFI	FT	FMS	00006	Overhead door clarification		10MAR97		RFI	NEW
				1) Door 264B is not shown on the elevation drwgs, please clarify.					
				2) Door 280B drwg A101.4 gives a rough opening of 10'-0", the door schedule shows 8'-0", please clarify. NOTE: I believe that this is the door that the custodian has questioned the size of.					
RFI	FT	FMS	00007	Elevator Clarifications		13MAR97		RFI	NEW
				Please review the enclosed RFI from our elevator subcontractor. The last (4) four questions could be clarified by (F.T.) Fletcher Thompson. If you have any questions please call.					
RFI	FT	FMS	00008	Steel Shop primer clarification		13MAR97		RFI	NEW
				Enclosed please find our steel fabricators RFI #7 for your action. Please call if you have any questions.					
RFI	FT	FMS	00009	N.I.C. Items		18MAR97		RFI	NEW
				Jerry, while I was making the list owner supplied items I came across some shelving in room 209 " Storage " that I think is supplied by the owner. Could you clarify this as there was no note on drwg A101.3					
RFI	FT	FMS	00010	Steel Clarification		26MAR97		RFI	NEW
				The enclosed RFI from our steel subcontractor needs clarification prior to our proceeding with the detailing in this area.					

Figure 6-1

With such a log, periodically updated, the status of outstanding RFIs can be reviewed at weekly job meetings and any overdue responses can be so noted in case future delay claims become necessary.

3. Shop Drawing Submissions. A system of transmittals when submitting shop drawings to the general contractor needs to be established and, similar to the RFI tracking log, one needs to be prepared to periodically review the status of all such drawings or samples sent to the general contractor for review and approval.

The contract specifications, most probably in the Division "0" section, will stipulate the amount of time allotted to the architect/engineer for review of shop drawings. Added to this must be the time for the drawings to reach the general contractor from the subcontractor or vendor, several days for the general contractor to review these drawings and transmit them to the architect/engineer and the travel time from consultant back to general contractor, back to subcontractor.

A Shop Drawing Submittal Log (Figure 6-2) should be reviewed at weekly job meetings and overdue returns noted in the job meeting minutes or by separate letter to the general contractor, or both.

4. Verbal Instructions/Directions from the general contractor. Written acknowledgment of any verbal instructions or directions issued by the general contractor in the field is another important procedure that must be implemented. If the general contractor has a habit of not issuing written confirmations, your project manager should do so, and do so promptly.

5. Extra Work Authorization. Confirmation of authorization to proceed with extra work will reduce the potential for future disputes and claims and should not be construed by the general contractor as a lack of confidence in their verbal authorization to perform work. If a lump sum agreement for extra work is not reached, work can proceed on a Time and Material basis based upon the procedures set forth in Article 7 of A.I.A. Document A 201—General Conditions.

- -

Today's Date   09SEP97

Submittals by Spec Section

- -

PACKAGE	SUBMITTAL	ITEM	FROM	TITLE REV.	DESCRIPTION	RECVD	SUBMTD	RETRND	FORWRD	STATUS	BIC
DIV. #09	09250A	00318	DRYWALL		G - P GYPSUM BOARD SELECTIONS	23JUN97	23JUN97	21JUL97	01AUG97	AAN	
				1	G-P GYPSUM BOARD SELECTIONS						
DIV. #09	09250B	00319	DRYWALL		USG GYPSUM PRODUCTS	23JUN97	30JUN97	21JUL97	01AUG97	AAN	
				0	U.S.G. GYPSUM PRODUCTS						
DIV. #09	09250C	00320	DRYWALL		ARMSTRONG CROSS TEE	23JUN97	23JUN97	21JUL97	01AUG97	APP	
				0	ARMSTONG CROSS TEES						
DIV. #09	09250CC	00137	DRYWALL		SW&J STUDS	23JUN97	30JUN97	12AUG97	13AUG97	AAN	
				1	S W & J STUDS						
DIV. #09	09250D	00321	DRYWALL		25 GAUGE STUD SPECS	23JUN97	30JUN97	12AUG97	13AUG97	AAN	
				1	25 GAUGE STUD SPECS						
DIV. #09	09250DD	00138	DRYWALL		1 1/4" STRUCTURAL TRACK	23JUN97	23JUN97	11AUG97	13AUG97	AAN	
				1	1 1/4" STRUCTURAL TRACK						
DIV. #09	09250E	00322	DRYWALL		6" Stud specs	23JUN97	30JUN97	08AUG97	13AUG97	AAN	
				1	6" STUD SPECS						
DIV. #09	09250F	00583	DRYWALL		7/8" FURRY CHANNELS/FLAT STOCK	23JUN97	30JUN97	21JUL97	01AUG97	AAN	
				1	7/8" FURRY CHANNELS/FLAT						
DIV. #09	09250G	00602	DRYWALL		Marino Flatstock-(P 9 brochure)	09JUL97	16JUL97	08AUG97	13AUG97	AAN	
				1	Marino Flatstock-						
DIV. #09	09250H	00672	DRYWALL		20 Gauge Studs	09JUL97	06JUL97	21JUL97	01AUG97	DIS	DRYWALL
				1	20 Gauge Studs						

Figure 6-2

Written confirmation of authorization to proceed with extra work should also include the method to establish the cost of that work.

This T&M process is made simpler if hourly rates have been submitted by the subcontractor and preapproved by the general contractor along with a clear understanding of what represents "costs." Hourly rate schedules such as the one illustrated in Figure 6-3 clearly defines all components of the applicable trade rate. Early in the project, a meeting can be arranged with the general contractor to establish the ground rules for T&M work—i.e., agreement on hourly labor rates, agreement on rates for equipment, materials to be billed at cost, and agreement on a small tool allowance as either a certain dollar amount per labor hour or a percentage of total labor. And, most importantly an agreement that the general contractor's representative will sign these daily extra work orders presented by the subcontractor's foreman. A sample of a typical Daily Work Order, usually available in multiple copy form is shown in Figure 6-4.

6. Accident Reporting. Forms and procedures for reporting accidents in accordance with OSHA requirements and company safety programs should be in the possession of the foreman, and all accidents should be reported, leaving it up to management to determine which ones are "reportable" to the insurance company and/or OSHA.

7. Delays—Real or Anticipated. It is a rare project that does not experience a delay, some of which are of no consequence (or at least it seems that way at the time) and some that are instantly recognized as being troublesome. Delays can be created by any party to the contract, and whenever they occur some form of documentation ought to be created.

Requests by the general contractor to delay work in certain areas, or deviate from the schedule of activities established by the general contractor's baseline schedule, or requests to work out of sequence should be presented to the subcontractor in writing, and if not forthcoming, the subcontractor must confirm such instructions from the general contractor. All of these requests carry with them the seeds for future disputes and claims and need to be documented in detail.

Delays created by other subcontractors should be brought to the attention of the general contractor when they occur, and noted in the Daily Log. These events are topics for discussions at the next job meeting and if these delays affect your company's performance,

SUBCONTRACTOR:	_____		LOCAL UNION NO. 24	
ADDRESS:	_____		CITY: NEW HAVEN	
	_____		STATE: CONNECTICUT	
TEL. NO.:	_____			

LABOR CLASSIFICATION: CARPENTER – JOURNEYMAN

EFFECTIVE DATES: 04/01/93 – 03/31/96

	%/HOUR	STRAIGHT TIME	TIME & A HALF	PREMIUM DOUBLE TIME
BASIC RATE		18.75	28.13	37.50
VACATION OR SAVINGS		0.35	0.35	0.35
TAXABLE EARNINGS SUBTOTAL:	100%	19.10	28.48	37.85
F.O.A.B. LIMITATION 7.65%		1.46	2.18	2.90
F.U.T.A. LIMITATION .8%		0.15	0.23	0.30
S.U.T.A. LIMITATION CONN 6.9%		1.32	1.96	2.61
S.U.T.A. LIMITATION N.Y. 3.1%		0.59	0.88	1.17
WELFARE FUND		2.70	2.70	2.70
PENSION FUND		1.30	1.30	1.30
ANNUITY FUND		2.55	2.55	2.55
APPRENTICE TRAINING		0.15	0.15	0.15
VACATION, HOLIDAY, SPEC., LIFE INS. MEDICAL		0.00	0.00	0.00
INDUSTRY PROGRAM		0.00	0.00	0.00
ASSOC. PROGRAM		0.10	0.10	0.10
WORKMAN'S COMP.		5.45	8.12	10.79
CT. W/C ASSESSMENT 9.4%		0.51	0.76	1.01
PUBLIC LIABILITY, BODILY INJURY, PROPERTY DAMAGE		0.94	1.41	1.87
SUBTOTAL:		36.33	50.82	65.31
C.O. SUPPORT:		0.00	0.00	0.00
OVERHEAD:		3.63	5.08	6.53
SUBTOTAL:		39.96	55.90	71.84
PROFIT		4.00	5.59	7.18
TOTAL RATE PER HOUR:		43.95	61.49	79.02

Figure 6-3

Before filling in section below, detach this sheet
or place a writing plate between this sheet and
carbon on other side.

JOB COST RECORD

DESCRIPTION	QUANTITY HOURS	@	MATERIALS	LABOR	OTHER EXPENSES	TOTAL COSTS
			TOTAL MATERIAL	TOTAL LABOR	TOTAL OTHER	TOTAL COSTS

REMARKS

TOTAL SELLING PRICE	
LESS TOTAL COST	
GROSS PROFIT	
LESS OVERHEAD COSTS ___ % OF SELLING PRICE	
NET PROFIT	

Figure 6-4

send a letter to the general contractor outlining the nature of the delay and their cost and time implication, if applicable.

8. Weather Conditions. Weather conditions such as severe rain or heavy snowstorms, or high winds or flooding or other Acts of God may disrupt or cause work to cease. If these adverse weather con-

ditions delay construction for any significant period of time, they need to be documented in the Daily Log, and, if necessary via letter to the general contractor. Although weather delays may be cause for a delay claim they are generally classified as Excusable-Noncompensable delays, which means the project completion date may be extended but no monetary damages will be paid. The chapter on claims and disputes will explain the various types of delay claims in more detail.

9. Product or Equipment Substitutions. Substitution of product or equipment may be necessary if the originally approved materials/equipment, for any number of reasons, are delayed to the point where the construction schedule is affected. If such a situation arises, a Request For Substitution form (Figure 6-5) should be quickly transmitted to the general contractor.

10. Differing Conditions. Site contractors frequently encounter site conditions considerably different from those indicated in the contract documents and these differences can result in significant extra costs. Most site contractors are aware of the procedures to follow in order to document and present their claims for differing site conditions, but other subcontractors may also encounter differing or unforeseen conditions.

When embarking on one of contracting's three Rs—Renovation-Remodeling-Rehabilitation, subcontractors may discover concealed conditions that vary from the contract documents, or they may uncover work that is at variance with the contract documents. When these situations occur, the subcontractor's field supervisor should immediately notify the general contractor's site representative, proceed to document the specific nature of the differing condition, and obtain agreement that the situation represents additional contract work, if that is the case. If these differing conditions present complex problems, written instructions from the general contractor on how to proceed should be requested and oftentimes an architect or engineer's sketch is required before proceeding with the work. Receipt of such a sketch may take days or weeks to receive, after which the added costs for this work must be prepared, submitted, and approved or written authorization is received to proceed on the basis of Time and Material work. A paper trail becomes essential in situations like this to document any delays resulting from this change/differing condition procedure.

And if a camera with date and time stamp is available it can prove invaluable in documenting the differing conditions as soon as

SUBSTITUTION REQUEST FORM

To: _____   Project:

    _____

    _____

    _____

===

Section   Page   Paragraph   Specified Item

_____ _____ _____   _____

The undersigned requests consideration of the following substitution:

_____

> Attached data shall include, in a tabular format to provide a line by line comparison – product description, specifications, drawings, photographs, performance and laboratory tests and the like with applicable portions of said data <u>clearly</u> identified.

FURTHER, The Proposed Substitution WILL (OR WILL NOT) Affect:

1. Dimensions indicated on the drawings? _____

2. Wiring, piping, ductwork, or other building services indicated on the drawings? _____

3. Other trades and abutting or interconnection work? _____

4. Manufacturer's guarantees and warranties? _____

5. The construction schedule? _____

6. Maintenance and service parts locally available? _____

> (<u>NOTE</u> – If Substitution WILL affect any item above, explain in detail.)

In addition to the above, the undersigned agrees to pay for –

1. Any and all changes to the building design, including structural, civil or electro/mechanical systems engineering (if any), detailing; <u>and</u>

2. Any and all additional construction costs caused by the requested substitution.

The undersigned further states that the function, appearance, and quality of the Proposed Substitution are equivalent or superior to the Specified Item.

===

SUBMITTED:	DESIGN PROFESSIONAL'S COMMENTS	
By: _____	_____ Accepted	_____ Accepted as Noted
Firm: _____	_____ Not Accepted	_____ Received Too Late
Address: _____		
_____	By: _____	
Date: _____	Date: _____	
Telephone/Fax: _____	Remarks: _____	

Approved For Subcontractor Submittal: _____

By: _____ Contractor: _____ Date: _____

Figure 6-5

they are exposed. If a redesign is required, the date when the condition was first discovered starts the "delay clock," if one is required. If this condition does occur, it is essential that a letter be prepared and sent to the general contractor outlining the situation and the problem it has created. (The writer has prepared a sample letter that can be modified to suit the situation at hand and this letter is included in Chapter 12—Sample Letters.)

11. Coordination Problems Involving Other Subcontractors. Mechanical and electrical trades are generally required to prepare coordination drawings to insure that all of the piping and equipment they are furnishing will fit into their allotted space. Drywall contractors and ceiling contractors are also involved in this process; however when the actual systems are installed, on-the-spot problems can surface and must be dealt with quickly by the general contractor.

    When these conditions occur and are not attacked promptly by the general contractor, other subcontractor work may be affected and such delays must be documented—the date when work was stopped and when work was able to restart. These conflicts may be just an isolated occurrence or part of a continuing problem that could have a serious impact on one or more subcontractor's schedule. Since it may be difficult to determine whether this is a one-time occurrence or the beginning of a series of delays, treat the first delay as though it is the first of many.

12. Job Meetings and Job Minutes. Job meetings are the forum in which the day-to-day problems encountered at the project can be discussed and afford the subcontractor an opportunity to talk about his or her particular problems, request information, or review construction scheduling.

    These meetings are usually conducted by the general contractor or the architect, who will prepare and distribute meeting minutes that become a part of the project's official documentation record.

    The last paragraph of the job meeting minutes will often contain a statement such as, "The above represents the writer's interpretation of items discussed and agreed upon, and if any changes or clarifications are requested they must be submitted, in writing, prior to the next meeting" (or sometimes this paragraph will limit response to 48 hours after receipt of the minutes).

    Some writers also include an "or else" clause—"or else all attendees will abide by the items as set forth in these meeting minutes."

    Since the meeting minutes represent an official reporting of events, it is important that all subcontractors read and agree with statements affecting their trade, and if they do not agree with the reporting, notify the general contractor, in writing, of their interpretation within the time constraint stipulated in the minutes.

13. When Liquidated Damages Are Included in the Construction Contract. Either specifications or the construction contract may include a Liquidated Damages clause which effectively requires reimbursement of costs incurred by the project owner if completion extends beyond the date stipulated in the construction con-

tract. When the general contractor's contract with the owner contains liquidated damages, even if the subcontract agreements do not specifically include this provision, by inference, the flow-through clause in the general contractor's subcontract agreement may be all that is required to enforce this provision.

It is important that the subcontractor document every delay as it occurs whether or not it appears that each delay or series of delays will actually affect his or her performance. A short note to the general contractor should follow with an explanation that although no claim for a delay is being expressed at this time, a record has been so noted in case a formal delay claim develops at some future date.

The writer knows all too well how easy it is to ignore isolated delays that appear to have little or no impact on one's work. Several years ago, his company was engaged as a subcontractor, by a large international general contracting firm to perform the site work, concrete foundations, masonry walls, and the cast-in-place concrete superstructure for a six-story office building. The contract between the owner and the general contractor and the subcontract agreement contained significant liquidated damages.

As the structure proceeded, the electrical subcontractor hired by the general contractor began to fall behind in the placement of underground and under-slab electrical conduits, which delayed the construction of the post-tensioned concrete slabs.

The writer, who was the project manager at that time, was charmed by the general contractor who kept promising that only the electrical subcontractor would be penalized if they were unable to accelerate their work—which they never did.

The project completion was delayed and the owner assessed the general contractor $700,000 in liquidated damages—and yes, the writer's firm was assessed $380,000 in turn. Lulled into a false sense of security, the writer did not fully document all of the electrical contractor's delays, which caused the delays in completing the foundation, superstructure concrete, and masonry work.

What to do?

Out of sheer desperation, the writer contacted all of the other subcontractors employed on the project and discovered that, in total, the general contractor had assessed the other subcontractors a total of $800,000 in liquidated damages; they were actually planning to make a profit on this situation!

Efforts to have the general contractor dismiss the $380,000 back charge, which they knew full well was not deserved, were to no avail. After discussing this matter with the company's legal counsel, a threat to commence legal action highlighting the general contractors profit-making scheme eventually made them drop their claim and issue final payment to the writer's company.

We learn from experience, and this escapade drove home the need to document every delay when liquidated damages are in effect—no matter what assurances are made by the general contractor!

14. Dealing with Hazardous Materials. Another problem inherent in Three Rs work is the potential for the discovery of hazardous materials. Depending upon the previous function of the building being renovated, remodeled, or rehabilitated, any number of hazardous materials may lurk undiscovered by the designers within walls, ceilings, or under existing floors.

   Look for lead paint in any building that was built before the 1970s, after which time the federal government mandated that the percentage of lead in paint be reduced to .06 percent. At about that time, latex and alkyd-based paints were introduced and the use of oil-based lead paints diminished.

   Asbestos-bearing materials are also likely to be found in older buildings, where as late as 1981, half of all asbestos consumption in the United States came from its use in roofing felt, felt-backed sheet flooring, vinyl asbestos floor tiles, asbestos-cement pipe, and equipment insulation and transite panels. The only way to effectively verify the presence of asbestos is to submit samples to a laboratory for analysis. Although visually, suspected materials may be assumed to be asbestos, microscopic inspection by a testing laboratory can ascertain its presence.

   If the building was previously used as a machine shop, the probability of encountering hazardous chlorinated degreasing solvents such as trichloroethylene or 1,1,1 trichloroethane is possible. If the building had been occupied by a dry-cleaning establishment, residues of perchloroethylene, a cousin of the two previous solvents, will, in all probability, be found somewhere in the building.

   If and when, suspected hazardous materials are encountered either visually or by detecting strong or unusual odors, the general contractor should be notified immediately verbally, followed by a written request to suspend work in the suspect area until it is determined to be free from hazardous materials.

   Exposing workers to hazardous materials, either knowingly or unknowingly can result in lawsuits of staggering proportions. When in doubt, suspend work in the suspected area and request written instructions on how and when to proceed.

During Project Close-Out

1. Partial Occupancy of the Building. Many owners request phased occupancy of a building in order to set up computer operations or install machinery or equipment in selected areas or begin to install office furniture. General contractors generally will usually oblige. Phased occupancy does have its pitfalls, however. Unless the area is "punched out" by the general contractor and the architect prior to occupancy, the question of who damaged floor, wall, or ceiling surfaces will inevitably occur and the question of responsibility for repairing damaged areas will undoubtedly create problems for those subcontractors who worked in that area.

   A walk-through with the general contractor's representative and/or architect prior to occupancy will create a record of the conditions of the space prior to move-in.

   If equipment has been installed in the area to be occupied and this equipment is to be maintained, the general contractor should relieve the appropriate subcontractor of that responsibility, in writing. And if this equipment is to be warrantied or guaranteed for a specific period of time, the warranty/guarantee period should commence upon the owner's acceptance of the space. This, too, needs to be documented by the appropriate contractor via letter to the general contractor.

2. Transmission of Close-out Documents. Depending upon the nature of the work, a subcontractor may be required to prepare multiple copies of Operation and Maintenance Manuals (O&M),certification that the Punch List has been completed, submission of "As-Built" drawings, and verification that "Attic Stock" per contract requirements have been delivered to the appropriate authority.

   All of these requirements should be accompanied by formal written transmittals which not only show what is being transmitted to the general contractor, but containing the signature of the receiving party. Equipment and product warranties will also be required and a quick review of the appropriate specification section will verify the format for these submissions.

3. Final Inspections. Each local and state government may have a slightly different procedure for final inspections by their respective departments, whether it is via a "Blue Book" sign-off or an official document indicating acceptance of the trade's work. Until all final inspections are received by the building department a Certificate of Occupancy will not be issued and therefore the project, in terms of contract obligations, will not have been completed. Since release of final retainage is generally triggered by the receipt of the

Certificate of Occupancy, if and when final inspections are required for specific subcontracted work, the general contractor should be notified by letter that these key inspections have been completed.

4. The Importance of Documenting the Last Date of Work. A record of the last date when the subcontractor worked on the project, whether it was to complete their contract work or to repair their work, may prove to be very important in the event that a mechanics lien must be filed due to nonpayment. The filing period for mechanics liens may vary from state to state, but, generally, liens cannot be filed after 60 or 90 days from the date the subcontractor last worked on the project. Payroll records may sometimes establish this date, but a separate letter slipped into the project file may be more effective.

The Chrono File

Not only is proper documentation essential today, but a system designed to locate and retrieve important letters and other documents quickly is also important. How many times has a letter been filed in a folder, but in order to retrieve it dozens of related folders have to be searched before it can be retrieved simply because no one can recall where it had been filed.

A chronological correspondence file may be the answer to this dilemma. By making a duplicate copy of that letter and filing it in a separate file arranged according to date typed, it is sometimes easier to determine when a letter was typed rather than where it was filed.

It is never too late to start to properly document a project. Stop and look at the methods now being employed and if they appear to be inadequate, reconstruct important past events now before proceeding on with the new system.

And remember when in doubt as to whether a situation warrants a letter to the general contractor, be on the safe side and send one.

7

Change Orders

Nothing has the potential to be more disruptive to the construction process—nor more certain to occur during the construction process—than the change order. And nothing can contribute more to the deterioration of the relationship between general contractor and subcontractor than the change order process.

But it doesn't have to be that way!

The American Institute of Architects (A.I.A.) A201 Document—General Conditions of the Contract of Construction, 1997 edition, Article 7 (Changes in the Work) sets forth a fairly complete definition of change order work. A Change Order is a written order prepared by the architect and signed by the owner, contractor, and architect agreeing to the following conditions:

- There has been a change in the contract work.
- This change may require a change in the contract sum.
- The change may also affect the contract time.

The same conditions would apply when the general contractor requests a change order proposal from the subcontractor, except that the general contractor instead of the architect initiates the change order.

Origins of Change Order Work

On a project of any size, it is inevitable that change orders will occur, and it is not unusual for disagreements over change orders to occur.

Change order requests arise from one or more of the following reasons:

1. Owner-Initiated Change Order. Revisions to the contract drawings and/or specifications at the owner's request often include additional work for which an adjustment in the contract sum is to be expected. These revisions can result in work being added to the contract sum, or changes may reflect deletion or elimination of scope of work, resulting in a decrease in the contract sum.

   Allowances included in the construction contract, when reconciled and adjusted, may result in costs greater than those included in the allowance section of that contract, thereby increasing the contract sum; the reverse may be true if the actual cost of the required work is less than the stated allowance and a deduct or credit change order will decrease the contract sum.

2. General Contractor-Initiated Change Order. On those occasions when the contract documents issued to the general contractor contain numerous errors and omissions these deficiencies become apparent as work progresses and the general contractor will prepare change orders for submission to the owner that include the additional costs to correct these problems. When this process accentuates design deficiencies, claims and disputes between contractor and design consultants are most likely to occur and the general contractor and the subcontractor may have difficulty in resolving them. Many of these types of change order requests are associated with differing interpretation of the contractor's obligations.

   Most contracts recognize the fact that unforeseen conditions may arise during construction and, depending upon their nature, may be cause for a change order increasing the contract sum.

   Depending upon the extent of restrictive clauses in the construction contract, the recovery of funds to compensate for additional costs incurred to deal with unforeseen subsurface conditions or concealed conditions may be difficult and will require some form of negotiation between all parties before acknowledgment and the final value of the change order is resolved—if, in fact, it is resolved at all.

   And, of course, delays caused by the owner or their consultants, job conditions, unanticipated events, or severe weather may generate a delay-based change order request.

3. Subcontractor-Initiated Change Orders. When owner-generated change order requests are issued to the general contractor, usually portions of this extra work involve subcontractors who will be requested to submit appropriate change orders. This form of change order request is probably the least complicated, as long as the subcontractor submits the proper cost breakdowns and backup docu-

mentation. However, when drawings have not been properly coordinated or contain inaccurate or incomplete information, change order requests initiated by the subcontractor and directed to the general contractor become more difficult to resolve. When subcontractors scrutinize their portion of the contract documents as work proceeds, these trade experts will uncover most of the errors and omissions in the contract documents, if any significant errors and omissions do exist.

Instead of becoming adversaries, the subcontractor and general contractor should discuss ways in which they can combine forces to resolve these problems since they both have a stake in an equitable resolution. Perhaps some value engineering suggestions can be presented to the architect/engineer, which if accepted would cancel all or a portion of the additional costs associated with the errors and omissions, and the architect and/or engineer may be more receptive to accepting these suggestions as long as they do not diminish the quality of the project.

If the general contractor's purchasing department has been less than thorough in buying out the job, they may not have awarded subcontract agreements that are all inclusive. When they discover that additional work is required, but was not included in the initial subcontract agreement, obtaining acceptance of this type of change order work will not be a simple matter. Since this probably highlights a shortcoming on the part of the general contractor's purchasing agent, settlement of any extra cost items will require some negotiation. But, once again, if a way can be found to propose any changes in the scope of the work that will result in savings to the subcontractor, eliminate the need for a change order, but still retain project quality, the general contractor may be inclined to pursue these changes with the design team to gain acceptance. This concept of "trade-offs" is a very effective way to deal with controversial change order requests.

Delays created by either the owner, architect, or general contractor may ultimately affect a particular subcontractor(s) scheduled work, and that subcontractor may feel entitled to request a change order incorporating costs associated with that delay. Depending upon the nature of the delay, both general contractor and subcontractor need to work together to produce the facts and costs related to these delays since both parties have a mutual interest in resolving these kinds of issues.

If the delay has been caused by the general contractor, the subcontractor should have already given written notice to that general contractor and must be prepared to fully substantiate their delay claim—and be ready for a battle.

Other causes for change order requests

When local building officials conduct their various project inspections, they often require changes to the work to comply with their interpretation of local building codes. If extra costs are required to implement these changes, the subcontractor should prepare a change order request to be submitted to the general contractor, who will, in turn, pass it on to the owner.

An owner's insurance carrier may require changes to the work in order to comply with their rules and regulations or in order to afford the owner lower rates.

The change in use of the building under construction requiring significant design alterations to the structure and its equipment is yet another reason to generate change order work.

Types of Change Orders

Lump Sum—this change order is one in which the scope of work is clearly defined and all costs associated with this change are clearly presented—when approved work will be paid for in accordance with the agreed lump or stipulated sum.

Unit Price—where unit prices have been included in the contractor or prenegotiated and only actual quantities are required in order to establish the cost of work. This form of change order is prevalent in public works projects, particularly when roadwork or site work is involved.

Although this may seem like a rather straightforward approach to change order work, when actual quantities vary substantially from the quantity initially proposed, the original unit price submitted by the contractor or subcontractor may present an opportunity to adjust that unit price. Various court decisions over the years have ruled in favor of the contractor requesting a change in unit prices on public works projects when actual quantities varied substantially from those quantities stated in the bid documents, but just as many court decisions have denied these requests.

Time and Material—often used when the actual scope of work is not easily defined or when work must commence immediately, or when neither party can reach an agreement on a lump sum.

This form of change order can create problems for owner, general contractor, and subcontractor unless the ground rules for the T&M work have been established beforehand and adequate documentation has been prepared and submitted with the change order proposal.

If the proper procedures are followed, Time and Material change orders can be processed promptly; if improperly prepared and documented, they can become a nightmare.

Pitfalls to Avoid When Working with Time and Material Change Orders

1. Establish as many acceptable costs as possible before starting the work.

   - Submit labor rates for all tradesmen that may be employed in the work. The breakdown should be complete and include a line item for each cost (Figures 7-1a and 7-1b).
   - If hand tools, or small tools that may be consumed partially or entirely are required for the work, establish a "cost" for these tools as either a percentage of work or an upcharge on the hourly labor rate.
   - If large pieces of construction equipment are required, submit a list of equipment rates to include all costs, except the operator's

BREAKDOWN OF HOURLY RATES

WORKERS TITLE:_____

	STRAIGHT	1 1/2 TIME	DOUBLE TIME
BASE WAGE RATE			
F.I.C.A			
F.U.T.A.			
S.U.T.A.			
GEN. LIABILITY INS.			
WORKER'S COMP. INS.			
WELFARE FUND			
PENSION FUND			
APPRENTICE FUND			
VACATION FUND			
ED. & CULT. FUND			
DEFERRED INCOME FUND			
PAID HOLIDAYS			
BOND PREMIUM			
INCIDENTALS			
OTHER:_____			

SUBTOTAL
OVERHEAD & PROFIT (15%)

Figure 7-1a

SUBCONTRACTOR: _____   LOCAL UNION NO. 24

ADDRESS: _____   CITY: NEW HAVEN

_____   STATE: CONNECTICUT

TEL. NO.: _____

LABOR CLASSIFICATION: CARPENTER – JOURNEYMAN

EFFECTIVE DATES: 04/01/93 – 03/31/96

	%/HOUR	STRAIGHT TIME	TIME & A HALF	PREMIUM DOUBLE TIME
BASIC RATE		18.75	28.13	37.50
VACATION OR SAVINGS		0.35	0.35	0.35
TAXABLE EARNINGS SUBTOTAL:	100%	19.10	28.48	37.85
F.O.A.B. LIMITATION 7.65%		1.46	2.18	2.90
F.U.T.A. LIMITATION .8%		0.15	0.23	0.30
S.U.T.A. LIMITATION CONN 6.9%		1.32	1.96	2.61
S.U.T.A. LIMITATION N.Y. 3.1%		0.59	0.88	1.17
WELFARE FUND		2.70	2.70	2.70
PENSION FUND		1.30	1.30	1.30
ANNUITY FUND		2.55	2.55	2.55
APPRENTICE TRAINING		0.15	0.15	0.15
VACATION, HOLIDAY, SPEC., LIFE INS. MEDICAL		0.00	0.00	0.00
INDUSTRY PROGRAM		0.00	0.00	0.00
ASSOC. PROGRAM		0.10	0.10	0.10
WORKMAN'S COMP.		5.45	8.12	10.79
CT. W/C ASSESSMENT 9.4%		0.51	0.76	1.01
PUBLIC LIABILITY, BODILY INJURY, PROPERTY DAMAGE		0.94	1.41	1.87
SUBTOTAL:		36.33	50.82	65.31
C.O. SUPPORT:		0.00	0.00	0.00
OVERHEAD:		3.63	5.08	6.53
SUBTOTAL:		39.96	55.90	71.84
PROFIT		4.00	5.59	7.18
TOTAL RATE PER HOUR:		43.95	61.49	79.02

NOTE:

Figure 7-1b

hourly rate. Any minimum billable hourly rates should also be included (Figure 7-2).

- Establish procedures for documenting the cost of materials. Will the general contractor require receiving tickets or actual invoices? How will actual material quantities be ascertained?

HEAVY DUTY CONSTRUCTION EQUIPMENT	DAILY	WEEKLY	MONTHLY
Compaction Equipment			
MBW	160.00	480.00	1,440.00
Plate	50.00	150.00	450.00
Jumping Jack	60.00	150.00	540.00
Rammax	250.00	750.00	2,195.00
Ingersol – SD 40D 5 – 10 ton	275.00	815.00	2,450.00
Duo Pact	200.00	600.00	1,800.00
Compressors			
Ingersol #185 CFM	80.00	240.00	750.00
Sulliair #185 truck mounted	90.00	270.00	810.00
Sulliair #250 CFM	110.00	325.00	980.00
Concrete Pump–Trucks – 80' to 120' booms w/operator & laborer	160.00 @hr.		
Grout Pumps – $65.00 @ hr. travel, 4 hr. minimum	105.00 @hr.		
Ditch Witch Model #6510 w/operator, by footage			
Excavators			
Kubota KH–91 mini excavator	220.00	900.00	2,700.00
Kubota KH–151 mini excavator	250.00	950.00	3,000.00
Cat 215 Excavator ($100.00 @ hrs.)	800.00	2,000.00	6,000.00
Komatsu 220 LC Excavator ($100.00 @ hrs.)	800.00	2,200.00	6,600.00
Komatsu 300 LC Excavator	900.00	3,100.00	9,500.00
Komatsu 300 LC Excavator w/hoe ram hydraulic breaker	1,650.00	6,100.00	18,500.00
Loaders			
Cat 953 truck loader ($90.00 @ hr.)	800.00	2,200.00	6,500.00
Cat 980 C rubber tire loader ($130.00 @ hr.)	1,200.00	3,600.00	11,000.00
Forklifts			
Komatsu Warehouse Forklift – 5,000 lb. Capacity	225.00	675.00	2,025.00
Lull Model 844 – 42'	400.00	1,050.00	2,800.00
Lull Model 844 B – 42'	425.00	1,100.00	2,900.00
Rubber Tire Backhoes			
Bob–Cat 743 B	175.00	525.00	1,550.00
Bob–Cat 743 B with Backhoe	250.00	750.00	2,250.00
Bob–Cat 843 B	250.00	750.00	2,250.00
Bob–Cat 843 B with Hoe – Ram Breaker Attachment	325.00	975.00	2,925.00
Cat 416 w/4–1 front bucket and extend–a–hoe ($85.00 @ hr.)	85.00 @ hr.	1,850.00	2,500.00
John Deere 710 w/4–1 front bucket ($85.00 @ hr.)	85.00 @ hr.	1,850.00	3,000.00
John Deere 710 w/hoe–ram hydraulic breaker			
Scissor Lifts			
24' Mark –Lift	135.00	355.00	1,050.00
30' Mark –Lift	160.00	435.00	1,275.00
36' Mark –Lift	225.00	550.00	1,550.00
Screening Equipment			
RD–90' Read Screen – All	750.00	2,275.00	6,825.00
Trommel Screen Royer 616 MP			7,500.00

Figure 7-2

- Daily work tickets should be used to document the number of workers employed, hours worked, task performed, and material consumed. (Figure 7-3).These tickets should be signed daily by the subcontractor's foreman and the general contractor's or owner's representative, as the case may be.

JOB INVOICE

3223

TO

TERMS:

PHONE	DATE OF ORDER
ORDER TAKEN BY	CUSTOMER'S ORDER NUMBER
☐ DAY WORK ☐ CONTRACT ☐ EXTRA	
JOB NAME/NUMBER	
JOB LOCATION	
JOB PHONE	STARTING DATE

QTY.	MATERIAL	PRICE	AMOUNT
DATE COMPLETED	TOTAL MATERIALS		

DESCRIPTION OF WORK

OTHER CHARGES	
TOTAL OTHER	

LABOR	HRS.	RATE	AMOUNT
		TOTAL LABOR	
		TOTAL MATERIALS	
		TOTAL OTHER	
Thank You		TAX	
		TOTAL	

Work ordered by

Signature
I hereby acknowledge the satisfactory completion of the above described work.

Figure 7-3

- Obtain agreement on allowable overhead and profit percentages to be applied to costs, if such a schedule has not already been included in the contract documents.

What Constitutes Cost?—Not As Simple As It Sounds

There are basically three types of "costs" as related to change orders:

1. Direct Costs—cost of labor, materials, equipment, tools, and other items required to perform or complete the work in the field.
2. Indirect Costs—costs associated with project management such as estimating time, secretarial assistance in preparing estimates, photographs, additional drawings required for the work, postage, shipping, phone calls, and other such administrative costs.
3. Consequential Costs—delays in performing base contract work due to introduction of this additional work into the initial construction schedule, and added impact on corporate overhead are two examples of consequential costs.

To paraphrase from Article 7.3.6 of the A.I.A General Conditions contract that refers to acceptable costs:

- Cost of labor, including social security, old age, and unemployment insurance, fringe benefits (either from collective bargaining agreements or otherwise, if the contractor is nonunion), workmen's compensation insurance.
- Cost of materials, supplies, equipment, including the cost of transportation. (A cost sometimes missed by a contractor is the cost to unload and distribute these materials or equipment.)
- Rental cost of machinery or equipment, exclusive of hand tools, whether rented from the contractor or from a rental company.
- Cost of insurance and bond premiums, permit fees, sales, and use taxes or other taxes or fees related to the work.
- Additional cost of supervision and field office personnel directly attributable to the change.

Although it may appear to be a simple question to answer, recognizable, acceptable "cost" may not be clear in the mind of the general contractor or owner.

What about the cost of reproduction of both plans and specifications required for office or field personnel or vendors in order to perform this extra work? Unless the general contractor is going to furnish sufficient copies of plans and specification revisions for the change order work, copies will be required for estimating by the subcontractor and for use in the office and in the field when the work is authorized. These costs can amount to hundreds of dollars for complex changes and the additional copies of revised plans and specifications must either be provided by the general contractor or included in the subcontractor's "costs."

Insurance and bond costs

Insurance and bond costs (where applicable) are often inadvertently excluded from the cost of work. A quick call to the company's insurance agent will determine whether the specific insurance requirements for the project will increase if the cost of the work increases.

If that is the case, a percentage can be established for each $100.00 or $1,000.00 of contract sum increase and added to the cost of the work.

When a subcontractor is required to furnish a labor and material or performance bond—or both—on a project, their bonding agent will audit the completed contract to determine if the cost of work as initially contracted for has either increased or decreased. Depending upon the completed contract sum, an adjustment will be made in the bond premium for that project.

There again, an increase in bond premium can be expressed as a percentage and added to the cost of work. But remember that the cost of the bond is affected by the total cost of your contract, which includes overhead and profit, so additional bond costs must be calculated after overhead and profit has been added.

The Constructive Change Directive

A.I.A. Document A201 provides for another approach to change order work, one referred to as the Constructive Change Directive (CCD), which can be employed when some extra work must be performed at the request of the owner, but there is either no time in which to review a change order proposal from the contractor or there is a disagreement over the costs for the extra work.

The architect will issue a signed CCD directing the contractor to proceed with the work, and reimbursement will be made based upon documentation of the following costs associated with that extra work:

- Cost of labor and all associated benefits and taxes.

- Cost of materials, supplies, equipment including cost of transportation.

- Rental costs of equipment and machinery, exclusive of hand tools, whether rented from the contractor or others.

- Cost of insurance and bond premiums, permits, fees, and taxes.

- Additional costs of *supervision* and *field office personnel directly connected with the additional work* (italics added by the writer to emphasis that architects recognize that additional supervision is an integral part of the cost of extra work).

A reasonable fee for overhead and profit is to be added to the above costs.

The construction cost-directive is basically an authorization to proceed with extra work on a time and material basis, but it is specific as to what constitutes "cost."

Change Orders—The Theoretical Approach

The textbook approach to change orders, if followed, would substantially lessen the number of disagreements surrounding the entire process, but this theoretical approach rarely takes place. In real life, an entirely different scenario takes place.

Assume the GC had just received verbal authorization from the architect to proceed with an owner-requested change and there is not enough time for the general contractor to prepare a proposed change order and submit it to the architect for review and approval, in writing—a process that could take weeks.

And assume that you, the subcontractor, have been requested by that general contractor to proceed with related changes to work already in progress or work being scheduled for the next few days.

Any delays in implementing the extra work will only add more costs to the change—so the GC issues a verbal request to your company to proceed with the work with either an agreed upon price or "we'll work it out" basis. In many cases that "we'll work it out" works—and in too many cases it doesn't. When those final costs are presented to the general contractor who presents them to the architect/owner there could be a difference of opinion as to the anticipated cost versus the actual cost. And guess who will be requested to accept a lesser amount?

This verbal authorization process is a common practice in the fast paced construction business today where good faith is often expected but just as often abused.

Long-term relationships with general contractors where considerable work has been satisfactorily performed on the basis of "we'll work it out" is one thing, but what about proceeding with work with a general contractor with whom the company has no previous experience, or working with one where results were less than satisfactory?

There are certain precautions that if taken, will lower the likelihood of disputes arising from the proposed change order work.

Obtain written authorization to proceed

Whether there is a long-term relationship or an initial relationship with the general contractor, requested change order work must be confirmed in writing from the outset. A handwritten note from the general contractor's field supervisor or project manager briefly describing the change is the bare minimum required. If the method of computing the final costs can be determined and agreed upon at that time so much the better. If an "order of magnitude" cost can be established and agreed upon that is another approach, or if a Time and Material authorization is included in the written change order request that is another safeguard against a future misunderstanding.

When the general contractor's field representative or project manager indicates that his or her company will issue written authorization for the changes upon return to the office, don't count on it. They may have had other more pressing matters (in their opinion) to do and may not issue the written authorization until weeks later, if at all.

Upon receipt of a verbal directive to perform "extra" work in the field, quickly follow up with a confirming letter such as:

July 14, 1997

John Logan   *Re: Edgehill Senior Living*
Acme Construction Company
122 Federal Street
Easton, Maryland

Dear John:

This will confirm your conversation with our foreman Joe Petrucci at the Edgehill site on July 14th whereby you directed him to extend the 2-hour-rated wall in Room 225 from the elevation of the proposed acoustical ceiling to the structure above.

We were advised to proceed with this work on a Time and Material basis and we will submit daily work tickets for this change to your superintendent for signature.

We would appreciate receiving your change order for this work promptly upon receipt of our Time and Material documentation.

(Mr. Subcontractor—Remember that in most cases, even though the change orders work has been approved by the general contractor, this work cannot be requisitioned until a signed change order is received from the general contractor.)

Very truly yours,

cc: Joe Petrucci

Pay When Paid and the Change Order

Most subcontract agreements contain the "pay when paid" clause which will also apply to change order work.

In the case of change orders, a roadblock to payment may surface. The general contractor cannot requisition the owner for change order work until they receive a change order signed by both architect and owner and the change order work may consist of proposals from any number of subcontractors which include their labor, materials, and equipment. If the architect or owner takes issue with any aspect of any subcontractor's portion of the change order, the entire approval process will be delayed until all such issues are resolved.

In the meantime, your proposal may have been acceptable to all parties, but the general contractor will not issue a written change order to your company until one is received from the architect for the entire change order.

In the case of general contractors who subcontract all of their work and do not perform any with their own forces, if the approval of a change order is delayed, their only costs may consist of estimating time, plus some corporate overhead, and, of course, their fee. This may not present much incentive for them to vigorously pursue resolution of the change order, but the subcontractors who have already expended payroll, material, and equipment costs may be "out-of-pocket" for thousands of dollars and require payment for the change order promptly so as not to adversely affect their cash flow.

Can anything be done about this situation? It may be difficult, but when negotiating the subcontract agreement with the general contractor, this subject should be brought to their attention. The contract could be amended to include a clause such as:

"When change order work is authorized, completed, and approved by the general contractor, the subcontractor will be allowed to request payment for the work on the next monthly requisition. Payment will be made by the general contractor within the same time frame that regular progress payments are made and will not depend upon the general contractor receiving payment from the owner for this work."

Preparation of a Proposed Change Order— Other Issues to Consider

There are a number of issues to be considered by a subcontractor when assembling an estimate for a proposed change order:

Will the work incorporated in the change order affect the completion time of my portion of the project? If there are liquidated damages in the contract between the owner and the general contractor and the "pass through" clause is included in the subcontract agreement, completion time becomes a very important component of the change order. If the work being requested is so extensive as to delay completion of the entire project, the general contractor should have alerted the owner to this fact and requested an extension to the completion date to avoid being assessed liquidated damages. And if the extent of your work will delay completion, a time extension so stated in the proposed change order is essential to alert the general contractor who, in turn, should notify the owner.

Even without the liquidated damages clause, if the nature of your work has increased dramatically, that is reason enough to include extended general conditions since the project will continue well beyond the initial completion date requiring more phone bills, more office and field supervision time, and so forth.

The overhead and profit applied to these extended general conditions will cover any additional corporate overhead costs.

Net cost

What is the net cost of this work (net cost = cost less overhead and profit)? Net cost is generally defined as cost of materials, including sales tax and delivery costs, cost of labor with all corporate and union fringe benefits applied, bond premiums (if applicable), insurance, equipment (either rented or company owned), tools (some expendable—i.e., small tools).

What other costs must be considered along with "bricks and mortar"? Remember the three types of costs: direct, indirect, and consequential.

Will additional supervision be required to implement this change order or can it be handled by the supervisor already assigned to the project? If the foreman's daily supervision activities will be significantly expanded by this extra work, his or her ability to properly supervise the "contract" work may be diluted and require another lead person to check layout, quality, ordering, and receipt of materials, and so forth. If this is the case, the general contractor should be advised so that justification for additional supervision can be documented and these costs accepted and included in the work.

What about additional project management time and related costs? This is a debatable item since the general contractor can argue that project management costs are "overhead," which is included in the subcontractor's overhead and profit percentage added to the net cost of the change order work.

The attached Change Order General Conditions Checklist (Figure 7-4) is a comprehensive guide to other costs to consider when preparing a

CHANGE ORDER GENERAL CONDITIONS CHECKLIST AND ESTIMATE SHEET

Project_____ #_____ Change Estimate No._____
Owner Bulletin No._____

	Material	Labor	Total

1. Supervision
    a. Project manager . . . . _____ _____
    b. Superintendent(s) . . . . _____ _____
    c. Project and Office engineer(s) . . . . _____ _____
    d. Field engineer(s) . . . . _____ _____
    e. Additional foremen . . . . _____ _____
    f. Accountant/time keeping/material check   _____ _____
    g. Home office supervision . . . . _____ _____
    h. _____ _____ _____
2. Temporary Facilities
    a. Field office(s) . . . . _____ _____ _____
    b. Material trailers/sheds . . . _____ _____ _____
    c. Temporary toilets . . . . . . _____ _____ _____
    d. Temporary roads . . . . . . _____ _____ _____
    e. Safety protection/equip-
       ment . . . . _____ _____ _____
    f. _____ _____ _____ _____
3. Field Support
    a. Office/first-aid supplies . . _____ _____ _____
    b. Blueprinting/copy-
       ing/photos . . . . _____ _____ _____
    c. Telephone . . . . _____ _____ _____
    d. Fire/theft alarm . . . . _____ _____ _____
    e. Insurances . . . . _____ _____ _____
    f. Home office expense . . . . _____ _____ _____
    g. _____ _____ _____ _____
4. Temporary Utilities
    a. Heat . . . . _____ _____ _____
    b. Light and power . . . . _____ _____ _____
    c. Water . . . . _____ _____ _____
    d. Elevators/lifting/moving . . _____ _____ _____
    e. Tests/inspections . . . . . . _____ _____ _____
    f. _____ _____ _____ _____
5. Construction Equipment
    a. Small tools (expendables) . _____ _____ _____
    b. Trash removal/light truck-
       ing . . . . _____ _____ _____
    c. _____ _____ _____ _____
6. Special Conditions
    a. Winter conditions . . . . . . _____ _____ _____
    b. Snow removal . . . . _____ _____ _____
    c. Cutting and patching . . . . _____ _____ _____
    d. Final cleanup . . . . _____ _____ _____
    e. _____ _____ _____ _____

Total change order general conditions $_____

Figure 7-4

proposed change order, based upon the nature of the project and the terms and conditions of the subcontract agreement.

Is the fee structure defined?

The fee structure for change order work will either be included in the base contract or set forth in the General, Supplementary, or Special Conditions portion of the specifications.

Some fee structures are based upon a sliding scale; the higher the cost of the work, the lower the allowable overhead and profit. These types of sliding scale schedules generally include maximum allowable fees to be applied to 2d, 3d, and 4th-tier subcontractors.

If no such overhead and profit fee structure is included anywhere in the contract documents, a reasonable percentage for overhead and profit must be negotiated with the general contractor prior to the submission of the first proposed change order. It is best to broach this subject at the initial project meeting so it will be one less hurdle to overcome once the project is underway.

When Change Order Work Involves Overtime

Extended periods of overtime reduce worker productivity. The Business Roundtable, an organization composed of executives from some of the country's largest corporations, conducted a series of studies relating to the construction industry in the 1980s.

Their study concluded that "scheduled overtime disrupts the economy of the affected area, magnifies any apparent labor shortage, reduces labor productivity, and may create excessive inflation on construction costs without material benefit to the completion schedule."

Their study also revealed that as more overtime work is scheduled, more time is lost through absenteeism. They also found that injuries increase as hours of work increase, not only in absolute terms but also in the rate of incidence.

And further, their studies found that "for hours above eight per day and 48 per week, it usually took three hours of work to produce two additional hours of output when the work was light. For heavy work, it took two hours to produce one hour of additional output."

The Business Roundtable study produced several charts plotting the loss of productivity when extended periods of 50- and 60-hour workweeks were encountered. Figure 7-5 reveals loss of productivity when workers worked 50 hours from periods extending from 1 to 2 weeks to 12 weeks. Figure 7-6 measures loss of productivity when 60-hour workweeks have been completed.

Scheduled Overtime

Decreases Productivity

Cumulative Effect of Overtime on Productivity 50- and 60-Hour Workweeks

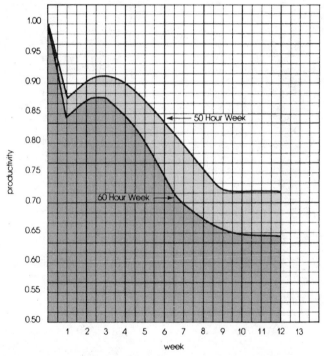

This represents the reduction in productivity normally experienced on projects operated on a basis of 50 hours per week and 60 hours per week. The data for these curves is from project operations in an area of tranquil labor relations and with excellent field management direction. The measure of productivity is a comparison of actual work hours expended for preplanned operations with a fixed standard base of calculated work hour requirements called a "bogey." These observations are on a weekly basis with all completed work recorded from physical count or measurement and the work hours expended obtained from actual payroll hours. The curves reflect the averages of many observations.

Figure 7-5

Ratio of Productive Return to Overtime Hours for 60-Hour Job Schedule

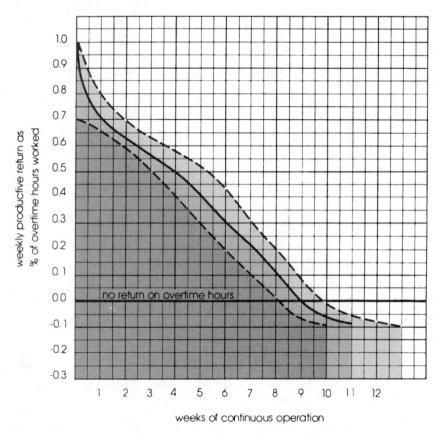

weeks of continuous operation

Direct comparisons of various data is difficult since all measurement of productive effort is not referenced to a Fixed Standard. The industrial firm's data on productivity is based on Fixed Standards, and a performance of 1.0 may not be the same as a performance of 1.0 referenced to some other standard of comparison. As a result, a 30 percent reduction of productivity in one set of data could compare with a 15 percent reduction reflected in another set of data due to this difference.

Figure 7-6

If the extra work being requested requires the subcontractors to have their crews work extended periods of overtime, their productivity units will decrease and a method to compensate for this lost productivity can not only be included in their costs, but also substantiated by the Business Roundtable studies.

For those persons interested in learning more about the various Business Roundtable studies, their address is 200 Park Avenue, New York, New York 10166.

Take the Agony Out of Change Order Work

Look at change order work from the perspective of the person to whom it is directed. If the change order request has been initiated because of a deficiency in the plans and specifications, the architect and/or engineer may be sensitive about these deficiencies, which will come to the attention of the owner who hired them.

If the general contractor's purchasing agent "missed" certain items or scope of work that should have been included in the initial contract, they will be very sensitive to the fact that they did not perform their job completely and will be resistant to agreeing to an increase in contract sum.

By recognizing the other party's concerns, a different approach may be used to obtain agreement on a proposed change. Look for trade-offs!

Are there ways in which the scope of work could be modified, without affecting the overall project quality, resulting in savings to offset these increased costs?

For example, will the architect accept another ceramic tile manufacturer who can provide similar quality, but at a lower cost to the subcontractor? If so, these savings could cancel the need for a proposed change order.

As another example are 18-gauge steel studs in a particular interior wall framing system not required structurally and would the substitution of 20-gauge studs be acceptable to the engineer? Such a change or changes may be sufficient to produce savings to offset all or a portion of the proposed change in question.

Here are guidelines to consider when issuing change order proposals:

- Prior to the issuance of that first change order proposal, thoroughly reread those portions of the subcontract agreement and the appropriate section of the contract specifications to ensure that the submission will comply with all of these guidelines.

- Advise the owner or general contractor, in writing, of an impending change order as soon as possible.

- When requested to submit costs for change order work, respond promptly and with sufficient detail and documentation so that a comprehensive review of the costs is possible.

- If errors and/or omissions are a source of the change order request, document completely those portions of the plans and/or specifications that are deficient.

- Obtain approval of labor, equipment rates, direct, and indirect costs early in the project and prior to any requests for change order work.

- When performing Time and Material work accumulate all documentation as the work progresses and request that the owner/general contractor's field representative sign daily work authorization tickets.

- Obtain written permission to proceed with change order work and an agreement on the lump sum amount.

- In the absence of written authorization from the owner or general contractor promptly submit a letter confirming the verbal agreement.

- Obtain a clear understanding of when change order work can be requisitioned and when payment can be expected.

- Proposed change orders should have an expiration date—i.e., "This proposal will remain valid until ("X" date)—or—"The subcontractor reserves the right to withdraw this proposed change order if not accepted within "X" days."

- If the proposed work will require the crews to work overtime, consider adding a percentage for lost productivity and also include premium pay for any supervisory staff.

- If the particular change order requires a substantial amount of estimating time and telephone calls to other subcontractors or suppliers, add some money to cover these costs and indicate them as costs required to prepare the estimate.

- Don't forget that when quoting an "add" cost, overhead and profit are included but when quoting a "deduct" cost, overhead and profit are excluded in the credit.

Schedules and Scheduling

The subject of scheduling could be equally at home in a chapter devoted to the mechanics of that subject or a chapter on effective management or, as in many cases today, a chapter on claims and disputes.

All three facets of the construction schedule will be addressed in this chapter. The principal reason for developing a construction schedule is to prepare a logical sequence of work tasks, with their durations, enabling the contractor to create a roadmap plotting the path of the project from start to finish.

Prior to the introduction of the moderately priced desktop computer, most contractors prepared a bar chart schedule by hand. Only the large, sophisticated builders had the resources and the necessity to create the much more complex critical path method (CPM) schedule.

However, the primary purpose for creating a schedule—i.e., to establish a time sequence for work tasks—in recent years has often taken a back seat to the use of the schedule as a document to prepare or defend against a claim for construction delays.

The Predominant Types of Construction Schedules

The bar chart

Often referred to as the Gantt Chart (Figure 8-1) after its originator, Henry Gantt, this type of schedule lists various construction activities in a vertical column on the left side of the chart, and a calendar—either by weeks or months—is spread out horizontally along the top of the chart. A horizontal line or "bar" is placed alongside each vertically listed activity extending out to the duration represented by the week or month across the top of the chart. From the early 1900s until the late 1950s, the Gantt or bar chart was the primary construction schedule.

The bar chart is relatively simple to prepare and is easily understood by professional and nonprofessional alike and was used extensively in the construction industry for many years. Most field supervisors, workers, and managers are familiar with its preparation and interpretation.

In large gatherings, either at an owner's meeting or building committee meeting, the simplicity of the bar chart schedule makes for an excellent visual presentation. But this does have its limitations.

The disadvantages of the bar chart are the following:

- It cannot graphically display a great deal of detail when large or complex projects are undertaken.

- It cannot adequately display the interdependence of one work task upon another.

- Updating cannot display "cause and effect" of delays on the entire project's completion.

- It cannot reflect the impact that a delay in one activity will have on other subsequent work activities.

The bar chart is often used during the bidding process to depict various milestone dates and start-finish dates for broad categories of work tasks, but in today's fast-paced construction projects where detailed schedules are generally required by contract and documentation of actual versus planned events are required to prepare for or defend against a potential claim, the CPM schedule is needed.

The critical path method (CPM)

The CPM schedule, in simple terms, is a graphic display of the start and finish of each work task, that task's dependence on previous activities—known as precedences—and the relationship with succeeding activities, referred to as successors (Figure 8-2).

With the availability of the relatively inexpensive desktop and laptop computers and the proliferation of moderately priced scheduling software, most contractors today have the capability to produce complex CPM schedules in house with their own staff. And most of their project managers are familiar with the preparation and updating of these schedules.

The CPM can be developed to display hundreds or thousands of interrelated work tasks.

PROJECT SCHEDULE

PROJECT __Turn of River Office Building__   LOCATION __Dover, Delaware__   DATE __December 18, 1998__

No.	DESCRIPTION	CALENDAR PERIOD	COMMENTS
		J F M A M J J A S O N D	
	Mobilization		
	Sitework		
	Concrete Foundations		
	Site Utilities		
	Structural Steel		
	Concrete Slabs		
	Exterior Studs/Sheathing		
	Punch List		

Figure 8-1

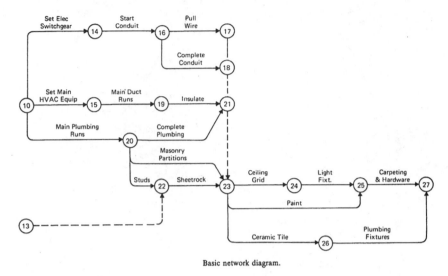

Basic network diagram.

Figure 8-2

The CPM Schedule can also be produced as a "milestone" schedule that is often a required submission in the original bid package (Figure 8-3).

A CPM schedule containing hundreds of work tasks will create a rather large graphic display requiring the use of a plotter to produce multiple printouts some as large as 36 inches by 60 inches.

With the use of a computer, changing logic or duration of any work task is not complex, and updating can be achieved rather rapidly. However, some adjustments become complicated when the initial (baseline) schedule needs to be modified due to significant changes in either logic, duration of an activity, or the proposed start or finish of an activity.

Along with the graphic display of the CPM Schedule as shown in the milestone schedule (Figure 8-3), detail sheets (Figure 8-4) can also be generated that list each work task, start and finish dates, and those tasks that must be completed (referred to as Predecessors) before other work can start, and whether or not the activity is on the critical path.

The number in the Predecessor column refers to the number of the task that is to be completed before the start of the related task number. For example, Task ID 478—Window Blocking is not to start until its predecessor ID 477 (CMU Veneer) has been started two weeks previously.

Although the CPM schedule has obvious advantages, there are some disadvantages.

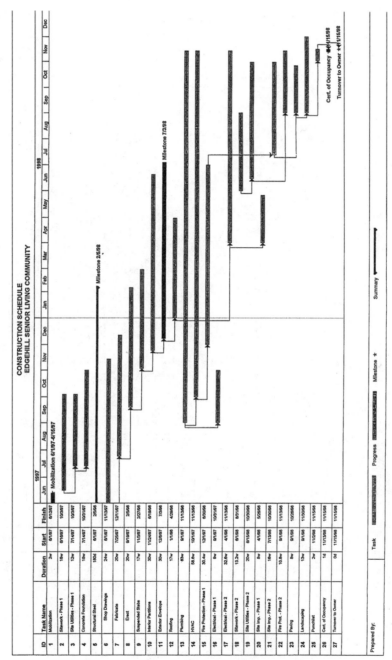

CONSTRUCTION SCHEDULE
EDGEHILL SENIOR LIVING COMMUNITY

Figure 8-3

151

ID	Task Name	Duration	Critical	Start	Finish	Predecessors	% Complete
469	Chimney Caps	2w	No	4/30/98	5/13/98	462SS+1w,270	0%
470	Flat Roof	1w	No	4/17/98	4/23/98	466,467,272	0%
471	Roof Shingles & Flashing	3w	No	4/17/98	5/7/98	466,467,273	0%
472	Frame Balconies	4w	No	4/14/98	5/11/98	459,276	0%
473	Spray Fireproofing	4w	No	3/24/98	4/14/98	277,460	0%
474	Ext. Steel Stud Framing	4w	No	3/24/98	4/21/98	460,462FF,278	0%
475	Insulate Beams	3w	No	4/15/98	5/5/98	476SS	0%
476	Ext. Sheathing	3w	No	4/15/98	5/5/98	474FF+2w,280	0%
477	CMU Veneer	4w	No	4/29/98	5/26/98	476SS+2w,281	0%
478	Window Blocking	2w	No	5/13/98	5/26/98	477SS+2w,282	0%
479	Sill Flashing at Stone Face	2w	No	5/20/98	6/3/98	478SS+1w,283	0%
480	Windows at Stone Face	2w	No	5/27/98	6/10/98	479SS+1w,284	0%
481	Downspout Supports	3w	No	5/6/98	5/26/98	476	0%
482	Synth. Stone	4w	No	6/9/98	7/7/98	477SS+1w,286,481	0%
483	EIFS	4w	No	6/23/98	7/21/98	482SS+2w,287,481	0%
484	Window Flashing at EIFS	2w	No	5/6/98	5/19/98	476	0%
485	Windows at EIFS	2w	No	5/6/98	5/19/98	484SS,289	0%
486	Flashing at Wood Siding	2w	No	5/6/98	5/19/98	290,476	0%
487	Windows at Wood Siding	2w	No	5/12/98	5/25/98	486SS,291	0%
488	Wood Siding & Trim	3w	No	5/26/98	6/16/98	292,486	0%
489	Aluminum Storefront	2w	No	5/6/98	5/19/98	476,293	0%
490	Custom Wood Windows	3w	No	6/3/98	6/23/98	295,476	0%
491	Window Glazing	3w	No	6/24/98	7/15/98	296,490,489	0%
492	Exterior Wood Doors	3w	No	7/22/98	8/11/98	297,483,482	0%
493	Caulk	3w	No	8/26/98	9/15/98	496FF	0%
494	Gutters & Downspouts	1w	No	9/16/98	9/22/98	482,483,488,299,496	0%

Updated 1/21/98 with revised sequence. Links removed and durations shortened to achieve 12/31/98 completion.

Figure 8-4

- A computer and software is required and, depending upon the quality of each, an outlay of $10,000–$15,000 dollars, or more may be required.

- Unless someone on the contractor's staff is computer literate, costly training sessions may be required before the operator becomes familiar with the software program and proficient in preparing and updating the schedule.

- Fully trained personnel need to keep practicing their computer scheduling skills or they will lose their proficiency rather quickly.

- Even a relatively simple CPM schedule requires considerable time to prepare initially and updates require periodic meetings with the general contractor, other subcontractors, suppliers, and field supervision personnel.

- When delays occur, a great deal of time and effort may be required to prepare a recovery schedule to incorporate the means, methods, and costs to compensate for these delays.

When used properly, a CPM schedule is a powerful management tool in assisting in the process of maintaining controlled job progress. It can be effective in highlighting those areas that must be micromanaged in order to either remain on schedule or recover lost time.

The program evaluation and review technique (PERT) schedule

Required by some government agencies, particularly the military, the PERT schedule focuses on the occurrence of milestone dates rather than the activities required to achieve the milestones. These types of schedules are often used by NASA and are more long-range project-oriented.

Although PERT schedules involve only time factors, when cost factors are added the program is known as PERTCO. PERT schedules are rarely, if ever, used in private industrial and commercial construction projects.

The Changing Role of the Construction Schedule

The schedule, in today's construction project, becomes a two-edged sword. Once it has been prepared by the general contractor and acknowledged by the owner, this schedule becomes the "Baseline" Schedule—the initially planned schedule of events required to complete the project.

Any significant changes—or, in some cases, minor changes in critical tasks—may be cause to revise the baseline schedule. And if these changes indicate that the completion of the project will be extended, but the owner or general contractor insists upon maintaining the original completion date, a "recovery" schedule will be generated to indicate how the general contractor expects to modify, accelerate, or otherwise change certain key operations to ensure an on-time completion date.

Once the general contractor issues the baseline schedule, and it is accepted by the architect and/or the owner, all participants to the construction process including subcontractors and vendors will be expected to comply with the logic and duration of all activities within that schedule.

If a subcontractor or supplier fails to meet its start and completion date and other trades are affected, the general contractor will be quick to notify that subcontractor or vendor of their noncompliance and its impact on the completion date.

The construction schedule and the construction contract

Many variations exist, but the primary function of a contract scheduling requirement is to ensure that the contractor adheres to the initial schedule when it is accepted, and if delays do occur, the owner will be advised of the cause and effect of any delays as well as the efforts required to maintain the initial or baseline schedule. Assigning responsibility for costs associated with delays is an entirely different matter.

The primary function of a construction schedule is to provide the project owner with a detailed description of the planned flow of work activities, but rarely does this initial, baseline schedule of events remain unchanged during the entire construction period.

Construction, being the high-risk business that it is, will be subjected to any number of "glitches" as work progresses—some created by the owner or design consultants, some brought about by the contractor or subcontractors, some by severe weather conditions, and some by events for which no one can be held accountable. But the project owner's contract with the general contractor will include sufficient restrictive clauses to protect their interests should delays occur.

And the subcontractor, bound by the terms of the owner's contract with the general contractor will certainly be held accountable if they are the cause for any delays.

Typical Contract Schedule Clauses

Typically, the contract with the owner will set forth the requirements for submission of the initial schedule, updates (often required with the submission of the monthly requisition), and methods by which the contractor is expected to implement to recover lost time if they fail to meet scheduled milestones.

A liquidated damages clause in the general contractor's contract with the owner, will, via the "pass-through" clause in the subcontract agreement, hold subcontractors responsible for any delays they may have created. The dollar amount of the liquidated damages an owner can assess due to late delivery of the project will be stipulated in the contract documents, and they can be substantial—$10,000 to $15,000 per day, or more, on a large project are not unusual.

Some contract requirements relating to adherence to the initial, accepted schedule can be rather stringent. For example, in one such project that the writer was involved with, the contract provided for the following:

"If any of the work is not on schedule, the contractor shall immediately advise the owner in writing of a proposed action to bring the work on schedule and shall submit two copies of a diagram showing changes. In such an event, the owner will require the contractor to work such additional time over regular hours—including Saturdays, Sundays, and holidays—at no additional cost to the owner, to bring the work back on schedule.

"If the contractor fails to take prompt and adequate corrective action to the owner's satisfaction, the owner reserves the right to perform such work as it deems necessary and back-charge the cost thereof against payments due the contractor."

Quite often the project delays can be traced to late deliveries of supplies and equipment and therefore the prompt submission of shop drawings by subcontractors and their vendors assume added importance.

The Shop Drawing Submission Schedule

Without approved shop drawings, not much equipment or materials can be incorporated into the work, therefore the prompt and correct procedures for submission of shop drawings becomes a critical part of any general contractor's schedule. And since the source of a significant number of these shop drawings originate with the subcontractors they engage, this stage of the subcontractor's involvement in the project takes on added importance.

At the construction project kickoff meeting, the procedure for the submission of shop drawings will generally be discussed, and subcontractors will be requested to submit their schedules of submissions. They will be requested to indicate the length of time for delivery of the material or equipment after the subcontractor receives an approval of that submission. Without accurate information from the subcontractor, the general contractor will have a difficult time preparing an accurate construction schedule.

More than one subcontractor has found themselves in trouble because they didn't properly prepare a realistic shop drawing submission schedule, and late deliveries of key equipment or materials created delays in their work as well as other trades who followed them. And the general contractor will be quick to advise the subcontractor that any costs associated with these delays will be billed to their account via a back-charge.

When a subcontractor takes too much time to purchase equipment or supplies because they are shopping around for the best deal, the time lost can be costly. What these subcontractors should also consider is the impact of late deliveries on the construction schedule and what costs may be assessed by the general contractor if these late deliveries affect other trades thereby causing the schedule to slip.

Another mistake subcontractors often make is assuming that a product being offered as an "or equal" to the one specified, will be accepted by the general contractor and the owner's architect/engineer. If the substitute product is rejected and additional time is required to purchase the specified product, obtain shop drawings, and accept late delivery, any savings that might have accrued by the substitution of an "or equal" may be eroded quite rapidly, and, in fact, may cost the subcontractor more money, particularly if job progress has been delayed by this process.

The importance of preparing a realistic shop drawing submission schedule cannot be overemphasized and the same can be said for participation in the preparation of the general contractor's overall project schedule—by providing them with detailed and accurate information.

The General Contractor's Preparation of the CPM Schedule

The preparation of a CPM schedule requires the assemblage of major and some minor work tasks to be undertaken by each subcontractor on the project and will include those activities to be completed by the general contractor's own forces if, in fact, they are to perform any work with their own forces.

The general contractor should be thoroughly experienced in the sequence of work tasks, but will usually require the assistance of subcontractors to furnish information relating to the time required to complete each phase of their work, taking into account the delivery of critical materials and equipment.

The GC must then evaluate which operation is to be completed before a subsequent one can start, or whether a certain amount of lead-time must be established before that next work task can commence. Or the GC may determine that some totally unrelated activities can commence and complete concurrently.

Once all of these activities are defined, the computer will be used to produce a rough draft schedule that may reflect a completion date in excess of that required by contract. The general contractor will then proceed to review the entire schedule, determine which activities need to be adjusted or changed in order to comply with the contract completion date.

So it is a long, tedious process that works best when all parties participate, establish realistic work task durations, communicate openly, and are willing to "tweak" certain tasks to complete them more expeditiously.

Since everyone will be expected to agree on their portion of the schedule and their interrelationship with other subcontractors and vendors, cooperation during the preparation of the first draft of the baseline of the schedule is all important. This first draft will, or should be distributed by the general contractor to each subcontractor to review, comment, change, or accept as issued.

When a general contractor, anxious to obtain a contract with an owner, promises to meet a project completion date that is either very aggressive or nearly impossible to meet, whom will they turn to, to assist in meeting these nearly impossible schedules? You, Mr. Subcontractor! Be particularly concerned if liquidated damages apply to this project.

Any tendency to bend to the general contractor's request to shorten the duration of the subcontractor's work beyond that which is considered reasonable ought to be avoided.

When the Baseline Schedule Has Reached Its Final Draft Stage

Subcontractors should expect to receive a letter from the General Contractor similar to the one below when the general contractor's baseline schedule is in its final draft form.

ABC Electrical
455 Old Court Road
Baltimore, Maryland

Gentlemen:

Attached are two copies of the baseline schedule for the Westover Elementary School project, dated April 15, 1998.

Please review this schedule and either accept or modify each of the following events:

1. *Shop drawing submission dates and approval duration.*
2. *Material/equipment and/or fabrication time, after receipt of approved drawings.*
3. *Activity durations.*
4. *Agreement on preceding work tasks that will allow your work to commence.*
5. *Agreement that your work tasks have been allocated in the proper sequence.*
6. *Any other comments regarding your schedule or the schedule of others.*

Please respond not later than April 22, 1998, and if this schedule is acceptable, acknowledge same by signing in the space allotted for that purpose.

> *Very truly yours.*
>
> *Tom Paine*
> *Mid Atlantic General*
> *Contractors, Inc.*

Remember, by signing such a document, your company becomes committed to adhere to this schedule, unless the general contractor permits your company, in writing, to deviate at either no cost, or according to any negotiated additional costs.

Beware the general contractor who does not bring subcontractors into the formulation of the schedule. It will be difficult if not impossible for this general contractor to prepare an accurate, workable schedule without the input of the trade specialists.

Also beware the general contractor, who after receiving subcontractor input prepares the schedule only to find that it produces a completion date substantially longer than the contract allows, and the general contractor arbitrarily reduces duration times for various subcontractor operations—without their agreement.

When the letter arrives requesting acceptance of a "forced" schedule, signing such a letter is similar to putting a loaded gun to one's head.

The resource loaded CPM schedule

Fine-tuning the CPM process further, some owners require the general contractor to submit a resource-loaded schedule. Once the activities are defined and durations are determined, the amount of each task's resources (i.e., manpower) will be required to be defined.

For example, if a concrete footing operation has a scheduled placement duration of two (2) days requiring one ironworker, two carpenters, and two laborers, manning and productivity are thereby established, monitored, and scrutinized utilizing these manpower requirements.

When resource loading is required, the distribution of workers over the entire project must be borne in mind by the subcontractor.

Once this resource-loaded schedule is accepted, the planned manpower for each task will be established and the respective subcontractors will be expected to provide workers accordingly. If they fail to do so and their work falls behind schedule they will be held accountable for all delays.

The cost-loaded CPM schedule

In addition to the activity, duration, and resource loading by incorporating the cost of all resources required to complete an activity, a cost-loaded schedule can be developed.

These cost-loaded schedules are of value in plotting the anticipated cost flow of the project on a monthly basis and the owner can anticipate the dollar value of future requisitions. But without monthly updates as the ebb and flow of construction activity proceeds, these cost-loaded schedules will be of little value.

A Word About "Float"

An inspection of some CPM schedules will reveal that some activities are listed with two starting and two finishing dates. These dates are indicated as "Early Start," "Late Start," and "Early Finish," "Late Finish."

All schedules need to incorporate additional time to compensate for unforeseen events, and these extra days are referred to as "float."

Float can also be defined as the number of days a noncritical operation can be delayed before it becomes part of the critical path. The noncritical path activities have some flexibility as to their starting and completion date. They can start at either the "early" or "late" start dates and consequently can finish as either the "early" or "late" finish date without affecting the overall schedule.

Questions often arise as to who "owns" the float. The contractors may, rightfully so, claim that they "own" the float—in effect, they must include some unanticipated delays in the schedule; however, the owners may indicate that they also require float to accomplish some work tasks or activities for which they are contractually responsible. For example, the owner may have elected to purchase all of the carpet and was advised by the contractor that the carpet must be on-site ready for installation by, say, August 1st. The owner may need some float time in case there are delays in the delivery of the carpet and therefore direct the contractor to provide them with an "Early" and "Late" start for carpet installation. This, in effect, removes some of the contractor's float time from the schedule. The GC may deny the owner any float time (not a good idea!), or negotiate some extension of time whereby one or two minor operations may be allowed to continue beyond the contract completion date.

These kinds of negotiations should have been concluded prior to the preparation of the baseline schedule, but if the owner's float time issues are resolved after the baseline schedule has been prepared, distributed, reviewed, and approved by all parties—including the subcontractors—someone's work durations may be shortened to accommodate the owner's float. Quite often the owner/general contractor contract will specifically indicate who owns the float and at other times the issue of float is addressed in the specifications.

When Schedules Are Not Met, Delays Occur

When schedules are not administered properly, or some significant unforeseen events occur, delays will not be far behind. The owner, by his or her actions or inactions, the architect/engineer by delaying approval of shop drawings or important inspections, and the general contractor and subcontractor for any number of reasons may create delays that affect the schedule.

When delays occur a recovery schedule will be required unless the owner will agree to extend the completion of the project.

The Recovery Schedule

When delays occur that affect the completion schedule, the reasons for these delays will be thoroughly investigated by the general contractor, particularly when liquidated damages may be assessed.

Were the delays created by the owner or their design consultants, by the general contractor, by subcontractors or suppliers, by Acts of God, or by the occurrence of unforeseen circumstances or conditions? When delays are brought to the attention of the owner they are probably the culmination of a series of events that have been occurring throughout the project for some time but were thought to be under control.

Whatever the cause, if the owner insists on maintaining the original completion date and accepts no responsibility for the delays, a recovery schedule will be required and all affected subcontractors and suppliers will be requested to provide their input in this schedule.

For example, the portion of a baseline schedule shown in Figure 8-5 and the recovery schedule (Figure 8-6) contain various fire protection, electrical, and mechanical work tasks.

		Continuing Care Retirement Community					8/12/97
ID	**Task Name**		**Duration**	**Critical**	**Resource Names**	**Start**	**Finish**
307	Infill stair treads		1w	No	Rogers	12/29/97	1/2/98
308	Fire standpipe		3w	No	Superior	12/22/97	1/9/98
309	Fire distribution mains		4w	No	Superior	12/8/97	1/2/98
310	Fire pumps & Equip. C-Wing		4w	No	Superior	12/8/97	1/2/98
311	Fire branch piping		4w	No	Superior	12/8/97	1/2/98
312	Plumbing hangers		1w	No	WRJ	12/11/97	12/17/97
313	Plumbing distribution mains		4w	No	WRJ	12/11/97	1/7/98
314	Plumbing risers		4w	No	WRJ	1/1/98	1/28/98
315	Plumbing branch piping		4w	No	WRJ	1/22/98	2/18/98
316	Plumbing equipment in 'C' wing		4w	No	WRJ	1/8/98	2/4/98
317	Elec. branch wiring - walls		4w	No	Acme	1/21/98	2/17/98
318	Elec. inspection - walls		0d	No	Acme	2/17/98	2/17/98
319	Elec. branch wiring - ceilings		4w	No	Acme	1/19/98	2/13/98
320	Elec. inspection - ceilings		0d	No	Acme	2/13/98	2/13/98
321	Elec. panels & distribution		4w	No	Acme	1/29/98	2/25/98
322	Switch & transformers		3w	No	Acme	4/2/98	4/22/98
323	Pull wire		3w	No	Acme	2/12/98	3/4/98
324	Systems wiring		4w	No	Acme	4/2/98	4/29/98
325	HVAC pipe hangers		5d	No	WRJ	12/8/97	12/12/97
326	HVAC risers		15d	No	WRJ	12/8/97	12/26/97
327	HVAC distribution piping		30d	No	WRJ	12/18/97	1/28/98
328	HVAC branch piping		30d	No	WRJ	12/18/97	1/28/98
329	Install heat pumps		2w	No	WRJ	3/4/98	3/17/98
330	Install cooling tower in 'C' wing		2w	No	WRJ	12/1/97	12/12/97
331	Boiler, heat Ex., pumps in 'C'		3w	No	WRJ	1/29/98	2/18/98
332	HVAC duct hangers		5d	No	WRJ	12/8/97	12/12/97
333	HVAC duct		3w	No	WRJ	2/9/98	2/27/98
334	RTU's		1w	No	WRJ	2/23/98	2/27/98
335	M&P roughin inspections		0d	No	Acme,WRJ,Superior	2/27/98	2/27/98
336	Elevator rails & platforms		1d	No	Eastern	3/12/98	3/12/98
337	Elevator doors		1d	No	Eastern	4/23/98	4/23/98
338	Elevator cabs		3w	No	Eastern	4/24/98	5/14/98
339							
340	**D Wing Finishes**		155d	No		12/18/97	7/22/98

Figure 8-5

	Continuing Care Retirement Community					10/28/97
ID	Task Name	Duration	Critical	Start	Finish	
312	Fire distribution mains	4w	No	1/29/98	2/25/98	
313	Fire pumps & Equip. C-Wing	4w	No	1/15/98	2/11/98	
314	Fire branch piping	4w	No	1/29/98	2/25/98	
315	Plumbing hangers	1w	No	2/5/98	2/11/98	
316	Plumbing distribution mains	4w	No	2/5/98	3/4/98	
317	Plumbing risers	4w	No	2/26/98	3/25/98	
318	Plumbing branch piping	4w	No	3/19/98	4/15/98	
319	Plumbing equipment in 'C' wing	4w	No	3/5/98	4/1/98	
320	Elec. branch wiring - walls	4w	No	3/25/98	4/21/98	
322	Elec. branch wiring - ceilings	4w	No	3/23/98	4/17/98	
324	Elec. panels & distribution	4w	No	3/26/98	4/22/98	
326	Pull wire	3w	No	4/9/98	4/29/98	
328	HVAC pipe hangers	5d	No	1/15/98	1/21/98	
329	HVAC risers	15d	No	1/15/98	2/4/98	
330	HVAC distribution piping	30d	No	2/12/98	3/25/98	
331	HVAC branch piping	30d	No	2/12/98	3/25/98	
333	Install cooling tower in 'C' wing	2w	No	2/9/98	2/20/98	
334	Boiler, heat Ex., pumps in 'C'	3w	No	3/26/98	4/15/98	
335	HVAC duct hangers	5d	No	1/15/98	1/21/98	
336	HVAC duct	3w	No	4/13/98	5/1/98	
343	D Wing Finishes	165d	No	1/29/98	9/16/98	
344	Apartments	155d	No	2/12/98	9/16/98	
345	Fireplace masonry	1w	No	2/12/98	2/18/98	
346	Flue liner	1w	No	2/26/98	3/4/98	
347	Set tubs	1w	No	3/5/98	3/11/98	
348	Hollow mtl.	30d	No	2/12/98	3/25/98	
369	D Wing Corridors	130d	No	3/5/98	9/2/98	
370	Trash chute	1w	No	3/5/98	3/11/98	
386	D Wing Garages	119d	No	1/29/98	7/14/98	
387	Hollow metal	2w	No	1/29/98	2/11/98	
388	Glass block	1w	No	1/29/98	2/4/98	
396	C Wing Finishes	230d	No	1/29/98	12/16/98	
397	C Wing SNF & ALF Rms.	149d	No	2/12/98	9/8/98	

Corrected Baseline with Soil, Rock, and Steel Delays   5

Figure 8-6

Noting Fire Protection activities Nos. 308, 309, 310, and 311 in the baseline schedule, all of these activities were to have been completed no later than January 9, 1998. Because of delays encountered by the general contractor, a corrected baseline schedule was published in October 1997, and this schedule shifts completion of these fire protection activities (ID 314-Fire Branch piping) to February 25, 1998.

Duration times for each activity have not changed, and none of these operations are now on the critical path, but does this mean that no additional costs will be involved in order to shift these tasks to a later date? Not necessarily.

When durations for various tasks are reduced, additional manpower may be required, or premium time work may be needed, both of which may impact the budget.

Recovery Schedule Checklist

Any recovery schedule proposed by the general contractor should be reviewed and the following questions asked and answered:

- Have duration of tasks changed and if so what additional costs are involved to meet these reduced duration times?
- Are these activities now on the critical path which means that they must start and finish on the dates so indicated with no float time available.
- Are there any logic changes, i.e., are different activities listed as predecessors or successors, and do they have any impact on the productivity of the task to be reviewed?
- Are other trades now required to work where previously other trades worked alone? (In other words, has trade stacking taken place, thereby reducing productivity?)
- Are activities now extended into times frames where collective bargaining agreements may expire creating a potential job action or wage/fringe pay increase?
- Will there be either additional material or equipment costs required to delay shipments already in progress or will additional costs be incurred because of price increases for these delayed shipments?
- Will the changed time frame for work start-finish dates have any impact on supervision/manpower requirements that were planned for other future projects currently under contract and scheduled to start soon?

Types of Project Delays

Delays and their impact on the construction schedule come in various shapes, forms, and severity, but no matter who was responsible or the reasons for the delays, they usually fall into one or more of the following categories.

- Excusable—a delay that justifies a contractual modification.

- Nonexcusable—a delay that does not justify a contract modification.

- Compensable—a delay that constitutes grounds for recovery of money damages.

- Noncompensable—a delay that does not constitute grounds for recovery of money damages.

- Concurrent delays—delays created by either the owner or the owner's consultants and the contractor, and these delays happen to run concurrently.

Procedures to follow to document and deal with these various types of delays are presented more fully and discussed in Chapter 9, Claims and Disputes.

Chapter

9

Claims and Disputes

The dictionary defines dispute as "to discuss, to argue; debate;" a claim is "asserting a right." The dispute occurs first and if not resolved, the claim will follow.

At one time or another your company may be faced with a disagreement or dispute over its contractual relationship with the owner of a project or the general contractor. Some disputes will quickly end after one or more negotiating sessions, but others will escalate to the next notch—the submission of a claim.

A learned judge described a large construction project in this manner:

> "Except in the middle of a battlefield, nowhere must men coordinate the movement of other men and all materials in the midst of such chaos and with limited certainty of present facts and future occurrences, as in a large construction project. Even the most painstaking planning frequently turns out to be mere conjecture, and accommodating to changes must necessarily be of the rough, quick and ad hoc sort, analogous to the ever changing commands on the battlefield."

General Patton—welcome to the construction industry!

What Triggers Claims and Disputes

Misunderstandings on the part of each participant's obligations and responsibilities in the construction process abound in the industry.

Although we work in an industry where we deal with contracts on a daily basis (hence the name contractor and subcontractor), how many of us have thoroughly read and fully understood our contractual obligations before signing that all-important contract? Only when we detect trouble over the horizon do we go back and revisit all of the contract language, only to find that there were clauses and stipulations that we should never have agreed to abide by. Or did we knowingly sign a contract with onerous conditions, anticipating that they would never be brought into play?

Not only are construction contracts full of language meant to transfer risk from one party to another, but the plans and specifications that form the nucleus of the contract obligations contain the seeds for future misunderstandings and disagreements.

The architect and engineer's interpretation of the "intent" of the plans and specifications may differ from the interpretation and "intent" as perceived by the contractor and, for any number of reasons, the plans and specifications may contain errors and omissions, not by intent, but there nevertheless.

The owner, in their attempt to solicit bids on their project as quickly as possible, not allowing the designers sufficient time for a full review and coordination of the bid documents, may have unwittingly taken the first step along the road leading to a project fraught with disputes and claims.

Drawings and specifications thus submitted to contractors for bidding purposes may contain several of the following shortcomings:

- Structural and architectural drawings that have not been fully coordinated and therefore there are dimensional differences between the two sets of drawings.

- Mechanical, electrical, and fire protection installations that will not fit in the space allotted to them, in either walls or ceilings; basically another manifestation of drawings that lack adequate coordination.

- A detail on one drawing conflicting with the way in which the detail is represented on another drawing.

- Door and frame schedules that do not agree with the door and frame details on the drawings.

- A Finish Schedule that does not agree with finishes designated on the drawings.

- Wall sections that do not meet the code requirements, that vary from large-scale details or various wall sections as shown on architectural drawings.

- A drawing that refers to a detail on another drawing but that detail either is missing or does not apply.

- Individual room and partition dimensions that do not add up to the overall floor dimension.

- Window or door schedule dimensions that are at variance with their corresponding openings as indicated on the drawings.

- Specifications that were obviously prepared for another project but have no relationship to the specifications required for the job in hand.

- Duplication of product requirements in two different specification sections, i.e., aluminum entrance hardware specifications in the aluminum door section and also in the hardware section. And based upon "risk transfer" language contained in the contract, the owner will expect to receive a credit for the deletion of one or the other product.

This is just a partial list of the problems that occur with some frequency on plans and specifications issued for bidding or for construction. And that is why when a contract or subcontractor agreement is negotiated requiring the contractor to complete the work in accordance with the "plans and specifications," what does this actually mean? Does it mean that the contractor is obligated to comply with the requirements shown in the defective plans and specifications or are they to comply with the intent of the plans and specifications? Or does it mean that the contractor or the subcontractor is expected to include all costs to correct all errors and omissions contained in the contract documents? The contractor's obligation lies somewhere in between these two extremes and the uncovering of any plan and/or specification defects, followed by prompt and equitable resolution of any problems will determine whether a project will proceed relatively smoothly or whether disputes, claims, and litigation is hovering just over the horizon.

Most disagreements between general contractor and subcontractor will occur for one or more of the following reasons:

1. During the contract negotiation stage, there was no definitive, mutual understanding of the scope of the work to be included in the contract. All that might have been mentioned was that the subcontractor was to comply with the requirements of the "plans and specs," whatever that means! Although the subcontractor may have been reluctant to discuss any plan/specification deficiencies that came to his or her attention for fear of losing the job, it is far worse to leave a negotiating session knowing that a firm price for the work has been reached, but there are significant plan and/or specification problems, with cost implications, that will need to be resolved. To lessen the impact of these unstated issues follow up with a written confirmation of price and scope and include items that fully define to the work to be performed, and, conversely, that specifically exclude the questionable items.

2. During the contract negotiation stage, a definitive scope of work and a corresponding contract sum will be established and include certain agreed-upon modifications to the "plans and specifications" standard. However when the contract is issued, the subcontractor may fail to read it thoroughly to confirm that all agreed-upon conditions are included.

   If the general contractor has either added or deleted other items not previously discussed and agreed upon at the time of negotiation, the subcontractor should take exception to these modifications and not rely on the general contractor's assurance, "Don't worry; it's company policy to include these items in the subcontract agreement, but we won't enforce them."

   As work progresses and the subcontractor begins to take exception to certain portions of the work, stating that they were verbally deleted when the subcontract agreement was negotiated, the general contractor may enforce the provisions of the contract requiring the subcontractor to perform the "deleted" work, as memories suddenly fail. The question posed by the general contractor at a time like this will undoubtedly be, "If you took exception to portions of the work, why did you sign the contract without requesting that these portions be deleted?" The lesson to be learned in, Don't rely only on good faith—personnel changes do occur; lapses in memory can prove costly.

3. The subcontractor did not have access to all of the contract drawings referenced in their subcontract agreement having been given only those drawings pertaining to their specific trade. However their contract includes compliance with all of the contract drawings and specifications. Even though the complete set of drawings may not have any impact on the subcontractor's scope of work, there really is no way of confirming that fact unless all drawings to be included in the contract have been reviewed. Don't agree to abide by the scope of work on all drawings unless you have reviewed all drawings.

4. The subcontractor did not receive any or all of the addenda issued during the bidding process, nor did the subcontractor receive any RFIs or RFCs generated by the general contractor or other subcontractors along with related responses from the architect or engineer. If the subcontractor was unaware of any addenda or RFIs or RFC issued during the bidding process, their proposal and subsequent contract with the general contractor should not include any reference to these documents.

5. The subcontractor agreed to an unrealistically low price for the work with the proviso that the general contractor would "make it up" either with change orders or by increasing the contract sum on a future project. What happens if the guy who "promised" to make up the shortfall suddenly departs from the company? Accept such offers at your own risk!

6. The subcontractor agreed to perform the work in an unrealistically compressed time frame. When a new contract is within reach and the general contractor's only bothersome stipulation is that the project must be completed in a drastically compressed time frame, address the issue at that time. Don't assume that things will work themselves out. If additional money is required to compensate for extended overtime or loss of productivity due to trade stacking, it is better to face these issues with the general contractor or else they will probably become the source of a major dispute later on if the schedule is not met.

7. The subcontractor had no previous experience with the general contractor and failed to investigate whether that GC had a reputation for treating subcontractors fairly or unfairly. General contractor's reputations are generally known in the trade, and all it takes is a few calls to other subcontractors who have worked with the GC or possibly a telephone call or two to some of the general contractor's suppliers to check on the GC's history of fair dealings, prompt payment record, and so forth. It pays to know whom you are dealing with and whether it will become necessary to take added precautions when working with certain contractors.

8. The subcontractor was not familiar with the owner of the project and did not know if the owner was financially capable of funding the work or whether they had a reputation of not making timely payments or unfairly withheld payments from time to time. Some owners are notoriously difficult to deal with and their relationship with the general contractor will filter down to all subcontractors— late payments, difficulties in obtaining agreement on change orders. If the owner's reputation is not known, make some inquiries. Has the same general contractor worked with the owner over a period of years or is each project awarded to a different GC? If the latter is true, contact some of these general contractors and inquire about their relationship with that owner. When unsure of an owner's record of timely payments to the general contractor, revise the "pay-when-paid" clause in the subcontract agreement requesting that the GC pay your firm within "X:" number of days of receipt of your monthly requisition.

9. The subcontractor was persuaded to proceed on the basis or an oral agreement before all matters of final contract sum and scope were resolved. Once the subcontractor has commenced work, most of his or her bargaining power will have evaporated. If the general contractor indicates that a contract will be forthcoming in a few weeks or so, confirm the agreement, in writing, being explicit as to scope of work and agreed-upon price. It is wise not to proceed with work until the general contractor acknowledges this agreement, or better yet, issues their subcontract agreement. When that subcontract agreement does not conform to the terms and conditions of the confirmation, resolve all differences immediately upon receipt of the contract and indicate that work will not continue until all significant differences are resolved.

   The longer work continues without mutual agreement on contract scope and sum, the more difficult it will be to obtain an equitable resolution.

10. When work is being offered that is substantially greater in both scope and dollar value than any project the subcontractor has worked on previously, the subcontractor should consider the fact that its weekly payroll will increase, in some cases dramatically. Greater amounts of materials will need to be purchased, and therefore late payments from the general contractor, coupled with an insufficient credit line may create a disastrous cash flow problem.

A company's growth results from seeking higher levels of work, but there are certain projects that may be offered along the way that could drastically affect growth and have the opposite effect. Large projects mean large weekly payrolls and the general contractor's payment cycle cannot be accurately determined before the job starts. Promises of prompt payment from the general contractor are not enough.

The general contractor should be requested to delete that pay-when-paid clause and substitute one that guarantees payment by a specific date. Large projects require large amounts of money in the bank, or a substantial line of credit. If both are missing, it may be wise to pass up that big job.

The Delay Claim

Claims for delays in completion of the construction project can become confusing and costly for the subcontractor unfamiliar with their complexity. As more and more owners compress the time frame for construction and require CPM scheduling for their projects contracts with the general contractor will generally include either liquidated damages or a more open-ended "actual damages" clause.

Whenever changes in a baseline schedule occur and timely completion of the project is in jeopardy, unless the owner admits causing the delay, the owner will, most likely, look to the general contractor to complete the project as originally scheduled. The general contractor will scrutinize the CPM schedule to uncover those activities that created the delay(s) and require the responsible subcontractors/suppliers to accelerate the work at no additional cost to either owner or general contractor. These responsible subcontractors/ suppliers may also be held accountable for costs incurred by other subcontractors/ suppliers to accelerate portions of their work.

The Liquidated Damages Clause in the Contract

Often the term "liquidated damages" is confused with the term "penalty clause." When a penalty clause for late delivery of a project is inserted in a contract, in order for it to be enforceable, the contract must also contain a bonus clause offering a specific sum of money to the contractor for early completion. No bonus clause—no penalty clause.

The liquidated damages clause incorporated into the construction contract represents the costs that the owner has determined will accrue if the project does not complete on time. These costs are generally expressed as daily costs. For example, if the project is an office building and tenant leases have already been executed and stipulate specific move-in dates, it is not too difficult to see that the owner will have suffered economically if the project completion date and subsequent tenant move-in dates are not met. When a school is being constructed and is not completed in time for the start of the school session, temporary classrooms may be required and costs associated with these rentals will be expressed as one portion of the contractor's liquidated damages clause.

Delay Claim Categories—Legal Terms

There are many legal definitions that apply when delay claims occur.

- Compensable Delay—a delay for which the contractor will be entitled to a contract sum increase and an extension of contract completion time due to some action or inaction caused by the owner or their consultants.

- Noncompensable Delay—a delay whereby the contractor is not entitled to either a contract sum increase nor an extension of project completion time and assumes all consequences for the delay.

Further, delays can be subcategorized as being:

- Excusable Delay—no party to the contract is determined to be responsible for the delay.

- Nonexcusable Delay—a delay for which the owner or contractor is deemed to be responsible.

Acceleration and Project Completion

From a legal standpoint the term "acceleration" occurs when:

- Contractors have been delayed in the completion of their project.

- The owner recognizes the cause of the delay but does not hold the contractor responsible.

- The owner directs the contractor to complete the project as originally scheduled and will compensate the contractor for the costs of this accelerated effort.

When all of these conditions have been met, the legal definition of acceleration has been achieved.

If the owner directs the contractor to accelerate, the contractor will require all subcontractors and suppliers to provide them with their additional costs to do so.

If the owner deems the delay nonexcusable and noncompensable, the general contractor will be required to absorb all associated costs to provide an on-time completion and will commence negotiations with all subcontractors and suppliers to receive the additional costs to do so.

The Overlooked Costs of an Accelerated Work Schedule—The Hidden Costs

Acceleration of a construction project generally requires more manpower as well as extended hours of work for tradesmen already assigned to the project. It may also involve "trade stacking"—multiple trades working in close proximity to each other creating loss of productivity or working on tasks out of normal sequence. Additional costs may be required to accelerate material and equipment deliveries and additional field supervision may be required to direct the added crews.

Inefficiencies will occur and since the subcontractor will be required to complete their work in a compressed time frame, albeit, at additional costs, these inefficiencies must be taken into account as the estimate for the accelerated work proposal is being prepared for presentation to the general contractor.

Overtime and loss of productivity

The Business Roundtable studies presented in Chapter 7 graphically display how extended periods of overtime reduce worker productivity. One such study concluded that four weeks of nine-hour workdays results in work that is 16% less efficient than four weeks of eight-hour workdays. Extended work hours lead to increased absenteeism and workers unwilling to continue working these long hours will result in replacement of workers in previously productive crews. The requirement for additional workers may necessitate supplementing existing crews with underqualified or unqualified workers.

All of these production shortfalls must be considered when an estimate for accelerated work is being requested by the general contractor.

There are also more subtle costs that will accrue during an intensive acceleration project.

The subcontractor's project manager may need to spend more time directing the flow of men and materials thereby leaving less time to devote to the other projects to which they have been assigned and possibly exercising less control over those other projects.

Larger weekly payrolls may place more pressure on existing lines of credit and the need to maintain a positive cash flow from all other projects. Perhaps part of the subcontractor's increased acceleration costs should include a stipulation that weekly or biweekly requisitions must be honored in order to maintain a satisfactory cash flow.

When delayed completion is acceptable to contractor and owner

There will be times when the project experiences a significant delay, however the owner of the project has no desire to accelerate completion. These kinds of situations can occur when a project in the public or private sector unexpectedly encounters hazardous materials either in an existing structure being renovated or in contaminated soils during excavation operations. Time required to identify, quantify, remove, and legally dispose of hazardous materials can be lengthy, and often all other work must cease until this operation has been completed.

Another example of a compensable delay may occur when a partial redesign of a project is required in order to accommodate a new product line or to meet the changed requirements of a major tenant just prior to move-in. In both cases the owner will recognize that additional costs are warranted and will request a fully documented cost proposal.

Will these kinds of delays affect the subcontractor and will additional compensation beyond the obvious "bricks and mortar" costs be warranted? The answer is—Yes!

Labor, material, and equipment escalation costs are obvious added costs, along with the extended rental period for such items as field office and storage trailers, scaffolding, air compressors, manlifts, etc. And extended project management and field supervision costs must also be taken into consideration.

There are other less obvious costs associated with these kinds of delays. If equipment is scheduled for delivery but must be delayed, there will be additional storage charges, but what about extended warranties?

Most equipment warranties commence with delivery of the equipment to the job site. The general contractor's warranty/guarantee obligations generally commence when the architect or engineer accepts the piece of installed equipment. When lengthy delays occur, the standard one-year guarantee can expire even before the equipment is installed. Unless the owner and general contractor agree to a shortened period of warranty, extended warranty costs will be a justifiable added cost.

But there are additional costs associated with delayed completion that are more complex, but do exist and are often overlooked. One such cost relates to how the delay has impacted the subcontractor's home office overhead—costs related to and recoverable if the Eichleay Formula is invoked. This term is most likely to be heard from the general contractor as they assess the cost of the delay, but it applies equally to subcontractor delay claims.

Claims For Consequential Damages—The Eichleay Formula

In 1954, the Armed Services Board of Contract Appeals resolved a dispute over the proper method of determining the amount of corporate overhead that a contractor could attribute to delays caused by the government during the course of a construction project.

The Eichleay Corporation, a general contractor, forced the answer to this question in a landmark case that hundreds or possibly thousands of contractors have used in their pursuit of claims resolutions with both private and public agencies.

The formula used to reach a settlement was thereafter referred to as the Eichleay Formula.

Whether or not this formula is actually used to compute the cost of "consequential damages," the theory behind Eichleay provides a valuable lesson in corporate management.

Every company strives to obtain a balance between the cost of overhead required to support a predetermined annual sales volume. Overhead costs that are consistently too high will reduce net profit; overhead costs that are too low may come about by "skimping" on adequately trained managers necessary to properly supervise the various company profit centers.

Eichleay focuses on the impact corporate overhead exerts on sales volume. When a company plans its projected sales volume for the coming year or years, it assumes that the overhead costs already in place or planned increases will be adequate to absorb the anticipated sales volume. If, for some reason, the projected sales volume is not achieved, the corporate overhead in place will not be fully absorbed; it will be underabsorbed by the lesser sales volume.

But even if the projected annual sales volume is reached and the corporate overhead fully absorbed, an extended delay in the progress of one or more major projects will impact the ongoing overhead costs. In other words, corporate overhead continues to be expended, but the anticipated revenue from the "stalled" project(s) is not available to offset these ongoing costs. Therefore corporate overhead becomes unabsorbed.

With the Eichleay Formula it is possible to actually quantify the impact a significantly delayed project exerts upon corporate overhead.

The "formula"

The formula is expressed as follows:

A. Contract billings ÷ Total billings for actual contract period ×
   Total overhead incurred during contract period =
   Overhead allowable to the contract

B. Allocable overhead ÷ Actual days of contract performance =
   Overhead allocable to contract per day

Figures 9-1 and 9-2 illustrate how this formula is prepared. It requires a month-by-month accounting of total company billings, actual billings for the delayed project, projected billings based upon the initial project schedule, and monthly overhead figures.

The Eichleay Formula has withstood the test of several court decisions over the years; however the 1997 revised A.I.A. 201 Document—The General Conditions—expressly excludes the contractor's ability to recover "consequential damages" such as the extended home office overhead calculated by the Formula. This apparently does not preclude a subcontractor's ability to include such costs when their contract does

Mo. # NTP 3/2/93	Month	Other A&A Billings	NH Yard Billings Actual	Total A&A Billings	NH Yard Per Contract CPM "0"	Adjusted A&A Billings	Monthly Overhead A&A		
1	Apr-93	$3,821,792	$476,000	$4,297,792	1,009,365	$4,831,157	$352,364		
2	May-93	$2,908,655	$112,690	$3,021,345	1,253,342	$4,161,997	$352,364		
3	Jun-93	$3,371,747	$288,339	$3,660,086	566,116	$3,937,863	$352,364		
4	Jul-93	$765,753	$84,884	$850,637	863,396	$1,629,149	$352,364		
5	Aug-93	$1,251,263	$280,237	$1,531,500	1,263,434	$2,514,697	$352,364		
6	Sep-93	$4,665,185	$434,781	$5,099,966	732,142	$5,397,327	$352,364		
7	Oct-93	$1,400,679	$373,660	$1,774,339	591,442	$1,992,121	$352,364		
8	Nov-93	$996,885	$339,647	$1,336,532	842,880	$1,839,765	$352,364		
9	Dec-93	$932,974	$524,479	$1,457,453	803,983	$1,736,957	$352,364		
10	Jan-94	$890,137	$391,415	$1,281,552	819,783	$1,709,920	$352,364		
11	Feb-94	$607,284	$249,691	$856,975	323,952	$931,236	$352,364	$3,876,003 Ceci/11	
12	Mar-94	$833,623	$140,092	$973,715	221,688	$1,055,311	$308,483	Avg =1994/12 Actual	
13	Apr-94	$804,576	$627,833	$1,432,409	275,236	$1,079,812	$308,483		
14	May-94	$719,071	$244,875	$963,946	257,155	$976,226	$308,483		
15	Jun-94	$1,684,041	$206,847	$1,890,888	529,440	$2,213,481	$308,483		
16	Jul-94	$1,330,985	$192,724	$1,523,709	143,700	$1,474,685	$308,483		
17	Aug-94	$1,759,226	$377,734	$2,136,960	380,888	$2,140,114	$308,483		
18	Sep-94	$2,053,225	$373,988	$2,427,213	1,427,847	$3,481,072	$308,483		
19	Oct-94	$1,599,410	$341,629	$1,941,039	611,115	$2,210,525	$308,483		
20	Nov-94	$1,431,972	$554,814	$1,986,786	508,114	$1,940,086	$308,483		
21	Dec-94	$933,166	$759,891	$1,693,057	919,014	$1,852,180	$308,483		
	Total	$34,761,649	$7,376,250	$42,137,899	$14,344,032	$49,105,681	$6,960,833	Actual Period O.H.	
	Deduct C/O Work		$4,116,357	$4,116,357					
3,77	Total W/O C/O work		$3,259,893	$38,021,542	Page 1				

1:41 AM

Where A&A Drywall is the subcontractor NH Yard refers to project– New Haven Railyard

Figure 9-1

176

Eichleay @ 1/95

MM Eichleay Calculation**:				
Unabsorbed Home Office Overhead During Period = (Planned Overhead - Actual Overhead):				
Planned Overhead:			Actual Overhead Contribution:	
(NH Yard Planned Period Revenue Per Contract)			(NH Yard Actual Base Contract Revenue for Period)	
(Adjusted FM&S Billings for All jobs over Period)			(Actual FM&S Billings for All Jobs over Period)	
	$14,344,032	Planned Revenue	Actual Revenue	$3,259,893
Divided by	$49,105,681	Adjusted FM&S Billings	Actual FM&S Billings	$38,021,542
Planned Billings would have paid	29.21%		Actual Billings Paid Only	8.57% Overhead
Therefore:	$2,033,297	$6,960,833 x % =	Therefore: $6,960,833 x % =	$596,808
	$96,824	Divide By Period Mos. =	Divide By Period Mos. =	$28,419
Credit Actual Cost/Mo. Paid =	($28,419)			
Subtotal	$68,404			
Overhead Cost for 20 Months Delay =	$1,368,084			

3/7/95

**Note MM Eichleay includes credit for earned revenue

Where FM&S is the contractor NH Yard refers to project– New Haven Railyard

Figure 9-2

177

not include the provisions of A.I.A. Document A201, 1997 edition. If such a claim is being considered, a conference with the company attorney is well advised.

Claims Avoidance Is Better than Claims Pursuit

An experienced construction professional can often develop a sixth sense as to when a dispute begins to escalate into a claim and when this occurs the best offense is a good defense.

At the first sense of trouble brewing, don't assume that it will pass.

- Review daily field reports and make their entries more extensive. Include other subcontractor's manpower, be more specific about where each subcontractor is working. Include observations of how the project is proceeding—are there more complaints from other subs about the way the general contractor is managing the project?

- When problems arise and are brought to the attention of the general contractor, document any conversations by either sending a memo to the GC or documenting the conversation in the daily log to include time and place where the conversation took place and any comments made by the GC's representative.

- Direct your foreman to take notes on any meaningful verbal conversations with the general contractor's on-site representative having to do with subcontractor performance, problems on the site, and scheduling concerns.

- Document all phone calls made or received relating to the dispute or impending claim.

- Take photos of the area or areas involving the disputed work.

- Scrutinize the regular project meeting minutes to uncover any statements that could be interpreted as assigning responsibility for any impending disputes. Respond if the problem appears to be directed to your company.

- Review the contract documents thoroughly to uncover any provisions that could be used to either strengthen or weaken your company's position if a claim is entered against it.

- Pay particular attention to onerous provisions in the contract. Is there a "no damages for delay" clause that will limit the ability to obtain compensation for delays? Does the contract contain specific written notification time for submission of a claim?

- Don't assume that you have lost before you have begun to fight. Remember—if the disputed matter appears to be unfair, it probably is!

If a dispute cannot be resolved amicably, there are other alternatives to litigation.

Alternate Dispute Resolution Processes

Litigation in the construction industry has become so costly and time-consuming in recent years that both lawyers and their prospective clients have sought alternate methods to resolve disagreements. Referred to as ADR (alternate dispute resolution), mediation and arbitration procedures and dispute resolution boards (DRB) have gained considerable popularity and spawned several new industries dealing in these matters. The Partnering concept, conceived and initiated by the U.S. Army Corp of Engineers, has spread throughout the public and private construction community and is an effort to resolve disputes quickly and keep them from degenerating into a claim.

When disagreements occur on the construction site, the subcontractor is presented with several methods to resolve these disagreements:

- Face to Face—one-on-one negotiations
- Arbitration
- Mediation
- Arb/Med or Med/Arb (if you prefer) a combination of both processes
- Litigation

Each procedure has its advantages and disadvantages.

Negotiations

Some disagreements are less difficult to resolve if they are dealt with promptly and between decision makers. Delaying resolution of a disagreement using "too busy" as an excuse is not an effective approach to a negotiated settlement. Effective negotiating requires prompt action, a meeting where each party to the disagreement is authorized to effect a decision, and there is a desire by each party to resolve the issue by compromising. Someone said that a successful negotiating session has ended when a resolution has been reached and neither party is entirely happy with the results.

Prompt resolution is the operative word. While facts are clear in everyone's mind, that is the time to resolve the disagreements. Long delays will only result in one or more parties becoming more entrenched in the correctness of their position and an unwillingness to accept a compromise, thus making closure more difficult.

Mediation

Mediation is very similar to negotiation in that it can only be successful if both parties to a dispute truly wish to resolve that dispute. The mediation process utilizes a third person, a professional mediator, who by using shuttle diplomacy will point out the strengths and weaknesses in each party's position in an attempt to effect a compromise. The American Arbitration Association provides mediation services and there are a number of other private organizations that can provide these services.

Costs are minimal and require the services of a professional mediator and a room or two in which the process can take place. It is not uncommon to have each party's lawyers present to offer the testimony of their client and witnesses. Generally, the mediation process can be completed in a day or two.

Mediation is voluntary and nonbinding. If one party is unhappy at any time with the way the process is being conducted, they can call an end to the procedure and elect to pursue another means of resolution, which may mean arbitration.

Arbitration

If mediation is not acceptable to all parties, arbitration—if not required contractually—is the next best alternative.

The American Arbitration Association, with chapters throughout the country, is an organization devoted to providing assistance in initiating the arbitration process. They can provide all the information and particulars about the process and related costs.

The arbitration process involves selecting one or more arbitrators, experienced in the field of the dispute, who will listen to both sides of a disagreement and render a decision. Although evidence similar to that presented in court cases will be submitted during the proceedings, and witnesses are sworn in, strict rules of evidence are not required. For example, hearsay evidence is permitted.

As each side presents its case, the arbitrators may question witnesses, document content, and so forth, and when the hearings are concluded, they will issue their findings, which unless specifically stated, are binding on both parties. If the aggrieved party does not receive the compensation awarded by the arbitrator's findings, they can apply to the courts for a judgment against the guilty party.

Costs associated with an arbitration proceeding can be obtained from either the American Arbitration Association or any of the private organizations offering these services. Generally, the advantages of arbitration are:

- Time required to commence an arbitration hearing is significantly less that that required to get on a court docket.

- Time required to complete an arbitration hearing is usually much less than in a court trial.

- Costs associated with arbitration may be substantially less than litigation.

- The facts in the case are heard by disinterested experts in the particular field being discussed rather than by a judge and/or jury of laymen not familiar with the industry in question.

A Word About Partnering

In 1988, the U.S. Army Corp of Engineers sought to find a way to settle claims quickly and more economically and, in the process, develop a less-adversarial atmosphere when working with contractors.

The partnering process that evolved out of this effort was based upon the realization that if all parties become more acquainted with each other at the start of a project, they would find that they all shared a common goal. By defining these common goals, attacking problems and resolving these problems equitably and promptly, successful completion of the project would be achievable.

Since 1988, any number of public agencies and private firms have embarked on Partnering projects. Common to all such projects is the use of a Facilitator, a trained professional needed to guide all participants through the process.

The owner, design consultants, general contractor, and all vendors and subcontractors are invited to the Partnering session. Each of these participants is requested to caucus with its own group and list its project objectives. When the facilitator combines all of these objectives, it becomes quite clear that common goals surface: prompt completion of the project, high-quality levels of construction, quick and equitable resolution of disputes, prompt payment, minimum number of change orders, and ability to make a reasonable profit.

Developing an atmosphere of working together to achieve these common goals is the key objective of the Facilitator.

One of the more important procedures created during this initial partnering session is that of prompt resolution of disputes and disagreements.

- Resolve simple problems at the lowest management level possible.

- Prepare a structured process for escalating an unresolved issue to the next highest management level until the issue is resolved.

- Agree to time frames for the resolution of disagreements/disputes at each level of the process and stick to them. For example, problems to be resolved at the supervisory level will be 24 hours; problems to be resolved at the project manager level will not exceed two days; problems presented at the executive level will be resolved in one week.

This problem-solving procedure may just be one of the most important by-products of the partnering process.

But whichever method is used to resolve disputes, one key word is Promptness. The ability to view a dispute from the perspective of the other party is another crucial element in the resolution process.

Just remember—the construction industry is an industry of contracts, and in order to deal effectively with claims and disputes, a thorough understanding of one's rights and obligations under the contract is the essential first step.

10

Dealing with Difficult General Contractors

As most businesses do, the construction business revolves around good faith on the part of all parties to the construction contract—the owner, the design consultants, the general contractor, and the subcontractor. Without mutual respect, trust, and a good-faith effort, the contract alone cannot offer full protection to a subcontractor working with a general contractor who does not wish to deal in good faith and fails to recognize trust as a part of the business relationship.

The greater majority of general contractors strive to achieve and maintain the same type of relationship with their subcontractors as they have with their own employees, fully aware of the knowledge that without mutual cooperation, the construction cycle can be much more difficult that it already is.

The Difficult Contractor

But there are a number of general contractors out there ready to take advantage of an unsuspecting subcontractor in any number of ways: by invoking various obscure parts of the subcontract agreement in order to extract more than their original bargain, withholding or delaying payment in exchange for concessions that exceed the obligations of the contract, or just making it more difficult to conduct business.

And there are some general contractors who withhold their best shot for last and bargain before remitting the final payment to the subcontractor, offering to release that last payment if the subcontractor will agree to settle for less than they are truly entitled to receive. Or the subcontractor may be requested to withdraw or substantially reduce certain outstanding change orders prior to receiving final payment.

And, lastly, there are those general contractors with "selective memory"—having verbally agreed not to enforce some restrictive clauses in the subcontract agreement, thereby luring the subcontractor into signing the agreement. These general contractors may have a sudden lapse of memory, and after threatening to enforce some of those restrictive clauses that they verbally agreed not to enforce, will question why the subcontractor signed an agreement without amending or deleting these offensive clauses in the first place.

Beware of the verbal commitment, "Don't worry; we'll work things out." These are the types of general contractors who subcontractors had best avoid in future dealings, or at best, take the necessary precautions prior to entering into an agreement with them.

Three Cardinal Rules

Dealing with difficult general contractors is made somewhat easier if three cardinal rules are observed:

1. Don't sign any subcontract agreement unless it has been read completely and all provisions in that agreement thoroughly understood. (Even if some objectionable provisions are ignored because this is a "must have" job, at least there will be an awareness of potential problems with the contract language and any necessary actions will be taken along the way in case these provisions are evoked by the general contractor.)

2. Don't accept any verbal directions or instructions from any party to the contract without promptly receiving or sending written confirmation.

3. Document everything whether or not it appears to be questionable or controversial at the time.

During the course of a construction project there will always be some disagreements that will be resolved through compromise, but when dealing with a difficult contractor "compromise" is not enough. Fire must sometimes be fought with fire.

How Disagreements Occur

The type of problems usually encountered when dealing with difficult contractors will probably involve the following:

- Interpretation of scope of work included in the specifications and in the drawings and the subcontract agreement.

- Progress payments that are delayed for no legitimate reason.

- Change orders/Extra work orders.

- Excessive/unreasonable back-charges.

- Punch list work.

- Final payment.

- Warranty items.

- Delay claims.

- Dealing with tough personalities.

- Threatening letters from general contractors.

Interpretation of scope of work

How many times has the general contractor generalized the scope of work as "per plans and specifications?" At first glance this would appear to be a reasonable approach in establishing the full scope of a subcontract agreement. But wait a second. Is your interpretation of what constitutes "plans and specs" the same as the general contractor's?

Most disagreements occur because of differing interpretations of what is to be expected to comply with these contract documents, and remember that the architect is the final judge of the intent of the contract documents. And the architect's interpretation of what is actually required may differ from that of the general contractor and the subcontractor.

If the plans and/or specifications contain details that are incorrect, is the contractor (whether general or sub) obliged to follow these defective details or are they obliged to construct the work so that it is workable? If there are obvious building code violations, is the subcontractor to call these violations to the attention of the general contractor during the bidding process or include the costs in his or her estimate to install the work in accordance with code?

If certain construction details are just plain wrong, are the contractors to follow these erroneous details? There is a legal term, "obstinate obedience," which refers to a condition where a general contractor or subcontractor proceeds with the work indicated by the plans and specifications knowing full well that the work will be deficient or defective. This is similar to the defense, "But I was only carrying out orders!"

When reviewing the plans and specifications during the preparation of an estimate, make notes of all errors, omissions, and questionable details uncovered in the process. Some subcontractors prefer to qualify their bids and exclude these questionable or ambiguous portions of the plans and specifications while others may include an "allowance" for those construction details that are vague. But however the subcontractor intends to negotiate the agreement with the general contractor, it is important to realize that merely agreeing to abide by the "plans and specifications" as the definitive scope of work may create problems when actual work gets underway, especially when dealing with difficult or unreasonable general contractors.

Delayed progress payments

Although most subcontract agreements contain the "pay when paid" clause, some general contractors will delay payment to the subcontractor after receipt of the owner's payment.

Some delays are justified and may occur while the general contractor waits for his or her bank to "clear" the owner's check, a process that may take up to one week and—in addition to the general contractor's accounting department—may take another week to process current requests for payment, so a two-week delay after receipt of an owner's check is not unreasonable. When wire transfers are used, the owner's bank electronically deposits the monthly progress check directly to the general contractor's bank, and these funds are immediately available for disbursement.

Some public works project specifications require the general contractor to disburse funds within 30 days after receipt of payment from that public agency. Therefore, if a "pay when paid" clause is in the subcontract agreement and the general contractor receives payment from the public agency within 30 days of submission of his or her requisition, the flow-through clause in the subcontract agreement may result in a subcontractor not receiving payment until 60 days from the time the general contractor receives his or her check. And this 60-day cycle will have been in strict accordance with the contract provisions.

But when the general contractor delays payment beyond the time stipulated in the contract, these funds could be used to pay debts on other projects, or the general contractor wants to "play the float" and receive a few days or week's interest on that large payment received from the owner.

Owners are often unaware of the general contractor's habit of late payments to subcontractors and vendors, and when this practice comes to their attention they do not look favorably upon such practices. After all their payment to the general contractor is for the sole purpose of paying for all work performed in their project during the corresponding period to time.

So when that general contractor consistently remits late payments to the subcontractor, the subcontractor needs to find a way to communicate this information to the owner. And one way to do that is to establish a relationship with the owner's representative as the project progresses. There will be several opportunities to talk with the owner's representative at various project meetings or when they tour the building on inspection visits. Stop and chat with them. Make them aware of who you are and the progress you are making. Explain some of the intricacies of your work and the fact that your company is quality oriented. As the relationship develops and you begin to establish a "first name" relationship, if the general contractor continues to issue late payments, a call to your owner contact will probably produce results. Make these calls sparingly; don't become a pest, but the owner is interested in whether or not the general contractor is dispersing funds promptly and properly, and unless your phone calls become annoying, an occasional telephone call to inquire about the date of payment to the general contractor will not be unwelcome.

Once armed with information about date of payment, the general contractor can be contacted to inquire when payment will be forthcoming.

General contractors do not appreciate subcontractors who contact owners concerning their payments, but they also don't want these owners to be aware of consistently late payments to subcontractors or vendors, and those late payment practices just might cease—at least for a while.

Change orders/extra work orders

Change order work involves recognition that additional work beyond the scope of the contract has been performed, and there is agreement as to the value of that work. If there is no agreement over one or the other of these conditions, trouble inevitably lies ahead.

Field change orders (those ordered at the job site), usually with some sense of urgency, can present major problems when dealing with difficult general contractors. No such work should be performed without a written order from the general contractor, preferably including a lump sum or "not to exceed" price. There should also be agreement that their field representative will sign daily work orders verifying the number of man-hours and description of work performed, especially if the work has been authorized on a "Time and Material" basis. This is the subcontractor's primary defense if the general contractor decides not to pay for this work.

The contract approach to change order work authorizes the start of work once a change order is signed by the owner (in the case where the contract scope of work is changed) or when directed, in writing, by the general contractor that changes are required by the general contractor, but no reimbursement for the cost of these changes will be forthcoming from the owner. This "by-the-book" procedure is rarely followed and "good faith" is the basis for the start and completion of most change order work. However, when the general contractor has a history of lack of good faith, the subcontractor must then rely on the terms and conditions of the contract—i.e., written authorization and agreement on establishing the cost of the work.

The subcontractor, when requested to perform extra work, in the absence of a history of general contractor "good faith," must not proceed with the work until a formal, written change order has been submitted by the general contractor and signed by the subcontractor.

Even this procedure may not be sufficient protection from an unscrupulous general contractor who may issue a signed change order, but once the work has been completed continue to negotiate the price even though it was established prior to the start of work.

If this occurs with any frequency one method of dealing with this situation is to refuse to perform any work beyond the scope of the original contract. That will certainly cause the general contractor some concern. If another subcontractor of the same trade is brought to the site to perform this extra work, warranty issues, among others, will arise. Who will warranty the entire assembly if two different subcontractors constructed it? And depending upon the trades involved, the requirement to obtain another permit (certainly in the case of an electrical or mechanical trade) will become an issue. A threat of refusal to perform extra work will generally get results and can be used repeatedly if the general contractor fails to honor its extra work commitments.

And this refusal to perform extra work will not be lost on the owner who will probably inquire as to the reasons why the general contractor is having these difficulties with a specific subcontractor.

Before taking such a position, read the contract thoroughly and in particular, the general, special, and supplementary conditions. Some of these special provisions may require the subcontractor to continue working and establish certain procedures for arriving at mutually acceptable costs for the work when completed.

And remember if your work is one component of the entire change order that is being disputed by an owner, it may take months for the general contractor to resolve all outstanding issues and receive payment. Situations like this can only be avoided by inserting a qualifying clause in the subcontract agreement during negotiations with the general contractor and prior to the start of work. A statement as simple as "Payment for all change order/extra work will be made within 30 days after receipt and approval of the work by the general contractor, regardless of whether the general contractor has received payment from the owner for said work."

Also be wary of those daily work tickets that are signed by the general contractor's superintendent that state "Acknowledgment of hours worked only." The general contractor's super may not have the authority to actually approve the work as "extra work" but you should at least get the project manager's agreement, in writing, that these extra work tickets do represent "extra work" and will be honored accordingly.

One further tip! All during the project, your foreman may have performed some minor additional work for the general contractor or maybe several extra work items on a "no charge" basis. Your foreman may even have performed work in excess of the scope of the contract in order to improve the quality of the job. Records should be kept of all of this "no charge" work, and at the end of the project, if the general contractor refuses to pay all or a portion of previously authorized extra work or wants to renegotiate the cost of a particular item, present the general contractor with a complete list of all of those previous "extra" items, with costs generously applied.

Excessive and unreasonable back-charges

Most back-charge issues concern daily or weekly cleanup operations when such requirements are dictated by the contract. Responsible general contractors become upset when subcontractor cleanup operations are not performed according to the contract and after their verbal or written notification remains unheeded they may engage a cleaning service and apportion back-charges to those subcontractors who have been negligent in their duties.

If the subcontract agreement stipulates that the general contractor must give the subcontractor 48 or 72 hours notice, or whatever, prior to engaging another subcontractor to complete the work, this will generally apply to cleaning as well.

Difficult contractors can be unreasonable when preparing back-charges for cleaning, adding costs to supervise the cleaning operations, charging exorbitant refuse removal and disposal fees, and often violating the written notice required to be sent to the subcontractor to clean before another service can be brought on site. And if a back-charge is issued by the general contractor without such written notice, it can be disputed, but until the dispute is settled, if ever, it will be cause for the difficult general contractor to withhold funds from future payments to the subcontractor.

When dealing with difficult general contractors perform all cleanup operations in strict accordance with the provisions of the contract in order to avoid back-charges often far in excess of actual costs. If requested to clean areas where it is obvious that the debris was generated by other subcontractors, take photographs of the area with close-up views of materials, labels, cartons, etc., that clearly prove that this trash was not generated by your trade.

There are other reasons that are cause for a general contractor to issue back-charges: costs to repair damaged work caused by the subcontractor, a subcontractor's refusal to perform work within the scope of the subcontract agreement when directed to do so by the general contractor, and costs incurred by other trades due to failure of the responsible subcontractor to adhere to the progress schedule, to name a few.

When back-charges are issued by the general contractor, take the following steps:

1. Acknowledge receipt of the back-charge but not responsibility for it. (Refer to Sample Letter in Chapter 13).

2. If there is disagreement over the nature or cost of the back-charge, be specific in the explanation of this disagreement in writing.

3. If proper notice was not given in accordance with the terms and conditions of the contract, i.e., written notice required "x" hours or days before the general contractor has the right to engage another subcontractor, this should also be included in the letter.

4. If the back-charge contains a specific dollar amount, request an itemized statement of charges with supporting documents.

5. Send all correspondence certified, return receipt required.

If the matter goes to mediation, arbitration, or litigation, the information requested from the general contractor and the information thus received will prove useful in settling the claim.

Final payment

The general contractor's final payment is contingent upon all vendors and subcontractors having satisfactorily completed their work and having submitted all close-out documents to the architect/engineer and accepted by them. Only then will final payment to the general contractor be released.

What about the subcontractor who has faithfully completed his or her work while other subcontractors have not and is patiently awaiting final payment? The general contractor may be frustrated because he or she too wants to obtain his or her final payment and close out the project.

The time to address such issues is when the subcontract agreement is being prepared. A subcontractor might attempt to insert the following clause:

"Upon completion of _____(subcontractor) work and acceptance by the architect/engineer (whichever is applicable) final payment will be forthcoming and will not be contingent upon the general contractor receiving final payment from the owner."

It will probably be very difficult to obtain such an agreement from the general contractor, but it may be a starting point in another direction—a concession to reduce retainage.

Some contracts include provisions to reduce retainage by 50% when 50% of the project has been completed. Other contracts allow reduction of subcontractor retainage upon written request by the subcontractor. Other contracts make no provision for reduction of retainage.

When negotiating a contract with a general contractor under conditions favorable to the subcontractor, the first proposal might be a request to release all retainage once their portion of the work is complete and accepted by the architect/engineer. A "difficult" general contractor may ask the architect/engineer to withhold approval because he or she doesn't want to reduce/eliminate retainage and remit payment to the subcontractor, and the consultants will comply with this request, since by contract they generally aren't required to provide partial acceptance of various trade work.

Punch list work

The creation and completion of punch list work can be a seemingly never-ending process. Although the architect is the authority designated to prepare the punch list, depending upon the size and complexity of the project, the issuance of a punch list may extend weeks or months—one list for one portion of the building, and then in a week or two another partial punch list, and so on. In the meantime, the general contractor's final payment and/or retainage will not be issued until all punch list work has been completed. And if one or more subcontractors delays completion of his or her punch list work, all other subcontractors must wait for their retainage.

The owner's representative will often prepare his or her own punch list independent of the architect, thereby adding more confusion to an already frustrating process.

What to do, especially if one is dealing with a difficult general contractor? First of all each subcontractor's foreman should "punch" out their work before they leave the project and correct as many items as possible. Secondly, when the punch list is distributed by the general contractor, it should be completed quickly. When the work has been completed a request should be made to the general contractor's site representative to have the architect "sign off" on all completed items. It is preferable to obtain the architect's approval and sign off because that is the only official one.

If additional punch lists are issued, adding items to the lists that were not indicated previously, write a letter to the general contractor protesting these late additions, and, under protest, complete all legitimate items quickly. Although this protest letter will probably have no effect, it may provide documentation if this situation persists, making it nearly impossible to receive final payment or release of retainage within a reasonable time frame.

Many general contractors do not pursue completion of punch list items as aggressively as they should because most of the retainage money received will be paid to the various subcontractors and vendors; the amount retained by the general contractors may not be significant, consisting of sums due for their general conditions only, if they have subcontracted all of the work. If the general contractor has front-end-loaded the schedule of values, chances are that the general contractor has already received his or her full fee as progress payments were received over the course of the project.

A subcontractor must read the construction contract to determine if there is a clause relating to reduction of retainage. The general contractor may be still withholding, say, 10%, when the contract with the owner allows a reduction to 5% at some predetermined percentage of completion. If that is the case, send a letter to the general contractor requesting reduction on retainage. If that doesn't work, send another letter and send a copy to the owner.

Warranty items

There is a distinct difference between punch list work and warranty work, and quite often funds are mistakenly withheld, not for incomplete punch list work but for warranty work. Some general contractors, quite frankly, don't understand the difference between these two terms.

Punch list work is that work required to complete the entire scope of the contracted work in a manner acceptable to the architect and engineer. Correction of damaged work, completing the installation of all work, and completing the work in accordance with industry quality standards is punch list work.

Warranty work is that which is required to replace or repair defective items or equipment during the period of time when that item is within the guarantee or warranty period. The specifications will define the warranty period for all components of work. The normal period for general construction work is one year, but selected items such as insulated glass and refrigerant compressors, to name a few, have five-year warranties.

This distinct difference between punch list work and warranty work assumes added importance when funds are withheld for incomplete "punch list" work that is actually "warranty" work and no cause to withhold final payment.

For example, if a lock set that previously operated properly suddenly fails to work, this is a warranty item and will either be repaired or replaced during the warranty period.

If the lock set had never been installed or installed but missing a part, replacement of the missing part or installation of the complete assembly is truly a punch list item.

If a punch list presented contains warranty items, a letter should be sent to the general contractor listing those warranty items. This may be of assistance in obtaining timely completion, approval of the actual punch list, and final payment. If the general contractor persists in withholding funds for warranty work send them another letter and send copies to the architect and owner.

Delay claims

Some contracts contain liquidated damage clauses that are expressed as a specific cost per day, per week, or per month, that a general contractor will be assessed, if the project is not completed in accordance with the initial or adjusted contract completion date. The liquidated damages represent the total cost of damages the owner will incur if the project is not completed on time. Costs such as loss of rental income if the project is an office building, interest on construction loans, lost production time (if an industrial plant is involved), and costs to renegotiate leases on an existing property are but some of the items included in the establishing of liquidated damages.

In the absence of liquidated damages in the contract agreement, particularly if there is a Time is of the Essence clause, costs may also be assessed against the general contractor who fails to complete the project on time. The contractor may be liable for actual costs or damages, which in some cases may be far in excess of liquidated damages.

When liquidated damages are included in the contract for construction, the owner's claim cannot exceed those daily, weekly, or monthly amounts included in the contract.

Some general contractors are overly optimistic about achieving timely completion of the project that experiences some delays in its initial stages. But don't be lulled into a false sense of security, particularly when dealing with a difficult general contractor. No matter what the general contractor says—that he or she will overcome the delays, that he or she will complete on time—if your trade is experiencing delays, send a letter to the general contractor describing the nature and extent of the delays in detail. And as more delays occur, send additional letters to the general contractor.

If the general contractor was correct in his or her assumption that the project would be completed on time in spite of early delays, no harm was done by sending these delay letters. But if no delay letters had been sent to the general contractor and the project completion date was delayed, this lack of documentation may prove fatal to the subcontractor when claiming additional costs for the delays or defending against the assessment of liquidated damages. And when dealing with difficult general contractors, rather than receiving their assistance in resolving the delay claim, they will be quick to place the blame on some subcontractor—possibly your company.

Dealing with tough personalities

We've all experienced working with an individual who is just plain disagreeable. They may use their position of authority to intimidate anyone they consider a subordinate, or they may have an adult tantrum on too many occasions. There are three types of aggressive personalities and if encountered when dealing with a difficult contractor each one can be approached differently.

First there are the Steamrollers, the "street fighter" types who are arrogant, angry, and vent their emotions on a nonstop basis, not allowing anyone to interrupt their tirades.

Never argue with the Steamrollers or respond by yelling back but attempt to defuse their anger without acting submissive. These types value strength and any attempt to back away will be viewed as weakness. When faced with Steamroller rage, try to respond after they have vented their anger with, "You know I feel the same way too, but can I ask you a few questions to make sure I've got the facts straight?" This will generally cause them to stop their tirade and wait for your questions, providing them with enough time to cool off or at least cool down a bit.

If one is being berated for a mistake, the surest way to defuse the Steamroller's anger is to admit the mistake, "Yes, I guess I really blew it." That will take the wind out of their sails because you are actually agreeing with them.

Then there is the Passive-Aggressive who is often sarcastic and sneaky, avoiding a direct confrontation with the individual responsible for the problem but the P/A will throw out barbs directed at the accused while in the presence of others.

Sarcasm should not be met with more sarcasm, which will only encourage more of the same.

The Passive Aggressive, not wanting to have a direct confrontation can be dealt with by bringing about a direct confrontation by announcing, "If you have a problem with my report (or whatever), let's discuss it now and see how we can resolve these issues." Deal with the Passive Aggressive's complaint when it surfaces and preferably in the company of others. Request a clear explanation of the problem and ask that it be resolved quickly so that it does not fester.

The Screamer may share some of the attributes of the Steamroller and should be allowed to "blow off steam." If the screaming persists for a considerable period, don't fight and don't walk away; follow the flow and the screamer will eventually calm down, at which point perhaps a calm discussion of the matter can be started. Try not to take these angry displays from the Steamrollers, Passive-Aggressives, or Screamers personally; in most cases they are merely a part of a stressed-out personality that must vent itself from time to time.

Threatening letters from difficult general contractors

We've all received threatening letters from owners, general contractors, and subcontractors, generally written on the spur of the moment, containing maybe not-so-accurate statements of fact and including threats if certain conditions are not met.

While it may be easier to ignore these letters, knowing they would probably not have been written had cooler heads prevailed, it is important that they not be ignored.

The individual writing that nasty, accusatory letter may leave the organization and his or her replacement, finding no response to the threatening letter could assume that there was justification for writing such a letter. Or the originator of the letter may be wrongly accusing your company to cover up his or her own mistake or shortcoming.

But of course if the threatening letter does state the facts correctly, even if written in an unprofessional manner, it must be answered promptly but in a professional manner.

If the situation, outlined in the threatening letter, continues or worsens and develops into a dispute or claim, any nonresponse may prove damaging. When responding to a threatening letter, try not to be influenced by its inflammatory nature but respond, point-by-point, to the statements in the letter, and put the matter to rest. In doing so, try to be conciliatory not argumentative and just try to state the facts.

There is another twist to this situation and that is where the general contractor fails to respond to a somewhat threatening letter from a subcontractor. This may occur when the general contractor verbally authorizes extra work, or accepts a no-cost change in the scope of work and agrees to issue written authorization or confirmation prior to start of that work. Without such written authorization or confirmation, the subcontractor will be "at risk" if for some reason the general contractor changes his or her mind. If sufficient time passes and no such letter of authorization arrives, and the subcontractor is planning to proceed with this extra work, a letter can be sent to the general contractor in sort of reverse English fashion.

"On (date)(name of individual who) verbally authorized our company to substitute 1-inch pipe insulation in all apartment demising wall partitions in lieu of the 2-inch specified on a no-cost basis.

We have not received your written confirmation of this change as of this date. If such written authorization has not been received by (date) we will take this nonresponse as authorization to proceed with this change on a no-cost basis."

Or in the case of the request for written authorization to proceed with extra work:

"On (date)(name of individual who) verbally authorized our company to construct all office demising walls to the structure above rather than to a height of 6" above the acoustical ceilings as indicated on (Drawing/Section, etc.). The cost of this work as accepted by your firm was $25,000.00. Although you indicated you would provide written authorization to proceed, as of this date, no such authorization has been received.

"We plan to commence work on (date), and request that your written confirmation be issued prior to start of work. Unless we receive written directive to the contrary, we will commence work as scheduled, at the agreed-upon price of $25,000.00."

These letters will document the situation in hand and will prove of value if written confirmation is not received from the general contractor, and/or the person(s) issuing the verbal request either disputes, does not recall the arrangement, or has left the firm.

The First Defense Against a Difficult General Contractor

Contracts, and their contents, assume a great deal of importance when dealing with difficult contractors. Most problems arise for one or more of the following reasons—each one having contract implications:

1. The subcontractor lacks proof or documentation verifying receipt of all bid documents sent to them by the general contractor. How can a subcontractor state that they did not, for example, receive Addendum #3 when they can't produce a document that reveals exactly what was transmitted to them for inclusion in the subcontract agreement?

   If the general contractor does not provide documentation concerning which bid/contract documents were sent to the subcontractor prior to the signing of a subcontract agreement, then the subcontractor must enumerate the documents received and the date(s) received and send a confirming letter to the general contractor.

   When a disagreement occurs over whether or not the subcontractor received a certain document, this confirmation letter will resolve this issue.

   And, of course, no subcontract agreement should be signed when it includes any documents that the subcontractor has not received and accepted.

2. A subcontractor must read and understand the complete scope of his or her work even if he or she is of the opinion that the general contractor will not require him or her to adhere strictly to the contract requirements. If exceptions to any provisions of the plans or specifications are proposed by the subcontractor and accepted by the general contractor, they should be negotiated prior to signing the subcontract agreement and included as amendments to the subcontract agreement. But in order to do so, the subcontractor must first read and fully comprehend the scope of work that he or she is expected to accept.

3. Instruct all field personnel to keep detailed notes on all "extras" whether they have been directed to perform this work by the general contractor or proceeded to make minor changes for the betterment of the project but did not plan to request an "extra."

   A brief description of the work in the daily log, or preferably on a work authorization form, referencing applicable contract plans/specifications and possibly a sketch of the work or detail involved is recommended. List all personnel involved in the extra work and copies of the weekly payroll reports should be attached to the work authorization form to document these labor costs. Any material or equipment costs should be attached with copies of receiving tickets on which the field supervisor writes the exact nature of the extra work and where these materials or equipment were used. Copies of invoices from vendors should also be included.

   A separate file for each of these extra work operations can be created in the office with the accumulated documents placed in the file. If the subcontractor is called upon to provide substantiation for any extra work item there will be no need to search through records that have been previously filed.

A difficult general contractor will often request more and more substantiating documentation months after a claim for extra work has been filed. This is generally a ploy by the general contractor counting on the fact that the subcontractor may have a difficult time accumulating all of the backup information and will eventually throw up their hands and negotiate a settlement on the claim or simply withdraw it altogether.

As exasperating as some of these situations can be, don't allow difficult general contractors to wear you down—because that is exactly what their strategy is. Negotiations often appear to be endless, but the trick is to stick with them, get through the resolution process quickly, and devote one's energies to more productive endeavors.

And then vow never to work for that company again, no matter how appealing the opportunity may appear!

4. Stand your ground if you are firm in your conviction. Don't back down beyond a certain point; don't cave in.

The writer's experience in such a matter will illustrate this point. During a walkthrough inspection of an office building, the owner's representative noticed a deviation from the contract documents.

Interior drywall partitions which were to be attached to the interior side of curtain wall aluminum mullions were to be joined to the mullions with an acoustical isolation strip—actually a 1/8" thick by 2" strip of open cell Styrofoam—probably worth $.25 for materials and a dollar or two for installation labor.

The owner's representative, while touring the building with the general contractor and the drywall subcontractor, noticed that fifteen such strips were not installed. The drywall subcontractor, who had a multimillion dollar contract on the project, was slightly embarrassed because he prided himself on performing quality work and voluntarily offered a credit of $35.00 for each missing strip—a total of $525.00. He further agreed to close the gap by applying clear silicon caulking. The owner's representative instantly rejected this proposal.

What ensued was a negotiating session. The owner said the credit was totally insufficient so the drywall subcontractor increased it to $45.00 per unit or a total credit of $675.00 even though he felt it was unreasonable. The bidding continued to $65.00 per unit but this price was considered insufficient by the owner, at which point the drywall subcontractor said, "(Expletive deleted) I'll tear down the walls and put the acoustical strip in and I withdraw my credit!" The owner very quickly accepted the $65.00 credit!

In this case it was the owner, not the general contractor, who was being difficult but, at times, standing up for what one believes is proper and may cause an unreasonable general contractor or owner to concede or back down in his or her demands.

5. If the project has been bonded and payments have been seriously delayed or payments for authorized change orders have been ignored by a difficult general contractor, a threat to "call the bond" can be very effective in bringing resolution to the problem.

The first step in this process is to request that the general contractor provide your company with a copy of its bond(s), which by contract, it is required to do. This request, by itself will notify the general contractor that you are considering contacting the bonding company to advise them that there is a potential default on either the payment or performance bond.

If there is no response from the general contractor, the next step is to send him or her a letter outlining your complaints and indicating that you will notify the bonding company in the event these issues are not resolved by a certain date. You may wish to copy the owner on this letter.

And if this letter is ignored the next letter will be sent to the bonding company stating the facts surrounding the disputed issues, including any appropriate documentation. Send a copy of this letter to the owner. All such copies should be sent certified mail, return receipt required.

Most difficult contractors will try to avert a meeting with the bonding company, but if this last letter fails to obtain a response, the bonding company will contact the general contractor and begin an investigation of the matter; however, most problems are resolved between general contractor and subcontractor before this last event takes place.

The Mechanic's Lien as an Effective Weapon

Each state has its own form of mechanic's lien law, but they all are enacted to serve one purpose—to hold the building owner liable for unpaid debts relating to the construction of his or her project. This responsibility is shifted to the general contractor, or in some cases, the subcontractor via appropriate provisions in the contract for construction.

Mechanic's liens can be filed by three levels of construction project participants:

1. By the general contractor if they have not been paid by the owner.

2. By the subcontractor if not paid by the general contractor (or owner if he or she has contracted directly with the owner).

3. By the material/equipment supplier who has supplied material/equipment to either general contractor, subcontractor, or owner (if the owner had contracted directly with that material/equipment supplier).

A mechanic's lien generally cannot be filed by a material supplier's middleperson. For example the supplier of an air-conditioning unit can file a mechanic's lien but the manufacturer of the compressor installed in that air conditioning equipment cannot.

A mechanic's lien is filed against the property owner and effectively places a claim against the property thereby preventing the owner from obtaining clear title to that property.

Since lending institutions require clear title to the property in case the owner defaults on his or her construction loan, he or she is particularly sensitive to having liens placed upon that property.

Therefore merely the threat of placing a lien against the property is sufficient to cause a difficult general contractor to pay an overdue invoice. If the threat fails, Step 2 is to send the contractor a letter stating an intention to file a mechanic's lien against the property and send a copy of that letter to the owner. If that fails to get results, contact an attorney and file the lien!

A general contractor can "bond the lien," in other words, obtain a bond in the face amount of the lien that will ensure payment for any legitimate claim if the general contractor does not resolve the matter. The owner and the lending institution will accept such a bond as assurance that the mechanic's lien will be satisfied or removed. These bonds usually are issued for the period of one year but can be renewed annually.

However, if the lien is not satisfied upon completion of the project, the owner may elect to withhold final payment to the general contractor (or subcontractor if he or she had contracted the work directly with the owner) even if the bond is still active.

The use of mechanic's liens is more prevalent in private projects since most government agencies have enacted laws prohibiting the filing of liens against their property.

Procedures for Filing a Mechanic's Lien

The filing of a mechanic's lien can be a complicated matter and is best done in concert with the company's attorney.

There are time restrictions that apply—i.e., liens can only be filed within a specified time from the last date significant work has been performed on the project, generally a period of 90 days.

The word significant is important! Some subcontractors, having completed their work months ago, not having received payment from the general contractor, may suddenly realize that their lien rights will expire in a day or two. So, in the case of a plumbing contractor, as an example, they may send a service man to the project and change a washer in a sink, or replace a belt on a fan. In the case of a carpenter or drywall subcontractor in the same situation, they may have one of their workers go to the project and adjust a door or patch a small hole in sheetrock.

If either of these subcontractor's believe that they have protected their lien rights they will probably be disappointed because many courts have disallowed the filing of liens on this basis, recognizing that this last minute work is merely a ruse.

The application to file a mechanic's lien must contain an accurate description of the property, with all "i's" dotted and all "t's" crossed. Many liens have been held invalid because a seemingly minor discrepancy existed in the property description.

One last important fact to consider regarding mechanic's liens. Some contracts between owner and general contractor or subcontractor contain a "no lien" clause.

When signing a subcontract agreement read it carefully to determine whether it contains a no lien clause, which will prohibit your company from filing an enforceable mechanic's lien. Consult with your attorney to determine if any "flow-through" clauses in the owner-general contractor agreement prohibiting the filing of liens will affect your ability to do so.

A Final Word

Throughout this chapter on Dealing with Difficult Contractors, one phrase has been repeated many times—"Put it in writing."

When working with difficult general contractors it becomes important to document all dealings with them, since it appears that their verbal commitments may not be honored or they may not even honor their contractual obligations without a fight.

Be prepared and assume the worst and assemble documentation for that arbitration or that court case that, hopefully, will never materialize.

11

Project Closeouts

When the project is nearing its closing days and all thoughts tend to drift to the new job that just came into the office, there is a tendency for both field and office personnel to relax their efforts to complete all closeout requirements. These tendencies are to be resisted because both the subcontractor's reputation and final payment are on the line.

The general contractor will begin to gather closeout documents from other subcontractors, along with the ones they are required to submit so they, too, can successfully complete the project, submit their request for final payment, receive all payments due from the owner, and in turn, dispense final payments to their subcontractors and suppliers—and move on to the next job.

One weak link in this chain of events will result in delays in closing out the entire project, and final payments to all parties will not be released by the owner to the general contractor. Because of the flow-through clause in most subcontract agreements, all subcontractors and vendors will have to wait patiently for their last payment, whether or not they were responsible for the delays.

Prompt attention to, and compliance with, closeout procedures separates the valued subcontractor from the mediocre subcontractor in their evaluation by general contractors and, as important, prompt attention and compliance will be rewarded with a prompt final payment.

Closeout Starts with Mobilization

Prior to the start of a project, a thorough reading of the section of the specifications dealing with closeout procedures is important. The time to start planning to close out the project begins when the project begins.

Do we need extra sets of drawings in the field so that daily entries on as-built conditions can be made? Are there inspections that must be made and documented during the project that require special forms to be sent to the field? When various products or equipment are shipped to the site, are the manufacturer's installation/operations procedures included in the shipment—documents that are often misplaced but are required to be submitted to the general contractor as part of the close-out package? These are all items that need to be addressed as mobilization efforts for the project begin and all field personnel become acquainted with all aspects of the project.

Although field personnel are required to become familiar with both the plans and specifications, it is easy to dismiss the General Requirements of the specifications on this new job as "boilerplate" and probably much the same as the last two or three projects. This assumption may prove costly.

Each architect and engineer prepares slightly different closeout procedures and it is important at the early stages of a project that a review of these "boilerplate" specifications be reviewed to make note of the important or unique requirements.

The preconstruction job meeting held in the subcontractor's office should, among other topics, touch on closeout procedures for the new project and the steps necessary for compliance as the project gets under way.

Creating a separate office file entitled "CLOSEOUT" during project mobilization and inserting the necessary documents as they are generated or received along the way will simplify matters at the end of the project, when all of this data can be sorted, coordinated, and packaged for transmission to the general contractor, along with a transmittal listing each and every document included in the package. As an added precaution, some subcontractors prefer to hand deliver these documents to the general contractor's project manager and obtain written confirmation of receipt.

The Closeout Specification Section

The most common requirements in the Closeout specification section are:

- Project record documents (as-built drawings).
- Coordination drawings (Required during construction but are converted to "as-builts" as the subcontractors involved in the coordination process make changes to the various systems as part of the coordination process).
- General contractor and subcontractor guarantees and warranties.

- Test reports.
- Inspection reports.
- Operation and Maintenance (O&M) Manuals.
- Keys, tools, spare parts.
- Attic stock.
- Preventative Maintenance Schedules.
- Charts—for valves, fire damper locations, other concealed controllable parts.
- Electrical panel circuitry directories.
- Final surveys.
- Record of Manufacturers Material Data Sheets (MSDS).

1. Preparation of record documents

Most trades will be required to submit "as-built" drawings to the general contractor at the end of the project. These drawings will contain:

- Approved changes made during construction.
- Location of underground or concealed work.
- Details that vary from those contained in the contract drawings.
- Relocation of any work—partitions, ceilings, mechanical, and electrical piping, conduits.
- Any dimensional changes.
- Access doors, "tack" locations of access points in accessible ceilings.
- Location of plumbing valves, HVAC fire dampers, other concealed parts that will require maintenance/periodic replacement.
- Footing depth elevations in relation to finished grade elevations.
- Any changes in floor elevations.
- Any structural changes.
- Any substitutions.
- Invert elevations of all underground utilities, manholes, and catch basins.

Depending upon the size and complexity of the project, these record drawings may be required to be submitted as sepias or Mylars or even in the form of Computer Assisted Design (CAD) diskettes in a format acceptable to the architect and engineer.

The subcontractor is frequently required to certify that the record drawings meet all of the criteria required by the contract. A sample certification would be:

These record drawings, prepared by:
_____*(name of subcontractor)*
*for*_____*(classification of work)*
have been reviewed by the undersigned and appear to be an accurate representation of the work incorporated into the project and are accepted as submitted in accordance with the technical documents.

This record document review made by this office is for determination of compliance to the requirements of the contract documents.

*Firm name:*_____

*Review date:*_____ *By:*_____*(name and title)*

Some general contractors and/or project owners will have their representatives periodically check the status of the as-built drawings as the job progresses and if they are not accurate or current may be cause to withhold payment to that subcontractor. When a subcontractor is responsible for the preparation of an "as-built" drawing, his or her project manager should review the status of such drawings during his or her weekly visit to the job site. This will also avoid problems associated with the final submission and acceptance of accurate as-built drawings at project closeout.

2. Coordination drawings

The process of developing coordination drawings varies depending upon the subcontractor's role in the project. Sheet metal, fire protection, HVAC piping, plumbing and electrical subcontractors will have the most important input into this procedure as drawings prepared by the "lead" subcontractor is circulated to others to create one final, approved drawing that verifies that all systems will fit into the areas designated to receive them.

Drywall and acoustical ceiling contractors will be called upon during this process if partition sizes or location changes are required, and, in the case of the ceiling contractor, if ceiling heights need to be lowered.

The final coordination drawings, approved by the general contractor and forwarded to the architect and engineer for comment and approval, do not relieve the general contractor or subcontractors of their responsibility for complete and proper coordination of all trades.

Even if the coordination of these drawings is approved by the architect/engineer, any conflicts that occur during installation of these systems remain the responsibility of all contractors.

These coordination drawings will require scrutiny of the following building components:

- Partition and room layout.
- Ceiling grid and tiles.
- Light fixtures—both wall and ceiling mounted.
- Access panels.
- Sheet metal, heating/cooling coils, grilles, diffusers, and other air distribution devices.
- HVAC piping and valves.
- Smoke and fire dampers.
- Waste and vent piping.
- Domestic and process water piping.
- Insulation for HVAC and Plumbing installations.
- Medical or industrial gases, if applicable.
- Roof drain piping.
- Major electrical conduit runs, panelboards, feeder conduits, racks of branch conduits.
- Above ceiling miscellaneous metals.
- Fire protection systems.
- Heat tracing of pipes and required insulation.
- Equipment supports, anchors, guides, seismic or vibration isolation devices.

A series of meetings are required to complete this coordination effort and prepare the final drawings that will fulfill the requirements of the closeout process. It is not unusual to find that some minor changes need to be made to the coordination drawings as actual installation work proceeds and it is important that these changes be properly documented so they can be incorporated in a revised set of record drawings.

3. Specific guarantees of materials and equipment

When the Closeout specification section is read prior to start of construction and important sections are highlighted, the requirement for extended or unusual guarantees and warranties will become apparent.

The standard warranty and guarantee requirement will read as follows:

> "The contractor warrants to the (Owner) that all materials and equipment furnished under this contract will be new and free of defects and that all work will be of good quality, free from faults and defects and in strict conformance with the Contract Documents for a period of one (1) year from the date of Substantial Completion _____."

There are exceptions. For example, the normal guarantee period for a lock set or a metal door or an aluminum window may be one year. However, the guarantee portion of the specifications may require a two-year guarantee for one of these items or a five-year guarantee on the insulated glass in that aluminum window. Any such extended warranties/guarantees are easier to negotiate, usually at a "no-cost" basis when the subcontractor is negotiating these purchases at the beginning of the project. Once a purchase order has been issued and the requirement for an extended guarantee is discovered, when the subcontractor does read the appropriate portion of the specifications, the vendor of that product may request a substantial up-charge to provide the additional warranty period.

Don't wait until incorrect guarantees/warranties are submitted and rejected by the architect/engineer at the end of the project. This is just another reason for a thorough review of the Closeout procedures prior to start of construction.

An important point to consider! Read the contract documents to determine when the warranty/guarantee period commences. It usually will take effect upon substantial completion of the project as defined and acknowledged by the architect/engineer. But suppose the general contractor is lax in obtaining a certificate of substantial completion from the architect and this delay affects your equipment/material warranties/guarantees? To avoid these kinds of problems send a letter to the general contractor requesting a copy of the project architect's acceptance of substantial completion in order to validate the start of your equipment/material warranties/guarantees. Or when the architect and/or engineer witness the startup of electrical or mechanical equipment and indicate their acceptance, send a letter to the general contractor requesting confirmation that the equipment has been inspected and approved by the architect or engineer and the guarantee/warranty period has commenced. Follow the guidelines for both situations included in the sample letter section of Chapter 12.

4. Test and inspection reports

Test and inspection reports may be required at various times during the construction cycle. Liquid or air testing of plumbing piping may be necessary to receive both design engineer and local building official approval. The design engineer may require copies of all such reports as they occur and a complete set of reports at project closeout. Inspections of insulation or sound batts may be required prior to the closing up of partitions or installation of ceilings. Floor and wall penetrations for both fire and sound transmission requirements may also be required to be inspected prior to enclosing those areas.

There may be a requirement for a Subcontractor's Daily Report (Figure 11.1) which is to be submitted to the general contractor each

SUBCONTRACTOR'S DAILY REPORT

PREPARE DAILY FOR THAT DAY'S WORK; SUBMIT TO JOB SUPERINTENDENT BY 8:00 A.M. NEXT WORKING DAY.

To:

Project: _____

Subcontractor: _____ Date: _____

Number of Subcontractor's Employees on Project:

        Superintendents: _____
        Foremen: _____
        Hourly Employees: _____
        Total: _____

Description of Subcontractor's work performed today (Give description, amount accomplished, and location):

_____

_____

_____

_____

_____

_____

_____

Remarks (Explain accidents, reasons for delays, etc.):

_____

_____

_____

_____

                                     _____
                                     Superintendent or Foreman

Figure 11-1

working or nonworking day and is to be accumulated into a complete file and submitted as part of the closeout requirements. If this is a contract obligation, these Daily Reports should be made as multiple copy forms, retaining one copy in the field, submitting one copy to the general contractor, and sending a copy to the office for retention in the "CLOSEOUT" file. (Even if there is no such requirement, as part of the project documentation, retention of these daily reports for at least one year is a good business practice.

When test reports are issued and approved by either building officials, testing laboratories, or the architect/engineer, they will be incorporated in the final closeout package. If a report indicates an unsatisfactory condition and there is no notation that a correction has been made followed by a satisfactory reinspection report, either an interim payment or final payment may be withheld pending receipt of that approved inspection. If any unsatisfactory conditions requiring reinspection are ignored by the subcontractor and do not come to the attention of the owner until the building or facility is occupied, any corrective action required by the subcontractor may be very expensive and could have been avoided if all required inspections and reinspections had been followed more closely as they occurred.

5. Operations and maintenance manuals

Most of the materials for the Operations and Maintenance manuals will originate with the vendor or supplier of the product or equipment. Collection of the brochures and data sheets that comprise the final O&M manuals must be done in a timely fashion. If the subcontractor waits until the end of the project to request the necessary manufacturers' documents, these materials may not be forthcoming promptly. Make the O&M requirements known to the vendor/supplier when the order is placed and request that they be submitted prior to invoicing.

6. Keys, special tools, spare parts

All keys for locks and equipment access are to be properly tagged when received to avoid being improperly identified and not accepted at project closeout. If duplicate keys came with the locks or equipment, it may be a good idea to send one of each to the office for safekeeping since these items often get lost on the job.

The requirement for special tools may allow the subcontractor to purchase the special tool(s) that can be used during construction, turned over to the owner, in used but serviceable condition upon project completion. In this way the subcontractor gains the benefit of using a tool that improves efficiency but one that they would normally not purchase.

When spare parts are required, these additional supplies can often be purchased at little or no additional cost when the initial order for the base product is placed. But when the subcontractor is not aware of the requirement for spare parts until the project is underway and a purchase order has already been issued, their vendors may request extra costs to provide these spare parts.

7. Attic stock

What is true of spare parts is also true of attic stock—those extra materials to be used by the owner if breakage or damage occurs after they have accepted and occupied the building—including the necessary attic stock materials in the initial vendor purchase order that should be considered.

8. Preventative maintenance schedules

These Preventative Maintenance (PM) schedules will be supplied by the manufacturer or prepared by the subcontractor after consultation with the product or equipment manufacturer. Once again, discuss the project's PM requirements with the vendor during initial negotiations to purchase the product. In this way, if there are extra costs involved they may be eliminated completely or substantially reduced during the purchasing process.

Operating instructions presented in video film format

Complex and sophisticated heating, cooling, and process equipment installations may require the subcontractor to provide video training tapes along with a specific number of hours of indoctrination training when this equipment is made operational. Once again, if manufacturer provided training sessions are extensive, or if the specifications allow the owner to spread the training sessions over an extended period of time, the cost of these sessions can be more effectively negotiated when purchasing the equipment.

Videotaping of start-up and operating procedures, if required, should be discussed initially with the supplier, who may be able to provide such services at a reasonable cost.

9. Certifications of specification compliance

Prior to final payment, some contract specifications require the general contractor and each subcontractor to certify that all products furnished and installed in the project meet the contract requirements. These certifications may also include statements attesting that no products or equipment furnished or installed contain hazardous materials.

The purpose of these certifications will serve to protect the design consultants and the owner if in the future it is determined that "off-spec" products or equipment or hazardous materials had actually been installed contrary to what had been previously certified. A sample Certification of Specification Compliance form is shown in Figure 11-2 and 11-2a.

10. Material Safety Data Sheets (MSDS)

Material Safety Data Sheets for all hazardous products are required to be shipped to the construction site prior to the arrival of the respective product/equipment. Although these MSDS are to remain on the site during the entire project since the storage, handling, and safety procedures contained therein may be required, too often they are either discarded or misplaced. If closeout requirements include the submission of MSDS for each product your company supplied for the project, make duplicate copies when received and keep in the Closeout file.

Punch List Sign-Off

There will be times when it appears that the punch list will never end as one architect/engineer's punch list is followed by another and additional punch lists are created by the owner. Although this procedure may be contradictory to the provisions of the contract documents, the subcontractor is best served by completing these additional items if they are minor ones.

And if the general contractor will not release final payment until all of these items have been completed, there is a way to obtain at least a major portion of the final payment while assuring the owner that the remaining items will be completed.

Make a list of the outstanding Punch List items and assign a value to each one. As each item is completed, the general contractor will remit a corresponding payment. Some contractors or owners will be agreeable to this process but will require the subcontractor to provide the actual cost to complete the outstanding item and then withhold double that amount. However if a great deal of money is being withheld because a half dozen or so minor items have not been completed, it is certainly worthwhile to propose this remedy.

CERTIFICATION OF SPECIFICATION COMPLIANCE

CORPORATE ACKNOWLEDGMENT

)SS.
)

On the _____ day of _____, before me came _____ to me known and who by me being duly sworn did depose and say that he resides at _____ that he is the officer of the said corporation executing the foregoing instrument, that he knows the seal of said corporation, that the seal affixed to said instrument is such corporate seal, that it was so affixed by order of the Board of Directors of said corporation and that he signed his name thereto by like order.

                                _____
                                  Notary Public

INDIVIDUAL ACKNOWLEDGMENT

State of
)SS.
)
County of

On the _____ day of_____, before me came _____ to me known and who by me being duly sworn did depose and say that he resides at _____ that he is the individual who executed the foregoing instrument.

                                _____
                                  Notary Public

PARTNERSHIP ACKNOWLEDGMENT

State of
)SS.
)
County of

On the _____ day of _____, before me came _____ to me known and who by me being duly sworn did depose and say that he resides at _____ that he is the partner in the firm of _____ doing business under the name of _____ and that he executed the foregoing instrument on behalf of said partnership.

                                _____
                                  Notary Public

                                       Certification

Figure 11-2

Final Inspections

Depending upon the requirements of the local building departments, some final inspections will be required, generally involving mechanical or electrical systems, and until the general contractor receives

```
CERTIFICATION OF SPECIFICATION COMPLIANCE

I/WE, the MANUFACTURER/SUPPLIER and INSTALLER of _____

_____

as specified in Section Number _____ of the Contract  Documents
prepared  by                                      Architects

such  Consultants   and   Sub-Consultants   retained  by _____
_____ to  participate  with  the Architect  in   the
preparation of these Documents.



do (does) herein`certify that -

1.   All materials furnished for said  project do fully comply  with
     all specification requirements  as stated  within the  Contract
     Documents;

2.   That no asbestos containing materials of any nature are used in
     the work;

3.   That execution of  the Work covered  by this certification  has
     been performed in accordance with the drawings prepared by  the
     design professional team.

CONTRACTOR: _____

CERTIFICATION BY: _____ TITLE: _____

ADDRESS: _____

CERTIFICATION DATED: _____

Distribution:

     Original and One Copy to:_____



                                  Att:
```

Figure 11-2a

proof of such inspections, the Certificate of Occupancy will not be forthcoming.

It is incumbent for each trade to determine which such final inspections are required by local and state officials and provide them to the general contractor as quickly as possible.

Special Requirements Related to Mechanical and Electrical Trades

Along with all of the above requirements, entire sections of closeout specifications may be devoted to plumbing, fire protection, HVAC, electrical, and equipment control subcontractors.

During the course of the project, various tests, inspections, and reports may be required as work progresses. Typically, air balancing reports (Figure 11-3) are required to be submitted and reviewed and approved by the engineer before final sign-off on the air-handling and distribution systems. Not only will various hydrostatic tests be required to meet building codes, but some design engineers require an entire series of other tests that ultimately will form a Testing-Inspection section in the closeout documents.

Figures 11-4 and 11-4a are typical hydrostatic tests required to be completed by the plumbing subcontractor witnessed by the general contractor and the design engineer. Figures 11-5 (Pump sign-off) and 11-6 (Exhaust Fan sign-off) may be required not so much as inspection reports but as Quality Control reports highlight the applicable sections to insure full compliance.

That last impression is usually the one that general contractors and owners remember as the project winds down and occupancy commences.

Prompt and efficient attention to closeout procedures will enhance the favorable relationships created throughout the construction project.

CFM TEST & BALANCE	DUCT LEAKAGE TEST		DATA SHEET #
	DATE	BY	

AIR SYSTEM_____   SPECIFIED TEST PRESSURE (P_T)_____
LEAKAGE CLASS (C_L)_____   DUCT PRESSURE CLASS (P_C)_____

DESIGN DATA				FIELD TEST DATA						
TEST SECTION	SURFACE AREA FT^2	ALLOWABLE LEAKAGE		DIAMETER		PRESSURE "wg			PERFORMED BY	ACTUAL CFM
		FACTOR CFM/100 FT^2	CFM	ORIFICE	TUBE	DUCT	ACROSS ORIFICE	DATE		

Figure 11-3

HYDROSTATIC TEST REPORT

DATE:_____   TEST REPORT NUMBER: _____
SYSTEM: STEAM CONDENSATE PIPING   SPEC. SECTION: _____
SYSTEM TEST PRESSURE: 200 PSI
LOCATION: _____   PRESSURE GAUGE READING:
START TIME: _____   START: _____
FINISH TIME: _____   FINISH: _____

COMMENTS:_____
_____
_____
_____
_____
_____
_____
_____
_____
_____
_____
_____

TEST ACCEPTED: YES   NO

WITNESSED BY:

        SIGN OFF:_____   DATE:_____

        SIGN OFF:_____   DATE:_____

          SIGN OFF:_____   DATE:_____

NOTE: THIS PRESSURE TEST REPORT MUST BE FILLED OUT EVERY TIME A TEST IS PERFORMED.
HydroSCP

Figure 11-4

HYDROSTATIC TEST REPORT

DATE:_____   TEST REPORT NUMBER: ____
SYSTEM: CHILLED WATER PIPING   SPEC. SECTION: _____
SYSTEM TEST PRESSURE: 200 PSI
LOCATION: _____   PRESSURE GAUGE READING:
START TIME: _____   START: _____
FINISH TIME: _____   FINISH: _____

COMMENTS:_____
_____
_____
_____
_____
_____
_____
_____
_____
_____
_____

TEST ACCEPTED: YES   NO

WITNESSED BY:

    SIGN OFF:_____   DATE:_____

    SIGN OFF:_____   DATE:_____

        SIGN OFF:_____   DATE:_____

NOTE: THIS PRESSURE TEST REPORT MUST BE FILLED OUT EVERY TIME A TEST IS PERFORMED.
HydroCWP

Figure 11-4a

QUALITY CONTROL SIGN-OFF
PUMPS

EQUIPMENT#: CHP-2

LOCATION#: EAST PENTHOUSE MECHANICAL ROOM

MANUFACTURER: PACO PUMPS

MODEL#: KP-8 X 10 X 15

SIZE/CAPACITY: 4800 GPM

ELECTRIC MOTOR

MANUFACTURER:

MODEL: A-1

SIZE/CAPACITY: 200 HP

VOLTAGE/AMPS ON LABEL:

COMMENTS:

SIGN OFF

INSTALLING CONTRACTOR:

Q/C COORDINATOR:

ENGINEER:

Figure 11-5

```
┌─────────────────────────────────────────┐
│        QUALITY CONTROL SIGN-OFF          │
│             EXHAUST FAN                  │
└─────────────────────────────────────────┘
```

EQUIPMENT#: E−1−82 _____

LOCATION#: _____

MANUFACTURER: BAYLEY _____

MODEL#: BI 200 _____

SIZE/CAPACITY: 4,400 CFM _____

ELECTRIC MOTOR

MANUFACTURER: _____

MODEL: A−1 _____

SIZE/CAPACITY: 5 HP _____

VOLTAGE/AMPS ON LABEL: _____

COMMENTS: _____

_____

_____

_____

_____

_____

_____

SIGN OFF

INSTALLING CONTRACTOR: _____

Q/C COORDINATOR: _____

ENGINEER: _____

_____

Figure 11-6

Marketing, Sales Development, and the Business Plan

It is the goal of most construction firms to negotiate contracts with long-term clients and seek less stressful and more profitable ways in which to conduct business. However, it is necessary to develop a company strategy to achieve this and other goals.

Marketing and business planning are two of the basic tools required to build a strong and long-lasting business. A marketing plan and a business plan go hand-in-hand. It's almost like the chicken and egg scenario—which should come first, or should they develop concurrently?

These two plans really require parallel development. Should the marketing and business plan fit the organization or should the organization be reworked to fit the marketing and business plan? Both of these plans have short- and long-term goals with minor, or possibly major, corrections required along the way.

Let's look at the marketing plan first because it may provide more insight into how the company's organizational structure and business plan are developed.

Developing a Marketing Strategy

Relying upon the various construction newsletters such as the Dodge Reports for notification of available bidding opportunities is certainly one way to seek business, but it may be spotty at best, usually highly competitive in nature, and subject to the ebb and flow of local business activity. It is a passive way to obtain work.

A marketing plan will point the way to a proactive approach to achieving the company's annual sales volume goal—a way to seek out work and let the world (at least the world that you are interested in!) know that you are out there and have definite services to offer.

Marketing requires self-analysis, carving out a segment of the market that best suits the company's strengths, and networking and advertising to advise potential clients of your organization and what you have to offer.

The self-analysis stage

What are proven company skills? Are they the ability to produce very competitive bids while still returning a decent profit? Is your company known for high-quality work and the ability to tackle difficult projects? Does the company have the reputation for working harmoniously with general contractors and, aware that not all plans and specifications are perfect, willing to abide by the "intent of the drawings" if minor corrections are required?

Does the company have the reputation for being able to meet compressed construction schedules while still remaining competitive pricewise, and does it have a particular expertise in a specific field such as hospital, medical, or pharmaceutical manufacturing or high quality interiors work?

The process of self-analysis should reveal the company's strengths as well as weaknesses because in this self-analysis process a matrix will develop to reveal the types of projects where the company excels and therefore should aggressively seek, and, conversely, the types of projects that the company should avoid, or at least improve its performance in, before attempting to increase its market share.

Review your market—past and present

Along with the self-analysis to uncover the company's strong and weak points, review the type of work that is ongoing and the type of work that was completed within the last five years. Which projects were the most successful—both from a profit and from a customer satisfaction basis? Which types of projects were not successful—and why?

All of these analyses might increase your company's awareness of that segment of the market in which you were successful and those past projects where you were less than successful. This type of analysis might point the way to what is known as niche marketing—finding that corner of the market in which the company excels and should be devoting more of its future marketing plan to that niche.

A guide to the self-analysis procedure

It is not too difficult to develop worksheets for this self-analysis process. The following forms may prove helpful in doing so.

Strength-Weakness Analysis Worksheet

What Are the Company's Strengths? (Be Objective!)

_____

_____

_____

_____

_____

What Are the Company's Weaknesses (Be Truthful—Even If It Hurts!)

_____

_____

_____

_____

_____

What Are the Company's Goals and What Time Frame Is Established to Achieve Them?

Goal	Achievement Date
_____	_____
_____	_____
_____	_____
_____	_____
_____	_____

What Kind of Work Has the Company Performed in the Past 3–5 Years?

Client	Type of Work	Value	How Obtained (Bid/Negotiated)
_____	_____	_____	_____
_____	_____	_____	_____
_____	_____	_____	_____
_____	_____	_____	_____
_____	_____	_____	_____

(This form will be as long as necessary to list all of these past projects)

What Kind of Work Is the Company Performing in the Current Year?

Client	Type of Work	Value	How Obtained (Bid/Negotiated)
_____	_____	_____	_____
_____	_____	_____	_____
_____	_____	_____	_____
_____	_____	_____	_____
_____	_____	_____	_____

These charts accentuate not only the type of work that has been performed, but also the type of client and ratio of hard bid to negotiated work. As an added exercise, assign "Satisfaction Values" to each project—one for the owner (were they satisfied with the work?) and one for the company (were you satisfied with the project?). Values of one to five can be assigned in both cases, with one being the least satisfied and five full satisfaction.

Competition Profiles—Identifying the Competitors

Competitor	Project	Reasons for Losing Job	Client Satisfaction
————	————	————————	————————
————	————	————————	————————
————	————	————————	————————
————	————	————————	————————

Since it is equally important to investigate why a sought after project had been lost to the competition, efforts should be made to determine the reasons for that unsuccessful bid.

Although it may not always depend upon price, there is no denying that most projects are lost because of competitive pricing. But those companies who constantly underbid the competition with estimates significantly below what is considered a "fair" or competitive price often do not remain in business for an extended period of time. These cutthroat competitors only drive down the profit margins for legitimate competitors until they eventually go out of business. The quality levels of these "low-ball" subcontractors might be less than acceptable, and postconstruction feedback for the owner, architect, or even other subcontractors may reveal client dissatisfaction with the subcontractor's work.

What Do I Need to Achieve the Company Goals?

Another checklist to better define goals is helpful

1. Organizational Changes—Do we need to make any? If so, list.

———————————————————————————————
———————————————————————————————
———————————————————————————————
———————————————————————————————
———————————————————————————————

2. Upgrade Internal Office Equipment (Hardware/Software/Management Tools)

_____

_____

_____

_____

_____

3. Physical Plant Changes (Increase office, warehouse, etc.)

_____

_____

_____

_____

_____

4. Resource Issues

Human Resources_____ (Probably the most important resource to reevaluate)

_____

_____

_____

Expand Line of Credit _____

Establish or Expand Bonding Capacity _____

Increase/Change Insurance Coverage _____

Review Capital Expenditures for Equipment/Tools _____

The Marketing Plan

Many subcontractors have no experience in effective marketing techniques and while they understand the need to start such a program they are unsure of how to take that all-important first step. The industry abounds with organizations that provide marketing expertise; some specialize in the construction industry.

Theresa Casey, President of On-Target Marketing and Communication in Columbia, Connecticut is one such firm and she states "For some subcontractors, marketing means printing business cards, placing an ad in the newspaper, or reviewing sales leads in the current Dodge Report. For most subs, however, these are just the basics. A successful marketing program involves making your company known to current and potential clients. Marketing can be viewed as the foundation for the sales process."

Terry Casey compares marketing to a three-legged stool consisting of (1) client relationships, (2) cost of the service being offered, and (3) reputation of the service provider (subcontractor). If one or more of these legs are missing a wobbly stool or shaky marketing plan will emerge.

Quality client relationships are not developed quickly or easily; they require implementing a time-tested, sustainable relationship and networking program.

Competitive price plays a significant role when soliciting that first job with a new client but from the client's perspective they are assuming a risk when contemplating a contract with a new subcontractor with whom they have had no previous experience. The importance of building a sound reputation based upon quality work, integrity, and, dependability, according to Terry Casey, cannot be overemphasized

Ms. Casey advises a comprehensive client relationship and networking program and low price is insufficient to ensure success. Quality work, attention to detail, and a professional approach to the project at hand is essential. A subcontractor's reputation for shoddy, incomplete, or untimely work will spread rapidly in the close-knit construction community, but a track record of having successfully worked with other clients will spread rapidly.

Cost of losing a client

Once a relationship with a respected client has been established, it is important to retain and build on that relationship.

A two-part equation helps quantify the cost of losing a client according to On-Target's experience in working with subcontractors: (1) the added cost of acquiring a new client and, (2) the lost revenue and profit from that client.

Benefits of continuing to work with a satisfied client

Add-on services—As clients become more accustomed to the subcontractor's services, they often buy more of their services without soliciting proposals from other contractors.

Clients prefer to work with the subcontractors they know and trust. In terms of cost and time, it is more efficient to continue working with subcontractor of proven ability.

Increased Efficiencies Experienced by the Subcontractor—An inverse relationship exists between the client's continued sole source of construction purchases and the subcontractor's operating costs. The subcontractor can develop more efficient systems by becoming more familiar with the client's demands, operating procedures, and personnel personalities. Terry Casey reports that one subcontractor reported a 60% decrease in operating costs after working with the same client during their second year,

Premium Fees—The confidence built through long-term relationships may often allow the subcontractor to charge slightly higher fees for their work since the client begins to recognize that these extra costs are justified by the consistently high-quality, dependable service provided by the subcontractor. However, this is not meant to be a license to arbitrarily increase the cost of future bids without ample justification to do so.

One never knows when a client may solicit competitive bids for a particular project to confirm their conviction that their reliable subcontractor's estimates remain reasonable.

And when a new management team replaces the one the subcontractor had previously worked for, it is not unusual for the new team to review all past subcontractor relationships and open bidding to the competition on future projects.

Performance, service, and relationships are the basic building blocks of an effective marketing plan.

Developing a Marketing Plan

On-Target suggests five steps to take in the development of a marketing plan:

1. Manage the process

   Include all company personnel in the discussions about marketing. Project managers and field supervisors who have worked closely with clients often have considerable insight into what the client expects of a subcontractor and what they do not appreciate. Prior to scheduling the first company meeting to discuss a marketing plan provides all attendees with an agenda, intended goals, and sufficient background material to review so that the session will be productive. Accurate notes should be taken and distributed and a date for the next meeting scheduled. It will require a series of meetings before a viable marketing plan is developed.

2. The SWOT analysis—Strength-Weakness-Opportunity-Threat

   Discuss the company's strengths and weaknesses, advises Ms. Casey. The company may have considerable experience in institutional work but may be less productive on commercial projects.

   What opportunities are out there and which ones does the company intend to pursue?

   What obstacles to obtaining increased business does the current competition present?

   Review the company's three to five year sales records, dividing them down into categories such as client type (general contractor, owners), construction type (residential, commercial, industrial) and industry type (biomedical, institutional, industrial) and profit level attained for each category.

The next step is to look at the firm's external environment. Has any new legislation been passed by federal, state, or local governments that would encourage or discourage growth in specific industries? For example, the Americans with Disabilities Act (ADA) created new opportunities for those firms that could perform the various types of retrofitting of existing buildings required by the Act.

Inquire about proposed economic developments in areas where the company operates. Are any towns planning to establish Enterprise Zones or target specific areas for growth?

3. Develop specific and measurable goals for the next one to three years
   Set specific, measurable goals, such as:
   - Increase sales by 10% over previous year

   - Agreement from five new general contractors to be placed on their bidders' list

   - Achieve reputation for competence in a construction specialty field such as biotechnological facility work

   - Acquire five projects directly from owners

   - Increase average project size to $1 million

4. Determine appropriate strategies
   Armed with the information from the three marketing planning process steps described above, identify the appropriate strategies or methods required to meet these goals, which may include the pursuit of any combination of the following:
   - Networking and team building (including professional association participation), a targeted sales plan

   - Restructuring the organization to ensure client satisfaction and service

   - Hiring a marketing/business development expert or contacting a firm specializing in these activities

   - Advertising and trade association program sponsorship

   - Public relations and promotion work (including attendance at trade shows)

   - Press releases and feature magazine articles in local publications

   - Brochure development including direct mail pieces

5. Tactics, responsibilities, schedule, budget

The key to implementing the plan is to list the specific steps that need to be accomplished and to identify a responsible person, a schedule, and a budget for each task.

Networking as a powerful marketing tool

Networking is one of the most powerful marketing tools available to the subcontractor. Active membership in local or state construction-related organizations will put your firm in contact with other specialty contractors, general contractors, owners, and design consultants. Keeping the company name in front of potential clients is important and business contacts in a social setting can be "door openers" when an interview or chance to bid on that new client's project is being sought.

Attendance at nearby trade shows affords the company an opportunity to see and be seen by competitors and potential clients—and also an opportunity to learn about new products and tools.

Seminars conducted by a variety of for-profit and nonprofit organizations present another opportunity to meet and socialize with one's peers and potential clients. And company attendance at such seminars will further the perception that the company is intent on growing professionally.

Membership in local civic organizations is another way to network— meeting people in the business community who are able to provide leads to future work.

The object of networking is to keep the company name in the forefront and when a general contractor or client is planning a project, your company will be invited to bid on that work—and that is what marketing is all about.

Along with a marketing program, don't forget some other basics that the clients expect and should be communicated to them:

- I can solve your problems; I won't create them.
- If I don't know, I'll find out.
- You will have no surprises. I will keep you updated.
- I will complete this project on time.
- I will maintain high quality levels.
- I will be responsible for my actions.
- I appreciate the opportunity to work for you.

The Business Plan

The business plan is a document that contains the goals the company will strive to achieve at some future date. By establishing priorities and goals a road map is created to guide the company along the path to a future destination—one of growth and profitability.

The business plan is somewhat like a road map with a starting point, a finish pointn and landmarks that must be passed along the way to reach one's destination. The first step is self-analysis of the company's workings.

The business plan Q & A

Questions such as, "What sales volume and corresponding overhead and profit levels are worthwhile goals to pursue in the years ahead?" need to be raised and answered.

Instead of operating on a day-to-day basis, the business plan will focus the company's energies in a controlled manner in order to achieve predetermined future goals.

The business plan will:

- Reduce to writing the future plans and goals that the company owners may have been discussing or thinking about but never formalized.

- Develop guidelines to achievable events in order to reach these goals.

Various pro forma financial statements can be created to plot "what if" situations.

- What if we want to increase our annual sales volume by 10% each year for the next five years? How long can we retain our current overhead before it must be increased?

- What if we achieve that volume in Year 2, but having increased our overhead, our volume drops in Year 3? What impact will this have on our net profit and what do we do about it?

- What if we lower our gross profit margin by 1% to attract more business, will the resultant net profit figures be too low to sustain us through a period when business is depressed?

- What if we miss our annual sales volume by "X" percent, how long can we sustain our proposed overhead? When would we have to reduce that overhead?

Based upon the company's average annual sales volume, corporate overhead, and actual gross profit margins, several "what if" scenarios can be created that will be helpful in developing a short- and /or long-term business plan taking into account changes in sales volume, overhead or operating expenses, and actual/proposed profit margins.

Establishing a business plan by focusing on the company's overhead

Another approach in the development of a business plan is to establish a desirable "overhead" figure and, based upon previous gross profit margins, plot the amount of annual sales needed to support this proposed overhead and return an acceptable net profit level. Several different yearly sales volume scenarios can be plotted against this overhead figure on a spreadsheet to display its impact on gross and net profit.

The contingency factor

Proper business planning in the construction industry must take into account the unanticipated variables. Public funds represent a significant portion of the construction market, and since these construction projects are generally funded on an annual basis, it is difficult to project a steady flow of funds. If the company is engaged in a substantial amount of public works projects, the vagaries of public funding must be considered. The surge in prison construction and school expansion programs which now appear to be past their zenith are two such examples.

Office building construction is subject to boom and bust cycles as witness such activities during the 1980s. Revitalization of the inner city in many parts of the country is largely responsible for the construction of 33 million square feet of office space in 1998, according to a BOMA/Cushman & Wakefield study. This is a substantial increase over the 12.9 million square feet built in 1996 and is evidence of the "swings" in commercial construction.

F.W. Dodge reported decreases in health care facilities and retail space in 1998 while projecting moderate increases in manufacturing and educational facility construction. Such ebb and flow in potential markets should be considered in forming business plan projections. Contingency plans ought to be prepared to focus on any prolonged downturn in the market—both public and private.

What Is This Thing Called Design-Build?

Design-build represents another approach to marketing a company's talents, and could become a very lucrative way to augment its mainstream business.

According to some industry sources, by the year 2005, more than 50% of all commercial construction projects will be awarded to design-build firms.

An entire chapter in this book has been devoted to the design-build process, an increasingly important project delivery system.

Developing a Value Engineering Capability— Another Sales Tool

The theory behind value engineering is to find a way to reduce the cost of construction without compromising design or quality. The value-engineering concept involves developing a systematic approach to the review of a project's design, or a construction component, or a building system to maintain the intent of the design, but at a lesser cost. Subcontractors are uniquely qualified to participate in a value engineering exercise because of their experience in assembling a project's systems and components—what works and what doesn't work.

And subcontractors may be more aware of new products, equipment, and tools since they are constantly in touch with the vendors of these products.

The subcontractor's experience in constructing similar types of projects or systems and overcoming design shortcomings that may have been encountered in the process affords them a basis upon which to comment on the potential for savings via value engineering suggestions.

Many general contractors have embraced the value engineering process as a method of negotiating a project with the client, either as a substitute for the competitive bid process or offering these services after a competitively bid process produced a project cost that exceeded the owner's budget. These general contractors tend to form close relationships with those subcontractors who have had the required experience and detailed database needed to provide value engineering assistance related to their particular trade.

The VE process is a "win-win" situation for all concerned. It allows general contractors and subcontractors to put their experience and expertise to work in order to bring a project within budget. This usually results in the general contractor being able to negotiate a contract with the owner and, in turn, negotiate agreements with those subcontractors with whom they worked during the value engineering process.

Owners and their design consultants also "win" in that the client is able to proceed with the project once their budget requirements have been met once the architect and engineer approved value engineering process has been concluded.

Pitfalls to Avoid during the VE Process

The value engineering process must be thought through completely to be effective. Savings resulting from one trade's VE suggestions may impact another trade and actually cause an increase in overall project cost rather than a cost reduction.

When general contractor and subcontractor are reviewing proposed VE suggestions, it is important to consider all aspects of the proposed changes, beyond those involving a single trade.

For example, an HVAC subcontractor may suggest replacing two roof-top air-handling units with one large one that may initially result in substantial savings relating to his or her trade. But what about the additional costs to add more structural support for the larger and heavier unit? Will there be an increase in the cost of electrical feeders or circuitry due to this change? And furthermore, instead of a smaller size duct system designed for each of the two air handlers, will a dimensionally larger system of risers be required, and, if so, will they fit into the interior wall framing system as presently designed? Only after considering all of these factors will the value engineering suggestion be considered complete.

Oftentimes these kinds of situations are not discovered until the VE suggestions have been accepted or even implemented, at which time the added costs in other trades are discovered and the owner is upset, to say the least, having agreed to a change that should have produced savings but may actually result in higher capital or operating costs.

These kinds of situations are to be avoided in order to preserve and enhance the reputation of both general contractor and subcontractor—and the way to avoid these potential problems is to carefully review the consequences of the changes under consideration before presenting them to the design team and the owner.

Remember—Value Engineering is not meant to compromise the quality of a construction project, but it is an activity designed to find alternative, more efficient methods of achieving the client's goals. When certain redesign suggestions are submitted by the contractor, they may be held legally liable for the integrity of the design, another reason to approach this process thoroughly and professionally. But once one's reputation for effective value engineering is established it can become a powerful marketing tool.

Another Marketing Tool to Be Mastered—The Oral Presentation

Many people find it difficult to prepare and carry out oral presentations, but today, the ability to effectively communicate a proposal to prospective clients is a skill that managers need to develop.

Even if the proposal is merely a review of price and scope relating to a negotiated contract, presentation is important and should convey assurance and professionalism on the part of the presenter.

A general contractor, from time to time, may request his or her major subcontractors to accompany him or her to a client presentation and be prepared to discuss his or her portion of the project and the subcontractor must be able to continue with the professional approach started by the general contractor. Having all of the facts at one's fingertips is only a part of the process.

There are a number of tips that will prove helpful when requested to make an oral presentation:

1. Select the appropriate level of company personnel to prepare and make the presentation. The presence of an owner at a presentation reinforces the company's interest in the project, and bringing along the estimator and possibly an operations person will add to the perception of depth of the subcontractor's staff.

2. The project manager and/or field supervisor that would be assigned to the project should also accompany the executives. Clients appreciate meeting the personnel that would be working on their project. These managers should be prepared to discuss their work experience in similar projects, if called upon to do so.

3. Learn as much as possible about the physical space where the presentation will take place. Will this be a small room or an auditorium? Some people, not accustomed to speaking in large rooms may be uncomfortable unless prepared to address a large audience. If audio-visual aids are going to be used during the presentation, the availability and location of electrical outlets, tables, and so forth will be important.

4. Rehearse—Don't wing it! A rehearsal prior to an oral presentation, in front of other company personnel unfamiliar with the subject matter may uncover some parts of the presentation that are unclear and need to be reworked. If several people are going to be involved in the presentation it is important to rehearse cue-ins so that the presentation flows smoothly and every participant gets a chance to rehearse his or her part, on cue.

5. Handouts are valuable if they fit the presentation. For example, an organizational chart is helpful to new clients and will explain the company's structure, personnel, and its responsibilities. If a breakdown of the estimate has been requested, this should be properly prepared in spreadsheet fashion. (And don't forget to proofread any documents to be presented to avoid being embarrassed by typos or arithmetical mistakes!)

6. Be prepared to answer questions that may not strictly apply to the main purpose of the presentation. Play the devil's advocate during rehearsal. Could the client request a list of references, previous projects, and yearly sales volume? Bring along other handouts that, if requested, can be presented at the meeting.

7. And lastly, if this is a new client try to learn as much about them as you can. What businesses are they engaged in, what products do they manufacture, or what services do they sell (if an owner)? If the client is a general contractor, what projects are they currently working on? What subcontractors have they worked with in the past? Who are the principals in the company? Does anyone have experience working with any of their personnel in the past when they were employed by another construction company?

It is important to establish a certain comfort level during the oral presentation and former associations can provide that comfort level.

Marketing is a skill that can be acquired and developed much the same as those technical skills the company possesses. Combined with a comprehensive business plan, the subcontractor will be ready to face many of the industry's challenges that lie ahead.

13

Design-Build and the Subcontractor

Design-build is neither a new concept nor a complex one. This project delivery system is similar to the concept of master builder practiced by the Egyptians 4,500 years ago during the construction of their pyramids. The master builder fixed sole responsibility for both design and construction in the hands of one qualified, experienced firm.

And so it is today as the design-build team of architect, contractor, and engineer provide the project owner with a single contract encompassing design and construction.

The future for design-build is bright indeed.

In 1986, approximately 3% of all construction project delivery systems were via design-build. By 1998, this figure had grown to 27% and, according to the Design-Build Institute of America, by the year 2005, 45% of all projects will be built utilizing the design-build concept.

Of What Interest Is the Design-Build Concept to the Subcontractor?

By its very nature, the design-build concept involves the formulation of a team composed of general contractor, subcontractors, architects, and engineers. This team offering the owner single-point responsibility for the design and construction of projects also offers the other participants to the process an opportunity to grow and prosper.

For those subcontractors familiar with the design-build project delivery system willing to devote more of their corporate energies seeking the work that these systems proffer, they will be readying their company to the challenges of the coming millennium.

Both general contractor and subcontractors need to become more familiar with design-build, not only because it represents the future, but also because it is a system that allows the contractor/subcontractor to enter a new market—one in which many such projects can be negotiated and where "low bid" is not the overriding factor. Although the competitive bid process is used extensively in public-sector work, many private-sector projects are negotiated. But no matter which system is employed, subcontractors who are professional in their approach, knowledgeable in their trade, in possession of a comprehensive database of costs, and steeped in the value-engineering process will find a receptive audience for their wares.

The Design-Build Team

The team of architect, engineer, and contractor form the basis of the design-build approach, with one of these members assuming the lead role.

Generally, the general contractor will assume the lead role and the architect and engineer will enter into a contract with the general contractor—not as a subcontractor but as a team member.

The design-build team will take on the responsibility to extract the project program from the owner, establish an estimate for the project, and upon the award of a design-build contract proceed to prepare the architectural and engineering drawings to encompass this program and then proceed to construction.

The Advantages of Design-Build

Combining design and construction in one contract relieves the owner of having to deal with two distinct entities—architect and designer—and shifts responsibility for both endeavors to one single source thereby relieving the owner of considerable management and coordination responsibility.

By combining design and construction, the adversarial relationships that often exist between architect and contractor are lessened substantially and usually disappear entirely.

Experience has shown that the number and type of change orders are substantially reduced as well as disputes and claims that often arise during the design-bid-build process.

And the design-build process results in both time and cost savings.

In a study sponsored by the Construction Industry Institute (CII), three project delivery systems were scrutinized—design-bid-build, construction manager at risk, and design-build. Researchers at Pennsylvania State University's College of Engineering looked at 351 projects in 37 states ranging in size from 5,000 square feet to 2.5 million square feet, and came to the following conclusions:

- Design-build project unit costs were 4.5% less than CM-at-risk projects and 6% less than design-bid-build projects.

- Design-build projects, measured in number of square feet constructed per month was 7% faster than CM-at risk and 12% faster than design-bid-build projects.

- Factoring speed of design into the equation, the design-build method was 23% faster than a design-CM at-risk system and 33% faster than the conventional design-bid-build process.

Similar studies conducted in England by the University of Reading Design-Build Forum revealed that the DB delivery system produced a 12% improvement in speed of construction and a 30% increase in overall project delivery. These British researchers also found that design-build resulted in a 13% reduction in unit cost and projects were more likely to be completed within a range of 5% of their original budget.

In terms of quality, the CII survey showed that design-build also came out ahead. On a scale of 1 to 10 with the low end representing significant difficulty in facility start-up and frequent callbacks, both DB and CM at Risk scored 7.5 while design-bid-build scored 6.

So we can see by these studies that design-build produces projects more rapidly, at lower cost, and higher quality.

However, there are certainly downsides to the design-build process:

- Responsibility from the owner and general contractor's perspective is too diffuse. The cultural differences between architect and contractor must be overcome since each may have a different agenda.

- The owner is placed in the position of a traffic cop, whereas in the conventional design-bid-build process, the architect acts as the owner's agent and controls the contractor actions to a degree.

- The cost savings generally touted as an advantage of the process is not always there.

- To some owners, general contractors, and architects, design-build is a venture into uncharted waters with all of the dangers that such ventures present.

- The checks and balances present during the conventional design-bid-build process are not present in the design-build process.

- Both surety and insurance concerns assume much larger roles in the design-build process because their experience to date has been somewhat limited.

Risk Allocation Using the Design-Build Process

Coupled with the responsibility to provide both design and construction services the design-build team will assume risks that are different from those associated with the more conventional design-bid-build process.

Because the roles of each player in the process change, risk allocation can become vague. The traditional role of the contractor who heretofore assumed no liability for design errors must somehow now assume that liability while not relieving their architect Team member of that responsibility. The same thing can be said for the bond process where the contractor would be requested to provide either a payment or performance bond, or both. The bonding company may now be requested to provide a bid bond or a payment and performance bond for a project that is not fully designed and may price the cost of these bonds accordingly. The entire process of risk allocation and responsibility changes dramatically when design-build is employed.

Risk Category	Traditional Design-Bid-Build	Design-Build
Geotechnical data	Owner	Design-Builder
Design criteria	Owner	Design-Builder
Design defects	Owner	Design-Builder
Constructability	Owner	Design-Builder
Coordination with utility companies	Owner	Design-Builder

Subcontractor Risks

The subcontractor may also be required to assume risks for which they may not have considered. If, for example, the mechanical-electrical-plumbing subcontractors (MEP) had been involved in their respective systems design and budgeting and if these systems, in final design, exceed the budget, the participating subcontractor may be required to deliver the system as designed but not to exceed their initial budget.

A subcontractor must be given the opportunity to monitor the designs for which they are to be held responsible if they have committed to a budget estimate. If denied this opportunity they may be assessed for any cost overruns.

The Design-Build Process — Building the Team

When a contractor and an architecture/engineering firm agree to submit a design-build proposal they will have to form a design-build entity. The general contractor may elect to issue a contract to the architect/engineer for design, and, theoretically this design team becomes a subcontractor. The general contractor may decide to form a joint venture where each participant becomes a partner, or a limited liability company (LLC) can be formed which limits the liability of each participant because it creates a "shell" corporation whose only assets may consist of the progress payments received from the owner. Incidentally many owners will *not* contract with an LLC recognizing that it has no assets and could default on the contract with little or no penalties.

The organizational structure of the design-build team will be of interest to any subcontractor joining the team. Absent the existence of a payment and performance bond, dealing with an LLC can be a sobering experience if they default on their contractual obligations.

The Teaming Agreement

During the proposal stage the preparation of a Teaming Agreement is important in order to memorialize the rights and responsibilities of each participant during this phase. If the proposal is accepted by the owner and a contract is awarded, the design-build team will use the Teaming Agreement as a guide in the preparation of a contract between each member of the team.

A typical Teaming Agreement will contain the following elements that form the basis of the team relationship and responsibilities:

Organizational Structure

1. A joint venture *or*
2. A Limited Liability Company *or*
3. A Prime-Subcontractor agreement where the general contractor is the prime and the subcontractor is the design team, or vice versa if the case may be.

Division of Responsibility Among Team Members

1. During the proposal stage
2. During the contract stage

Proposal Preparation Phase

1. Which party will prepare the technical and design work necessary to comply with the Request for Proposal?

2. What functions will the architect perform? Will an engineer's services be required at this stage? What about the need for geotechnical services?

3. How will the costs for the proposal preparation be shared?

4. When and if confidential information must be shared by the team members, how will this confidential and proprietary information be protected?

5. Exclusivity and Noncompeting clauses need to be addressed so that one party or the other cannot withdraw from the process and team up with another competing design-builder.

6. Establishment of penalties if one party or another withdraws from the proposal process and the remaining members have to seek other participants or abandon their submission.

Post Award Stage

1. Agreement on a contract format for the design-build team, i.e., lump sum, GMP, Cost Plus?

2. Agreement on the scope of participation and who will perform those services.

3. Establishment of construction and design fees.

4. Establishment of contingency for both the design and construction phase of the project.

5. Procedures for coordination of the design with the construction budget and how adjustments will be made to comply with the budget without sacrificing the integrity of the design.

6. Participation in savings in both design/construction stages, if such a clause is being considered.

7. Indemnity, bonding, and insurance considerations and responsibilities and how they are to be relegated.

8. Warranty, errors and omissions, and faulty construction issues; how responsibility is to be affixed and who pays for correction.

9. A Standard of Care provision which deals with intent; a sample of such a provision is set forth below:

DESIGN/BUILDER shall perform design professional services and related services in all phases of the project. The standard of care for all such services

*performed or furnished under this Agreement will be the care and skill ordi-
narily used by members of the engineering/architecture profession practicing under similar conditions at the same time and locality.*

Termination of the Teaming Agreement

1. By mutual agreement
2. When one or more parties is in default

Some Contract Provisions Unique to Design-Build

The Design-Builder's contract with the owner will contain some clauses
unique to the process and if the contractor/subcontractor agreement
allows the subcontractor to obtain a copy of that agreement, it is a document that should be read and understood.

Some of the provisions to look for:

The *Intent* Clause

The Intent of the contract documents is to include all of the work required
to complete the project except as specifically *excluded*. It is acknowledged
that as of the date of the contract the plans and specifications are not complete, but define the scope and nature of the work and are sufficient to
establish the contract sum. No adjustment shall be made in the contract
sum if, as a prudent contractor, contractor should have been aware of or
anticipated such additional work as may be required to produce a first
class (office or whatever) building.

The *Increased Scope/Delay* Clause

If causes beyond the contractor's control delay the progress of the work,
then the GMP (or Lump Sum) for design/construction services, the contractor's fee and/or the date of substantial completion shall be modified by
change order as appropriate. Such causes shall include but not be limited
to: changes ordered in the work, acts or omissions of the owner or separate contractors employed by the owner, the owner preventing the contractor from performing the work pending dispute resolution, hazardous
materials, differing site conditions, adverse weather conditions not reasonably anticipated, fire, unusual transportation delays, labor disputes,
or unavoidable accidents or circumstances.

The *Hazardous Materials* Clause

To the fullest extent permitted by law, the owner shall defend, indemnify, and hold harmless the contractor/architect/engineer, subcontractors

and the agents, officers, directors and employees of each of them from and against any and all claims, damages, losses costs and expenses, whether direct, indirect or consequential including, but not limited to attorney's fees, costs and expenses incurred in connection with litigation or arbitration, arising out of or relating to the performance of work in any area affect by hazardous materials. To the fullest extent permitted by the law such indemnification shall apply regardless of the fault, negligence, breach of warranty or contract or strict liability of the indemnitee.

The *Deviation from Owner's Program* Clause

Design-builder's proposal shall specifically identify any deviations from the owner's program, which indemnification shall be set forth on a separate exhibit in the proposal identified as "Deviation List." In case of any inconsistency, conflict or ambiguity between the Owner's program and the design-builder's proposal, the inconsistency, conflict or ambiguity shall be resolved in accordance with the following order of precedence:

Deviation List

Owner's program

Design-builders proposal (excluding the Deviation List)

The Design-Builder's *Contingency* Clause

The GMP (or Lump sum) includes a contingency in the amount of $ _____, which is available for the design-builder's exclusive use for costs that are incurred in performing the work that is not included in a specific line item or the basis for a change order under the Agreement. By way of example, and not as a limitation, such costs include trade buy-outs (in the case of a GMP contract *writer's comment*), overtime, acceleration, costs in correcting defective work, damaged or non-conforming work, non-negligent design errors or omissions and subcontractor defaults. The contingency is not available to the owner for any reason, including changes in scope or any other item which would enable the contractor to increase the GMP (or Lump Sum) under the agreement. Design-builder shall notify owner of all anticipated charges against the contingency.

The Role of the Subcontractor in the Design-Build Process

A design-build team will often assemble a select group of subcontractors and suppliers during the proposal stage and the actual design stage.

Most contractors, architects and engineers recognize the value that experienced, quality subcontractors can bring to the table during the many stages of a project's development. The subcontractor's intimate knowledge of cost, constructability, what works and what doesn't work is invaluable to both builder and designer whether developing conceptual estimates, discussing design considerations, proposing value engineering options or establishing schedules.

The drywall contractor may be called upon to comment on the difference in cost between an 18 gauge and a 20 gauge curtain wall system and the span that will accommodate 25 gauge studs for interior work instead of 20 gauge metal studs.

The mechanical subcontractor may be requested to provide costs associated with one HVAC system over another. How much will a DX system cost per square foot of building as opposed to air-to-air heat pumps? What about the use of fan coil units? What will long-term maintenance costs be for alternate systems and what could the owner anticipate in the way of yearly utility costs?

The concrete subcontractor may be invited to join a discussion about structural design and asked to provide costs per square foot of building for various types of cast-in-place concrete systems. If the construction of the structure will take place during cold weather, what additional costs should be added for winter protection?

At the outset of these meetings, the design-builder will generally state his or her intention with respect to subcontractor participation in the project.

They may simply state, "Work with us during this design development/ budgeting stage. If we get the job, so do you."

Or they may express their desire to competitively bid each portion of work but will treat all subcontractors participating in the design development process in some preferential way.

It is important to determine the design-builder's inclination in this respect, but even if all work will be competitively bid, the design-build team cannot avoid looking favorably upon those participating subcontractors.

Changing the "Contractor" Mind-Set

Involvement in design-build requires a much different perspective than that of the design bid-build process.

The individual shield that a general contractor/architect, engineer or subcontractor raises during the design-bid-build process to ward off responsibility for design errors and omissions, dimensional or coordination problems must be lowered when joining a DB Team.

It is the responsibility of the Team to prepare a complete set of design documents to fulfill the owner's project needs.

The process of give-and-take is an integral part of the design-build development review process which will be ongoing until 100% complete documents are issued.

Hopefully the interaction between general contractor, architect, engineer, and subcontractor will be such that a "more than one project relationship" will be established. There should be more willingness to "give" because it may be possible to "take" on the next negotiated project.

If the Team fails in its efforts to completely understand the owner's program, fails to ask the right questions, and upon being awarded a contract, does not produce the design to meet the owner's needs, they may be bound by the "intent" of the design-build agreement and be required to provide such additional scope as may be necessary to fulfill the owner's needs with no increase in the contract sum.

In fact the design-build contract with the owner will probably contain a clause similar to the one below:

> "The intent of the contract documents is to include all of the work required to complete the project, except as specifically excluded. It is acknowledged that as of the date of the contract the plans and specifications are not complete, but they define the scope and nature of the work and are sufficient to establish the contract sum. No adjustment shall be made in the contract sum if, as a prudent contractor, contractor should not have been aware of or anticipated work as may be required to produce a first class (office or whatever the project is) building."

If the Team concludes a successful project from a profitability, marketing, and working relationship standpoint, the current project will most likely be parlayed into future projects utilizing the same "team members."

Those subcontractors who can provide these services will be sought out by design-build firms, and if they prove themselves, will be afforded opportunities to establish long-term relationships.

The DB team is charged with the responsibility of extracting the owner's program and creating a set of plans and specifications that incorporate that program.

Pitfalls to Avoid During the Design Development (DD) Stage

When a subcontractor is brought on board the design-build team, he or she is expected to bring with him or her experience in a number of areas: cost, constructability, scheduling requirements, and to some degree design mainly as a function of cost or value engineering.

During the design development stage the architect and engineers will prepare interim design drawings for review by the owner and the contractor; the owner in order to insure that the design is developing according to his or her needs; the contractor to insure that the design is developing within the parameters of the estimate. The design team will also prepare a set of outline specifications, possibly including specific equipment and materials based upon the subcontractor's input into their respective components of construction.

At each stage of the design's development, the contractor must review the drawings to insure development-estimate compliance after which the drawings will be presented to the owner. The contractor should review each drawing with the owner explaining each one in detail and projecting what the next phase of design development drawings will reveal.

All participating subcontractors should be part of the contractor's review before presentation to the owner. These subcontractors must perform the same ritual—are the drawings being developing as they anticipated, does it appear that the design will meet the budget? These review meetings should be memorialized by the preparation of detailed meeting minutes, prepared not only by the contractor-design, but also independently by each attending subcontractor. Exceptions taken to the design development (DD) drawings must be noted so that if future drawings fail to incorporate these comments, a record of having voiced concerns or even objections will be documented.

If the outline specifications are being fleshed out during the design development stage, each participating subcontractor must review them thoroughly and issue his or her comments to the design-builder.

This review process should continue until the proposal stage is complete and a final presentation to the owner has been made incorporating the exact drawing dates of the proposal plans and the sections and preparation date of the outline specifications. These two documents will be incorporated in any forthcoming contract and along with the "Intent" paragraph mentioned above and will define the working relationship, duties, rights, and obligations of the design-build team.

"Intent" versus Owner Changes During Construction

The plan and specification review process, in the words of Yogi Berra, "ain't over until its over."

During construction it is not unusual for an owner to request changes to the plans and/or specifications. The design-build team must determine whether these changes fall within the context of fulfilling the owner's *intent* or whether these changes truly represent increases in scope of work. There is often a very fine line between these two situations. At the point in time when such owner requests occur, all concerned subcontractors should meet with the design-build team to determine whether "they should have known" to incorporate this work whereby all such changes must be made to comply with the *intent* of the owner's requirements at no cost to that owner. Conversely, if it is apparent that the requested changes clearly exceed the *intent* and *scope* of the design-build agreement then two approaches can be pursued; the design-build team can prepare a Proposed Change Order for submission to the owner, or can proffer changes to the contract documents which would offset the additional costs of the owner's requested change at no appreciable decrease in the quality of the project.

If any changes are not handled in this manner, as soon as they occur, the design-build team will find themselves in a quagmire when the actual construction work starts. The writer experienced one such situation that illustrates the point. While having been involved in design-build projects with another firm for about two years, he often discussed developing design-build capability with his current employer. And he convinced them to propose this project delivery system to a long-term client who had a history of making numerous changes to construction in mid-stream. The client was a medical instrument manufacturer on the cutting edge of technology and their space needs changed rapidly as their product line changed and as manufacturing priorities changed to meet sales demands.

The writer cautioned the project management-design team time and time again about the need to document all changes after the initial plans and specifications were approved by the owner and a contract was awarded.

The project involved demolition of the interior portion of two floors of an existing office building, creating an enlarged marketing department, new product display areas, and several conference rooms where doctors could inspect these new products and view medical instrument demonstrations performed on mannequins.

After demolition, steel partition work was to proceed rapidly followed by electrical, mechanical, acoustical ceilings, fire protection, drywall and all finishing trades.

After demolition had been partially completed, the drywall subcontractor began to lay out their partitions and the owner's representative confirmed the layout. However once actual metal partition work began, the newly appointed manager of the marketing department decided that several offices, including his own were much too small and had to be enlarged. These changes had no appreciable cost impact and were made and the drawings changed to reflect not only the partition change but the MEP and sprinkler changes as well. All previous drawings were discarded, only one set was retained in the field (and the architect, using computer assisted design (CAD) electronically erased the original design and continued to do so as additional changes were made).

Further changes were made by several mid-level managers and the design-build team succumbing to pressure to "push the job faster," incorporated the changes not really pausing to determine whether they were within the intent category or exceeded this standard.

As work proceeded further, the Chairman of the Board walked through the area and declared that this design was totally inadequate and directed the contractor to demolish major portions of the work already in place and completely change the design of the balance of the floor. Who is going to argue with the Chairman?

But, the design-build team, forgetting one of the basic principles of this or any other project, failed to stop, re-design, assemble costs to re-work, and incorporate the cost of all other scope changes.

Time was of the essence and that was one of the reasons why the owner had agreed to a design-build delivery system in the first place.

The project was finally completed at a cost of $3.5 million, but the *contract sum was* only $1.750 million. The one set of original design drawings left at the job site were so worn and ragged that they were worthless in determining initial "contract" scope.

Retracing design changes, arguing about which changes were in the *Intent* category and which ones were true scope increases took approximately nine months. By that time both subcontractors, contractor ,and designers were willing to discount costs in order to resolve these issues which were tying up valuable human resources due to the owner's request to review each and every item in minute detail at weekly meetings lasting six hours or more. (Perhaps this was the owner's wear-'em-down strategy.)

The lessons to be learned apply to design-bid-build as well as design-build except the *intent* factor takes on more importance in design-build. All parties in a design-build mode must fully understand the difference between *intent* and *scope* changes, which, in some cases, is not a simple matter, but dealing with reasonable people should make the process a little easier.

Another lesson to be learned is when embarking on a new method of doing business, learn as much as you can about the process. Talk to an experienced practitioner and heed his or her advice. Thirdly, **never** destroy previous issues of drawings even after the project has been completed because one ever knows when they will be called upon to retrace the sequence of construction and the changes in scope.

Design-build may well be a twentieth century fad that falls short of its twenty-first century hype. But any project delivery system that controls costs, raises quality levels, reduces claims and disputes, and shortens completion time should have a bright future.

14

Developing an Effective Management Team

The construction industry has been criticized over the years for its slow acceptance of modern management methods, but a closer look at the makeup of the industry offers some insight into this problem.

Of the more than 5.7 million general contractor, heavy construction, and specialty contracting businesses in the United States, as of 1992 Department of Commerce census, most are small firms. Witness the 4.6 million total employment for these 5.7 million firms, which averages just 1.2 employees per company.

The majority of these companies are closely held or family businesses too often focused on day-to-day operations rather than planning for the future.

As construction projects become more complex, they take longer to complete, and the slow decline in productivity in the industry and the scarcity of highly trained workers has also had an impact on completion time.

With the increase in competition, construction companies must begin to realize that the need to develop and embrace effective management systems becomes more critical, not just to maintain or increase net profit percentages, but to survive!

The Owner versus the Manager

In the small to midsized construction firm, the owner will, more than likely, also assume the role of the manager—but these functions are distinct and separate and the transition from entrepreneur to executive is often difficult to achieve.

The owner's primary role in a contracting company is to assume responsibility for establishing the goals and objectives of the company and create the business philosophy by which the firm will operate. In addition, an effective management team must be created to implement these goals and objectives and ensure that the company philosophy as established by the owner is carried out.

With this team in place, owners will then be free to concentrate on what they do best—foster the entrepreneurial spirit in the company they created, establish procedures for accountability, and monitor the effectiveness of the management group.

Too often, owners of these closely held or family contracting businesses firmly believe that since they created the firm, only they are capable of operating it on a day-to-day basis. While they are capable of doing so, will this ensure long-term stability and growth?

Owners tend to believe that as long as everyone is working hard and working long hours, everything will be O.K. And they also hold to the opinion that it is nobody's business but their own how they run their company, without giving proper recognition to their key personnel who allow them to remain in business.

This attitude may prevail for the near term, but if there are any thoughts of perpetuating the business, ensuring growth, maintaining profitability, and properly rewarding those individuals in the company that helped to make it the success it is, modern management techniques must be employed.

The owner's primary function in the small to midsized firm should be to:

- Build a strong management team
- Establish the moral and ethical philosophy of the company (and practice what one preaches!)
- Develop short- and long-term business goals and objectives—the business plan
- Periodically review, update, or revise these business plans
- Create a system of accountability and monitor the system on a regular and consistent basis
- Objectively review the performance of the company's employees and reward them accordingly

The Board of Directors

Most closely held or family businesses, particularly if they are organized as corporations, will have a Board of Directors, generally a rubber stamp affair composed of Uncle Louie, Aunt Fannie (who also helps out the bookkeeper on a part-time basis), and possibly some other family members who will always vote the way they have been instructed.

But more and more small businesses are discovering that a "real" board of directors composed of a banker, a marketing or public relations executive, a representative from the manufacturing sector, possibly a lawyer or accountant has real value. The purpose of a Board of Directors is not to run a business, but to bring together a team of experienced business professionals who can objectively review and comment on current and future business practices and plans. Creating an "outside" Board of Directors should be at the top of the list of an enlightened owner's management agenda.

Once a decision is made to create an outside board of directors, it may not be too difficult to find and recruit a competent group of responsible individuals. Prospective candidates can be sought from business acquaintances, friends, and professionals with whom the company currently does business—its lawyer, its accountant. The usual composition of a Board of Directors for small firms will include five board members, or slightly more if so desired, always maintaining an odd number so that a majority vote can be achieved when necessary.

Board meetings are generally held three or four times a year; however emergency sessions may be called when the need arises. Compensation for board members is often based upon the size of the company and the number of meetings they are requested to attend.

Some management consultants suggest compensating each board member $300 to $500 per meeting, if the company sales volume is less than $10 million and for companies with greater annual sales, compensation can be increased accordingly.

Tips to More Effective Managing

To those who say that managers are born, not made, professionals in the field would reply that while some managers do have an intuitive management aptitude or talent, others can easily learn to be effective leaders. Seminars, lectures, trade association courses, books, and videotapes on management techniques abound, and anyone with a desire to learn or increase their knowledge of the subject can avail themselves of these resources.

Here are a few tips culled from the experts:

1. Get to know the interests, strengths, and shortcomings of your people. People perform best when they are doing something that interests and challenges them. When assigning projects, try to match the person with the project instead of randomly assigning work with no such thought in mind.

2. Give your people a sense of independence while not compromising accountability. Let them use their initiative; let them know that their new ideas will be accepted, reviewed, and commented upon. Give them some space in which to operate.

3. View promotions and salary increases on the basis of accomplishment and worth to the company. Don't merely use seniority as the basis for promotions.

4. Let your people know that you accept mistakes as part of a learning process, as long as the individual involved does not continue to make the same mistake. Too often a mistake is met with comments from the manager that either instills a fear of loss of job security or demeans one's self-respect. Such a message may lead to having mistakes covered up, and when disclosure comes, as it always does, it comes at a higher price—to all parties.

5. Let people know that it is safe to disagree with you as long as there are well-thought-out reasons for doing so. Dissent is healthy as long as it is productive and not contrite dissent. Although it may be ego building to surround oneself with "yes" people, they have been the downfall of scores and scores of companies.

6. Learn how to listen and make eye contact. Let the party who is speaking finish before commenting; interrupting may be perceived as rudeness, and it can also disrupt the other person's train of thought.

7. Avoid personality conflicts. Keep work-related encounters just that. When arguments do occur, particularly when it is with someone who is not your favorite person, criticism should be task-related, not personality or ego related.

8. When explaining an existing or new policy or work rule, present background or rationale for the policy or rule, which will make it easier to accept. Explain why exceptions to that rule or policy cannot be easily accommodated.

9. Praise in public; correct in private.

10. Establish an atmosphere that says you are interested in solutions to problems, not merely interested in assigning blame.

11. In order to create an atmosphere of integrity, mutual respect, and encouragement of self-esteem, managers must practice what they preach.

Achieving Increased Productivity—One of the Keys to Profitability

The 1990s will probably be best characterized as an era of increased industrial productivity accomplished in part by corporate downsizing, mergers, and acquisitions. The United States emerged as the world leader in manufacturing productivity. Increased productivity is the goal of every manager and there are some steps that can easily be initiated to improve that bottom line.

Productivity in the construction industry has a dual focus: productive managers and office support staff and productive field supervisors and workers.

Renewed interest in focusing on productivity has led many managers to take a hard look at their current operations to determine what works and what needs fixing.

Some thoughts to consider:

- Review employee training procedures to evaluate their adequacy. Are there new safety and environmental rules and regulations requiring additional instructional sessions? Do weekly manager/supervisor meetings include training aids, and if not, can they be changed to incorporate more training sessions?

- If not already in place, create an accountability system whereby employees can be held accountable for their performance and measured against those standards. This can be accomplished with office staff by instituting annual or semiannual performance reviews in which goals and achievements are openly discussed and agreed upon. Accountability in field operations can be achieved and monitored periodically by reviewing daily/weekly productivity reports.

- Develop the Teamwork approach to problem solving and achieving defined goals. Although many companies give lip service to the teamwork concept, an effective manager must wholeheartedly commit to the concept and actively promote it. Encourage suggestions from those persons with hands-on experience in their field when addressing issues in their department.

- Periodically review goals as they relate to productivity, safety, and quality to determine if these goals have been met or were unrealistic to begin with and need to be revised.

- Instill the idea that everyone in the company is a salesman for the company and should be client-oriented.

- Emphasize QUALITY in all areas of operations. Strive to be the best. Everyone is proud to be part of a team that is known for producing a quality product.

- Safety programs effectively administered not only make good business sense from a bottom-line perspective, but let employees know that their managers are concerned for their personal well-being.

Accountability

Establishing a yardstick by which performance can be measured will be welcomed by manager and worker alike and it becomes an indispensable tool to the owner.

Yardsticks can be developed to measure both field and office productivity levels, the former being reasonably objective in nature, while the latter may be more subjective.

If performance accountability measures are just beginning to be introduced in the company, one large meeting followed by several smaller ones are needed to fully acquaint everyone with the program. As questions arise during its implementation, everyone should be sent intercompany memos stating the question asked and the response given. It is possible that many employees may have had the same question but were too timid to request clarification.

The job description—accountability for the office-based employee

There are two ways for employees to view their job descriptions—either from the narrow perspective of "If it doesn't include a specific task, I am not obliged to do it," or the more broad approach, "The job description is meant to be a guideline and, within reason, does not restrict my work activities to only those items included in that description." The job description may be viewed as the "intent" and specifics, to be worked out between manager and worker, may result in a slightly amended job or expanded description.

Job descriptions written by the employee can be somewhat enlightening to the manager in that it may contain tasks that the employee had been performing that they should not have been doing and, conversely, not performing tasks that they were obligated to do.

An employee's job description written by the department head coordinated with the one written by the employee will produce the best results.

One's reporting authority is an important aspect of any job description. Everyone should be familiar with the organizational chain of command and who reports to whom so that job-related questions, requests for vacation time, medical leave, late for work calls, and sick time can be relayed to and authorized by the appropriate manager.

Empowering the manager to document and evaluate performance

Many companies have annual or semiannual performance reviews at which time they conduct interviews with the employees in their department in an atmosphere of an open dialogue. The manager may refer to a written form on which certain topics are listed so that employee performance can be rated on a numeric scale where "1" may be the low end of the scale and "5," the high end. A sample Performance Evaluation form is shown in Figure 14-1. Modifications to this basic form can be made to customize it to fit an individual manager's requirements.

During the review process, an open conversation must ensue so that the manager can relate his or her view of the employee's performance during the preceding period. This is generally followed by the employee's response to the ratings assigned by his or her manager or supervisor. Constructive dialog is the key to a successful performance interview and the manager should discuss the employee's weak points, offering suggestions for improvement while also pointing out the employee's strong points and value to the company.

This is the time when the employees should comment on their goals and aspirations, both short-term and long-term.

At the end of the interview, both manager and employee should reach agreement on what past performance levels were attained and which ones need more improvement prior to the next review period. New goals can be established at this time if mutually agreed upon.

The manager or supervisor must strive for objective and truthful performance ratings that will form the basis for future promotions and salary increases and which will also serve to document poor performance.

Each reviewing manager or supervisor must overcome the tendency to convey to each employee the impression that he or she has done a good job, when, in truth, some were performing well below acceptable standards. Realistic evaluations, while difficult to verbalize at times, are critical to both the interviewer and interviewee's professional growth.

In this day and age, reviews must also be made with an eye to potential lawsuits. If a continually poor performing employee is dismissed, but past performance reviews reflect adequate performance, the discharged employee's lawyer may be knocking on the door shortly after that pink slip has been signed.

Daily production control—accountability for field personnel

Tracking, recording and tabulating work-in-place costs is a critical part of any construction company. Cost-reporting serves many functions:

Employee name:_____   Date:_____

Performance Appraisal System
Mid-Year Employee Performance Review

I. JOB PERFORMANCE FACTORS

Review the performance factors and definitions. Using the rating scale, the supervisor should circle the performance level that is appropriate for each factor.

1 = Unsatisfactory   2 = Needs Improvement   3 = Competent   4 = Exceeds Standards   5 = Outstanding

Performance Factors	Performance Rating
Quality of Work: Work is done accurately, thoroughly, and completely. The work is done according to the job goals. The work results are dependable, even when there is a heavy work load or unusual job pressures.	1 2 3 4 5
Quantity of Work: Under normal conditions, a reasonably amount of acceptable work is done each day.	1 2 3 4 5
Knowledge of Job: Understands the job and the assigned tasks. This understanding was gained through work experience, education and/or special training.	1 2 3 4 5
Planning and Organizing: Avoids crisis situations by planning and preparing in advance. Follows plans through to completion. Handles work assignments in an orderly way.	1 2 3 4 5
Performance in Emergencies: Recognizes when a problem is critical and needs immediate attention. Able to use judgment and decide on a reasonable action for solving the problem.	1 2 3 4 5
Accepts Direction: Follows instructions. Accepts supervision, suggestions and guidance with a positive attitude.	1 2 3 4 5
Initiative: Able to carry on with duties without being told to do so. Suggests new ideas on ways for doing the job better. Shows willingness to work.	1 2 3 4 5
Dependability: Can be counted on to perform the job without constant supervision. Comes to work regularly and on time. Shows reasonable judgment. Stays in work area.	1 2 3 4 5

Figure 14-1a

- Creates a database for estimating future projects
- Provides cost updates to cross-check or correct the current database
- Measures worker productivity in the field
- Establishes a performance curve for individual field supervisory personnel
- Provides basis for development of conceptual estimating capability

Database for Estimating Future Projects

This is a fundamental use for field-generated cost and productivity data. By breaking down a work task into its component parts, and creating a cost-code system to assign codes to each of these tasks, the field supervisor will track each individual work task, also reporting the quantity

Interaction with Others: Communicates with coworkers and the public in a positive way. Is considerate and courteous to others. Avoids lengthy personal conversations during work hours.	1 2 3 4 5
Flexibility: Able to accept in a positive way changes in work assignments or conditions of work.	1 2 3 4 5

II. OVERALL PERFORMANCE RATING

C.   Carefully review the criteria for each of the performance levels identified below and circle the rating number which best describes the employee's overall performance for the evaluation period.

1 = Unsatisfactory 2 = Needs Improvement 3 = Competent 4 = Exceeds Standards 5 = Outstanding	1 2 3 4 5

<u>Unsatisfactory:</u> Performance is unacceptable and requires improvement in order to retain the position.
<u>Needs Improvement:</u> Performance is not consistent and falls short of the expected on most factors.
<u>Competent:</u> Performance generally meets supervisor's expectations on most performance criteria.
<u>Exceeds Expectations:</u> Performance exceeds the supervisor's expectation on nearly all performance factors.
<u>Outstanding:</u> Exemplary overall performance deserving special recognition.

Comments:_____

_____

_____

_____

_____

III. APPROVALS

TO BE COMPLETED BY EMPLOYEE'S SUPERVISOR
I have discussed the contents of this appraisal with the Employee during a scheduled appraisal on this date.

_____   _____
Supervisor's Signature   Date

TO BE COMPLETED BY EMPLOYEE
I understand that my signature below only indicates that I have read and discussed the contents of this appraisal with my Supervisor; it does not necessarily imply agreement with the appraisal.

_____   _____
Employee's Signature   Date

Figure 14-1b

GOALS FOR NEXT PERFORMANCE PERIOD

Employee _____   Period covered _____

Department _____   Reviewing Supervisor _____

Listed below are goals created jointly and mutually agreed upon by the Employee and by the Supervisor for achievement by the target dates indicated. They will be considered in completing Section "A" of the Employee's next Performance Appraisal.

GOALS	ACTION STEPS TOWARD REACHING GOALS	WHEN WILL PERFORMANCE BE SATISFACTORY? (DATE)	WERE GOALS SATISFACTORILY MET? (YES/NO) EXPLAIN

Employee's signature _____   Supervisor's signature: _____

Figure 14-1c

installed during a normal work period. As the accounting department prepares payroll from the task code and quantity information on the daily time sheets, a cost per unit of work is quickly established.

Different projects have differing degrees of difficulty and repetition. For example, an eight-foot-high steel stud partition installed in an uninterrupted fifty-foot (50') line in a new building project should generate lower unit costs than another fifty-foot (50') framed wall installed in a renovation project, where this wall must be interrupted every ten feet (10') to accommodate existing steel columns.

To include both of these framing costs into one work task database may be misleading, so some method should be developed to segregate work tasks that are similar in nature, but installed under differing conditions.

Not only will these segregated costs present a more accurate base for estimating purposes but will also provide a clearer picture of worker performance.

Cost Updates

As new crews are formed or modified, as new tools or procedures are introduced to the field to increase productivity, the current database needs to be updated to account for any significant changes due to one or more of these factors.

Not only will the estimating department have an interest in database updates, but managers will be able to obtain tangible proof of productivity increases that may have been caused by technological improvements or improvement in worker productivity created by increased worker motivation or changes in management procedures.

Measuring Productivity

Increases in productivity resulting in a decrease in unit costs should be investigated by the project manager. It is just as important to understand why unit work task costs have been decreasing as it is to be concerned about increases. Any number of reasons may be attributable for a decline or increase in unit prices. The manager's task is to uncover the reasons and then react accordingly.

Performance curves

Why are some field supervisors able to attain higher rates of productivity than their peers? By comparing one supervisor's performance accomplishments with another, a measure of managerial ability will emerge. A field supervisor achieving consistently high ratings may be raw material for the project manager's spot that may be opening in a month or so. Promoting from the ranks has obvious advantages. It creates incentives for workers who can see that additional responsibilities and increased pay await those who perform. Promoting from the ranks also improves company morale when workers can see that good performance is recognized by management and rewarded.

Conceptual estimating

A comprehensive database is a useful tool in the creation of a conceptual estimating capacity. The ability to translate unit costs into systems costs or component costs can become a powerful marketing tool for management.

How often do clients—owners or general contractors—place a call to your office requesting "ballpark" figures for some system, or some square foot area, when they are assembling a preliminary budget for a project? The specialty contractor that can respond accurately and quickly may well be invited to join the "team" if the project is being negotiated with the owner. The ability to estimate conceptually, that is, from sketchy, incomplete drawings or even a verbal description of the project makes that specialty contractor a valued participant when design-build projects are under consideration.

Meetings! Meetings! and More Meetings!

Your voice mail builds up—10, 15, 20 messages. Stacks of mail are on the desk. Shop drawings remain in limbo and where have you been for the past two days? In meetings!

According to a source reported in the December 8, 1997, issue of *USA TODAY*, the average number of meetings jumped from seven per week to ten per week between 1981 and 1995. Too many meetings accomplish nothing but waste a manager's valuable time. Workers asked to rank emotionally-charged situations on the job indicate meetings as a top problem, the *USA TODAY* survey reports.

One reason for the increase in meetings is the increase in the team approach, requiring periodic meetings to maintain communication between team members.

Meetings can be more productive if the right approach is taken: when scheduling meetings, it is important to keep the agenda moving along and end them as quickly as possible.

- First of all don't call that meeting unless there is a real need to conduct one. Without an agenda or a purpose or a goal, no meeting should be scheduled.

- Prepare for the meeting—set the agenda and do it in writing.

- Distribute the agenda to all attendees ahead of time.

- Give participants as much advance notice as possible. Hopefully, all participants will be able to determine what is to be expected of them and come prepared. If this doesn't happen, let them know in no uncertain terms that they will be prepared for the next meeting.

- Limit attendance to those with a need to know and either conduct the meeting yourself or appoint another leader when the agenda is distributed.

- Keep a clock in the room and announce a time limitation to the meeting. And keep it!

- Encourage everyone to participate while keeping strictly to the agenda. Worthwhile topics not on the agenda but advanced by a participant should not be dismissed but met with, "That's a good point, but let's you and I meet (after the meeting)(next week, etc.) to discuss that issue separately." To do otherwise will stifle other ideas.

- Encourage vigorous debate and if any member appears to be shy or otherwise reluctant to talk, try to bring them into the conversation.

- Visual aids are very effective for certain kinds of meetings. Presentations, in particular, are 43% more effective when visual aids are used.

- Meeting minutes should be written after all meetings and promptly distributed to all interested parties. When assignments are made to individuals, or various members are requested to take action on a topic or topics, the meeting minutes should so state, along with the time required for this response.

- If additional meetings are required, they should be scheduled at the conclusion of the current meeting and all attendees requested to be prepared to respond as required.

- If at all possible, try to limit meetings to 30 minutes.

The Employee Handbook

Even small businesses can profit from developing an Employee Handbook. It has a number of advantages. When interviewing prospective employees, a well-prepared, comprehensive handbook will familiarize the interviewee with all of the pertinent information about company benefits, rules, regulations, and procedures that they can review in the privacy of their home.

For the interviewer it offers assurance that even though all benefits and procedures may not be reviewed, inadvertently, the interviewee will note them after reading the handbook.

In this era of "quick to litigate," the handbook offers some protection to the company if some disgruntled employee initiates a lawsuit claiming they were unaware of certain rules and regulations that ultimately led to their discharge.

An employee handbook can be interpreted as a contract between company and employee and as such should be reviewed by the company attorney while in draft form.

The handbook should contain, as a minimum, the following provisions:

1. A brief description of the company, its history, and its mission.

2. Normal working hours and recognized company holidays. The subject of overtime should be addressed—who is eligible to receive overtime pay and who must authorize it.

3. A statement regarding pay and salaries. If the company policy has been to award yearly increases based upon government published cost-of-living increases and other performance rating, these procedures should be clearly defined. A statement that all wages and salary increases are based upon the company's ability to pay such increases is an important sentence to add and places the employee on notice that yearly wage increases are not automatic.

4. A list of all company benefits should be included, such as paid vacation policies, allowable paid sick days, excusable absences due to the death of an immediate family member, absences for personal matters or doctor's appointments, and possibly a complete, separate section on pension/profit-sharing plans, including 401(k) if offered by the company.

5. Drug, substance abuse, and any no-smoking policies are to be addressed, as well as the disciplinary action for violators.

6. Sexual harassment has been getting a lot of media attention nowadays and a company policy regarding this issue is important. Some companies provide training sessions that not only identify the act of sexual harassment, but also address how it is to be reported and the action to be taken upon receipt and investigation of such a report.

7. It is necessary to elaborate on job attendance policies. Even though hours of attendance is included in another section of the handbook, company policy as it relates to lateness or requests to leave work early should be set forth in a separate section .

8. Disciplinary action is another topic to be carefully thought out and inserted in the handbook. A list of conduct that will not be tolerated and the consequences of such behavior ought to be spelled out loud and clear. For example, violence and/or theft may be cause for

dismissal. But be careful of the word "immediate" dismissal. In some cases there may be no need for any investigation, such as when several employees witness another employee punching the boss in the nose, but in other cases, further investigation may reveal that the facts as previously presented are not quite the way they were presented, and premature, immediate dismissal may result in a major lawsuit.

9. Job and office safety procedures need to be spelled out.

10. Grievance procedures is another topic that requires some thought and may result in the establishment of a Grievance Committee to review and comment on real and alleged complaints.

11. A statement relating to crude or rude language should be crafted along with the company policy reinforcing the need to respect the dignity of every individual in the company.

What Is This Thing Called TQM?

Total Quality Management was one of the buzzwords of the 1980s and 1990s, and although there is much talk about it, there were varying opinions of what constitutes TQM.

Does it mean the ability to consistently produce high quality work? Does it mean improving the quality of management? Does it mean rethinking corporate philosophy? TQM encompasses all of the above.

In simple terms, TQM is a business philosophy focusing on an attitudinal change in a company's culture. TQM is a continuing process of improvement involving all aspects of the business. The goal of TQM is to prevent mistakes before they happen, a process to seek error-free work, both in the field and in the office.

TQM will yield the following benefits:

- Increase client satisfaction
- Create greater efficiency
- Result in larger market share by being able to market the company as a proven quality-oriented contractor
- Reduce rework and warranty work
- Ultimately achieve higher profits
- Improve the company's reputation among peers and the entire construction community
- Lower insurance costs
- Build increased corporate morale

TQM is not a program; it is a management process whereby a commitment is made to deliver a quality product on a continuous basis. It involves every aspect of the company, from that telephone operator who answers the phone with an electronic smile, to that worker in the field who installs that plumb wall, to the accounting department who gets its monthly requisitions out to the owner on time, in the proper format, and with all required documentation necessary to obtain prompt payment. That is the essence of TQM.

Creating the TQM process

The first step involves the awareness of a need for such a process, a total commitment to the program by top management, and a statement of policy—a mission statement that describes the organization's values, guiding principles, purposes, and vision.

This mission is to be presented to all employees in a clear concise manner informing everyone that from henceforth the company's commitment is to strive to be the best of the best. Just as there are numerous books, seminars, and courses pertaining to effective management principles, so are there numerous books, seminars, and lectures devoted to the practice and implementation of Total Quality Management for contractors. Managers interested in instituting a TQM program will find easy access to a multitude of reference sources.

A synopsis of the TQM process involves the following:

Management's clear statement regarding TQM   Key executive managers must be involved in the formulation of a TQM policy. The policy statement should encompass all parts of the organization. The statement should be ambitious and easily understood. The first part of the statement should include the quality objectives; the second part should contain the specific commitments necessary to achieve these quality objectives. As an example:

> It is the policy of the Acme Construction Company that we will strive to provide the highest quality product and services to our clients by (the second part of the statement—specific commitments to achieve these goals).

or

> It is the policy of the Acme Construction Company to achieve and maintain a position of leadership in providing the highest quality product and services to our clients by (second part of the statement).

This second part of the TQM statement can include a number of specific objectives, such as:

- Work closely with vendors to obtain source materials and equipment that meet or exceed the contract specifications.

- Assurance that all actions of the company recognize the responsibility to maintain an accident-free work environment.

- Reduce and finally eliminate the need for any punch list or repair work.

A series of goals, which are to be specific in nature, can also be included in the statement:

- Reduce rework in the field by 5% in the next half of the year.

- Increase cash flow by 5% by monitoring Accounts Receivables

- Ensure that all project management job status reports are complete not later than the 5th of every preceding month.

Establishing the TQM team Executives and managers from each department within the company will form a Steering Committee. Field managers will be represented as well as office managers. These managers will be charged with developing a quality improvement plan, including its implementation and communication throughout the company. Training and education activities for all departments are to be included in this quality improvement plan. Quality teams will be created to study needed improvements for targeted processes and Quality benchmarks will then be created along with a system to monitor and measure progress. Employees working in a specific activity will be trained to monitor that activity and will be empowered to effect continuous improvements.

Creating a quality awareness Benchmarking is one way to expand one's awareness of Quality. Identify other outstanding companies in the industry that have mastered a process or achieved certain goals and strive to duplicate their achievements. In other words, uncover and implement the "best practices of the trade"—that's the concept of benchmarking.

All participants in the process are to be encouraged to submit suggestions for improvement without concern for embarrassment or reprisals. Remember that as W. Edwards Deming, the father of Quality Control, stated so well—workers with hands-on experience producing the product are management's best source of ways and means to improve quality.

Management must be committed to encouraging these suggestions, recognizing good ideas when presented, and implementing them when accepted.

A recognition program should be instituted to communicate to all company personnel when someone's quality assurance suggestion has been accepted by the company. Awards can take many forms—cash bonuses, dinner for two, a plaque honoring the recipient, perhaps just a pat on the back and a "well done" by the boss, when the occasion arises.

Not only should internal company team members be recognized for their efforts in promoting TQM, but the other members of the construction team—the general contractor, the owner, the architect, and engineers—should be commended for their assistance in achieving high quality standards during the construction project.

Providing a training and education process   No need to tell management that good people are hard to find, but even good people can benefit from on-the-job training and education. This is evident in the field of computer software where effective new programs require employee training before they can be put into effect. New project management software takes time to learn, but once learned can produce much more effective management controls. McGraw-Hill's *Engineering News Record* magazine reports that the scarcity of trained workers is becoming more acute. In their January 26, 1998 issue, an article in that publication warns contractors that the lack of sufficient numbers of trained workers may have an impact on industry growth for the current year. And both union and open shop labor organizations have stepped up their training programs in order to avert the acute shortage of trained workers that appears to be imminent. Available labor must be continually trained, educated, and motivated so they can be as productive as possible.

Review and evaluation of the process   Every employee in a company embracing TQM must be aware of the company vision and quality policy. Post-project analysis is an excellent method to use to review what went right and what went wrong. TQM carries this process somewhat further by using charts, critical performance analysis, and benchmark comparisons to emphasis the results of the review.

Measurement charts must be simple and easy to understand and graphically display the results of efforts to employ TQM in each department having a hand in the project.

TQM is a never-ending process. It is a continuous review and evaluation of ongoing operations with an eye to improving these operations.

All companies practice TQM in some form or fashion. All companies make an effort to please their client in the hope of obtaining repeat business. All businesses are upset when costly mistakes are made in the office or in the field. TQM provides a method whereby these mistakes are not only noted, but there are procedures to investigate the reasons for the mistakes and take steps to not only avoid them in the future but to find ways to improve the entire process.

Consider Ten Effective Management Strategies

1. Create a marketing plan and a business plan.

2. Review estimating procedures. Have they been on the mark, or have they been consistently too low or too high? It is time to consider new estimating software?

3. Know your costs when assembling a bid. The estimating department should develop actual costs and leave any adjustments to management prior to submitting the bid.

   Backup for all costs is critical in case there is time to review the bid prior to that all-important negotiating session with the general contractor or owner.

4. Develop an effective safety program. Implement it and monitor it. It will pay dividends:

   - Increase productivity
   - Reduce worker's compensation costs resulting in lower overhead
   - Reduce direct and indirect costs of accidents
   - Increase company morale and reduce human suffering

5. Conduct preconstruction meetings with all personnel involved in the project.
   - Review the estimate—its strong and weak points and problem areas
   - Review profit goals and pitfalls to avoid in order to achieve them
   - Review construction details with the field people and solicit any suggestions and recommendations that may improve productivity and quality
   - Discuss any labor, material, or equipment concerns

6. Conduct interim meetings to review each project. Rather than conduct one weekly meeting in which all projects are discussed, consider setting aside time each week to review every project separately, inviting the field supervisor, project manager, and accounting people to participate.

7. Stress minimization of claims losses. Poor or incomplete documentation is the No. 1 reason why claims are lost and profits are reduced. Effective means of documenting potential claims should

be discussed at the preconstruction conference and reviewed at the weekly review meetings. At the postproject meeting, any disputes and/or claims that occurred during the project should be reviewed.

8. Conduct end-of-job meetings. Review what went right and what went wrong. It is just as important to determine why profit goals were exceeded as it is to review why profit goals fell short of expectations.

   Discuss those events that were controllable and those that were not. Review relations with the general contractor and owner. Were they satisfactory or not—and the reasons for it.

9. Think cash flow. Prompt billings to general contractors and owners and prompt follow-up on receivables is the lifeblood of a construction company. But cash flow considerations begin much earlier. Before signing that subcontract agreement, consider if billing and payment terms are acceptable or ought to be changed. What about retainage? Can it be reduced by 50% when the project, or your work, is 50% complete? Think about that punch list and take steps during the negotiation stage to control cash flow. Try to obtain an agreement to assign a value to each incomplete punch list item to avoid withholding the entire final payment until all such work is complete.

10. Consider the importance of strengthening the company's financial statement.
    - Financial institutions and bonding companies will base their rates on the strength of your financial statements.
    - Increased credit lines, necessary to grow the business result from improved financial statements
    - Some clients may require copies of certified statements before considering an award of that all important, prestigious project.

Most construction companies end the year with net income that is less than 2% of sales. Implementing more effective management procedures will provide opportunities for your company to run ahead of the pack.

15

Effective Writing Techniques

You know the feeling—sitting with pencil and paper or in front of a word-processing computer trying to gather your thoughts to write that letter of introduction to a prospective client, respond to a threatening letter from a general contractor, or compose a letter to employees to explain a new company policy. Although you may have thought you knew exactly what to write, when it came time to do so, it became a daunting task.

What to many people is a frustrating experience needn't be!

Let's take a look at various approaches to preparing for and writing concise but effective letters, and you will find that they all employ much the same basic methods.

General Guidelines to Writing a Letter

Don't expect that your first draft will produce the final letter. A first draft allows you to put your thoughts on paper and accept the fact that revisions will be needed. This will relieve some stress, since most people do not produce their final letter the first time it is written. In fact, some letter writers may create as many as six revised drafts before they are satisfied that their letter contains all of the thoughts it was meant to convey. So don't feel discouraged if you have to redraft and revise your letter several times before it conveys the message to your intended reader.

Another helpful tip could be called the "Put-it-away-for-another day's review" technique.

Whenever writing a letter explaining a complex situation or when writing a letter in a pique of anger, it is always helpful to write the draft, put it away for a day or two, reread it, and determine whether, in the first case, it was clear and concise, and, in the second case, whether you really wanted to say those awful things.

Seven Basic Letter-Writing Principles

1. Before beginning a letter, establish a clear purpose for the letter—"What do I want to accomplish by writing this letter?" Do you wish to advise someone of a potential problem, clarify a questionable matter, deny responsibility for certain actions, propose a solution to a problem?

2. Learn to write as you would speak. Pretend you are having a conversation with the person to whom you are writing. Would you speak like any of those form letters you have seen? The answer is probably not. Now you can begin to write in a more conversational manner. Obviously that doesn't mean you should use the word "ain't," even if you use it in conversation, or that you should use the word "dummy," even if that is really what you want to say (find another word that is less offensive and more diplomatic!) Writing as you would speak lends a more credible tone to your letter, which will not be lost on the reader.

3. Be concise. Your letters should be concise; express a statement in as few words as possible. For example, when sending a letter to a general contractor indicating that a forthcoming addendum was not received when promised, you might have written: "As we discussed last week, you indicated that we would receive a copy of Addendum No. 3 on June 5th, 1998, however we did not receive it on that date." A concise sentence stating the same facts would be, "We did not receive Addendum No. 3, as you promised, on June 5, 1998." Instead of using 27 words (exclusive of dates) as the first sentence illustrates, the same message was conveyed by the 11 words.

4. Don't use hackneyed expressions or trite or overused expressions such as "enclosed herewith" when just plain enclosed will do. Don't use "submitted for your perusal;" use "for your review." (Would you actually use "perusal" if you were talking to someone?) Other expressions to avoid, as an example (try to think of others):
   - Thanking you in advance—How do you know they want to be thanked? They may wish you never sent that letter!
   - To be perfectly honest—Does that mean that you usually are not honest?
   - As you are well aware—How do you know the person to whom the letter is being addressed is aware of the situation? And even if they are, isn't this like talking down to them?

5. The first sentence of the letter should be a "grabber" and express its purpose. Instead of writing, "After reviewing your letter of May 5th in which you state that we are late in the delivery of Sheetrock to the Church Street project we beg to differ with the facts as set forth in that letter." Why not just state, "Sheetrock was delivered to the Church Street project, as agreed, on April 30th." Try to set the tone of the letter in this first sentence and create reader interest.

6. Keep paragraphs short. Research has shown that long paragraphs cause the reader to lose both interest and comprehension. Several short paragraphs are much better, and for added impact, try a one-sentence paragraph to attract the reader's attention.

7. Readers tend to focus on "bullets" and, if appropriate when presenting a list, use a bullet to draw the reader's attention to these listed items.

The Three C Method

Clarity, correctness, and courtesy are three important guidelines to follow when writing letters, so says one writing expert.

Clarity means that short, familiar, everyday conversational words should be used. Clarity also requires sentences to be effectively constructed and incorporated into effective, short paragraphs. Examples can often be used to introduce clarity into a sentence or paragraph.

Clarity has to do with being able to choose words that are familiar including technical terms that are part of your everyday business vocabulary. It is not necessary to consult a dictionary to impress the reader with the use of "big" words which neither the writer nor the reader would use in conversation. The goal in pursuing clarity is to write a letter that contains effective sentences and paragraphs that clearly express the writer's thoughts.

Correctness refers to proper spelling and punctuation—the mechanics of letter writing. Facts or figures contained in the letter should be checked for correctness and if the letter contains numbers or calculations they should be checked and verified arithmetically.

Courtesy is the third "C" and means exactly what it says. No matter what the content of a letter its tone should be courteous—it should not irritate, hurt, or belittle the reader. Depending upon the nature of the letter, sincerity, tact and thoughtfulness are all concerns that the writer should consider.

Another writing consultant adds a fourth "C"—completeness.

Obviously, if the letter is responding to a list of questions, all questions should be addressed and answered. When considering "Completeness," the Five W Formula familiar to news reporters and investigators should come into play when reviewing the completeness the writer's response.

- Who—To whom is this letter directed?
- What—What is to be accomplished by the writing of this letter?
- When—When did the events referred to in the letter take place or when are they expected to take place?
- Why—Why is this letter necessary?
- Where—Where were events to occur, or where did they occur?

Some Tips to Writing Effective Letters

1. Establish a purpose for the letter. Writing is an important business task and like most important tasks requires adequate preparation. Some letters deal with matters that could produce serious consequences and therefore should be approached with the same businesslike thoroughness as other critical company activities like estimating and cost control. Other letters may be more or less routine and would not require the same degree of preparedness.

   But in either case, the writer must ask themselves questions similar to the five Ws
   - What is the purpose of this letter?
   - What will be the reader's needs in relation to the subject mater?
   - What is going to be the scope of the letter? Will a great deal of research material readily at hand be required or is this letter of a general nature?

2. Research before writing. In most cases letters are written to establish a position or respond to a position taken by others. Either the initiation or response letter will most likely require some research to explain or elaborate on the issues to be incorporated, and this data or reference material ought to be assembled prior to the writing of the letter.

   The writer must ask, "What other facts or documents do I need in order to prepare this letter?" Unless these facts or documents are readily at hand as the first draft is being prepared, precious time will be lost in searching out this information as it is needed, and most importantly, one's train of thought will be interrupted and those concise statements that were being formed in the writer's mind, but not yet reduced to writing, may be lost.

   Those little yellow stick-ums can be used to flag the correspondence, daily logs, or other documents to be referred to during the preparation of the first draft and a highlighter might be used to further assist the writer in focusing on pertinent research data.

3. Organizing the letter. Organization of the letter is important. How is the letter to be developed? What facts will come first, second, and third? Where and how will any substantiating material be inserted into the body of the letter?

    Preparing an outline first is an easy way to organize the content of a complex or lengthy letter and enables the writer to define the important elements requiring emphasis along with lesser important points.

    When a word processing program is used to write a letter, the outline created can serve as a skeleton to be fleshed out and expanded.

    If a response to a previous letter is being prepared, it is sometimes helpful to write notes alongside those issues or points in that letter to insure that each issue will be addressed in the response.

4. Writing the letter in draft form. It is a difficult task to clearly and concisely express all of the points that need to be included in the very first draft of a letter; everyone develops "writer's block" at one time or another. The draft approach to letter writing somehow puts the mind at ease because the writer knows that he or she is not under a self-imposed obligation to produce the final form of the letter at the first sitting. They can be more relaxed in their letter writing approach knowing beforehand that it will be revised before reaching its final form.

    Often important facts come to mind after the first draft is written and with the use of a computer and word processing software, insertion or deletion of sentences or complete paragraphs is a relatively simple matter.

    The draft of the letter should be prepared in sufficient time to allow for review. Too often important letters are written in haste and the writer doesn't allow enough time for them to be properly proofread. Letters with typos, missing words, incomplete sentences, arithmetical mistakes are not only ineffective but display a degree of carelessness on the part of the sender which is certainly not lost on the recipient.

5. The final revision stage. Many professional writers revise their drafts frequently before they are satisfied with its final form—and even then they may revisit the draft in a day or two and make even more changes.

    So is it with business letter writing except for the very few who can write the perfect letter on their first attempt Once a draft has been revised, if time permits and urgency is not required, put the letter aside for a day or two and then read it anew. This fresh look may reveal key issues that lack the intended clarity, or a new thought or fact that must be added or perhaps the tone of the letter that appeared to be proper a day or two ago is too harsh or, conversely, not strong enough.

This setting aside of a letter for a day, particularly when it is a harsh or accusatory one, will allow the writer to calm down and possibly to tone down some of its inflammatory statements.

And, of course, when critical dates, mathematics, or arithmetic figures or calculations are included in the letter, they should always be checked for accuracy. With spell-check software it is a simple matter to check for correct spelling; without such an electronic aid, be sure to do so manually.

Lastly, check the addressee's name and title to insure that they are correct. Misspelling one's name or listing an incorrect business title is a sure turnoff for anyone receiving a letter. No letter should be signed by the writer unless it has been proofread. Make this a cardinal letter writing rule.

Instead of—You Might Consider

Certain expressions appear from time to time in letters we have all written or received; look at the checklists below and see how many you've used in the past. Try to avoid using these cliches in the future.

Not too good	Better
If we are not mistaken	We believe
In accordance with your request	As requested
Your early attention to this matter will be appreciated	Please act promptly on this request
In an equitable manner	Equitably
We are not in a position to	We cannot
Let us hear from you in response to	Write us concerning
Will you please arrange to send	Please send
We would therefore ask that you kindly investigate	Please investigate

Write as you would talk.

Instead of	Use more conversational phrases
Hold in abeyance	Wait
Pursuant to your request	As you requested
Prior to	Before
Subsequent to	After
Conceptualize	Think of
Due to the fact that	Because

Instead of	Use more conversational phrases
At an early date	Soon
Take into consideration	Consider
Ascertain the data	Get the facts
At this point in time	Now

Use as few words as possible

If you want to say	Why not shorten it to . . .?
Engaged in conducting a survey	Conducting a survey
Long period of time	Long time
Enclosed herewith	Enclosed
Decide at a meeting to be held on Monday	Decide at Monday's meeting
During the year 1999	During 1999
There is one point that is clear and that is	One point that is clear
The cost was higher than I expected it to be	The costs was higher
That is the situation at this time	That is the situation
During the course of the meeting	During the meeting
Throughout the entire week	Throughout the week
The trouble with the compressor was that it was too noisy	The compressor was too noisy

It is difficult to shed old habits and cultivate new ones, but since written communication in general, and letter writing, to be more specific, is such an important part of our day-to-day business life, with patience and practice everyone can produce concise, clear, and correct documents.

Chapter 16

Sample Letters

The sample letters included in this chapter are meant to serve only as guides, since individual requirements may necessitate considerable modification to any of these letters.

But the goal of each letter is the same:

- Be concise and precise.
- When referring to various drawings, details, or specifications of contract obligations, be specific and include exact plan numbers (and issue/revision dates), detail number and related drawing, specification section, paragraph, and subsections, if applicable. When referencing contract provisions, include the contract date and the article or section in question.
- If action is required, name the party to whom this responsibility is to be assigned and include a date by which the action is to take place.
- Address correspondence to a specific person in the organization, never to just "Gentlemen" (First of all the gentlemen might be a woman!)
- Be timely in the execution of writing the letter. If it weren't important, there would be no need to write the letter. As they say, "Timing is everything."
- In some cases, a telephone call to the person to whom some letters are to be sent is an act of courtesy and prepares the reader for what is, in all probability, not a nice letter, but a necessary one.
- Check all important letters for proper spelling of the recipient's name and title, spelling, and grammatical errors, and for arithmetical errors, if applicable.

- Don't forget those "ccs," by now an outdated designation for "carbon copies." Who else should receive a copy—the boss, field personnel?

- Letters that may precipitate or become part of potential legal action should be sent certified mail so there is proof of receipt by the recipient.

- Don't forget to put that nasty letter aside for at least overnight, when cooler heads may prevail the next morning.

A diskette containing all thirty (30) sample letters is included in a pouch inside the rear cover of this book and will permit the readers to "bring up" any letter on their computer screens and modify it for their particular needs. The diskette format is Microsoft Windows 95— Microsoft Word.

Index to Sample Letters:

1. Introduction to client or general contractor requesting placement on bidders list.

2. Response to verbal request to proceed with Change Order work.

3. Response to direction to accelerate your work.

4. Response to general contractor's Stop Work order.

5. Response to general contractor's request to stop work in one area and continue to proceed with work in other areas.

6. Request to general contractor for interpretation of plans and/or specification questions.

7. Letter expressing disagreement over general contractor's interpretation of plans/specifications.

8. Letter to general contractor requesting overdue payment.

9. Letter to general contractor requesting reduction in retainage.

10. Notification to general contractor of delay in receiving shop drawings previously submitted.

11. Notification of delay in receiving response to Request for Information (RFI) or Request for Clarification (RFC).

12. Response to general contractor's revised construction schedule.

13. Request for punch list.

14. Request to establish cost for incomplete items in remaining punch list work.

15. Request to general contractor for "sign-off" on punch list.

16. Request to general contractor to review condition of work in area to be occupied by owner when partial occupancy is being considered.
    a. Letter to general contractor notifying him or her of damage to your work by others in areas that have been completed and turned over to owner.

17. Notification to general contractor that by its actions/inactions, subcontractor is being delayed in ability to start to perform their work.

18. Notification to general contractor that other subcontractors are affecting their ability to perform work efficiently and according to general contractor's schedule.

19. Request for submission/acceptance of "or equal" product or equipment.

20. Confirmation of verbal or telephone directive/instruction from a general contractor/owner.

21. Letter to general contractor who has a history of ignoring previous correspondence.

22. Claim letters:
    a. Notifying general contractor of circumstances that could create delay.
    b. Notifying general contractor that delay has occurred.
    c. Notifying general contractor of intent to file delay claim.

23. Response to general contractor's letter that subcontractor does not have sufficient manpower on job, which may create delays.

24. Request for payment of materials/equipment stored off-site.

25. Request to have architect/engineer inspect work and accept it.

26. Letter to general contractor requesting copy of bond and intent to notify bonding company of nonpayment.

27. Letter to general contractor advising them that subcontractor has encountered unforeseen conditions or uncovered work not indicated in contract documents or encountered "differing conditions."

28. Letter to general contractor stating that due to delay in obtaining architect/engineer certificate of substantial completion, warranties/guarantees on equipment/ materials will expire prematurely.

29. Letter to general contractor disputing backcharges.

30. Letter of intent.

LETTER No. 1   Introduction to client or General Contractor requesting placement on Bidder's List

Heading to either owner or general contractor

(*Note:* Don't address such a letter to "Gentlemen"; make a call to determine the individual to whom such a letter should be written and his or her title. Double-check for correct spelling—no one likes to have his or her name misspelled!)

Dear Mr. General Contractor/Owner,   re: Project "X"

Our firm has been engaged in the mechanical (or applicable trade) subcontracting business in Elkton, Maryland (or wherever you are located) for more that (x) years. We pride ourselves on being competitive, quality-oriented, and completing our work on time.

We wish to be considered as a qualified bidder for the mechanical (or applicable trade) portion of the office building (or whatever) you are planning to construct for (client) in Chesapeake City, Maryland.

Enclosed are our company brochure and a list of recently completed projects with related references. We would very much appreciate an opportunity to meet with you and present our company's credentials.

I will be calling your office on (date) to arrange an appointment at your convenience.

> With best regards,
>
> James Subcontractor
> Vice President—Operations

LETTER No. 2   Response to verbal request to proceed with Change Order Work

Dear Mr. Contractor/Owner,   re: Project "X"

On May 5, 1999 we were authorized by your project manager, John Glenn, to proceed with the extra work as set forth in Drawing SK-3A, dated April 30, 1999, prepared by Triangle and Square, A.I.A.

Mr. Glenn directed our foreman, Joe Bologna, to perform this work on a Time and Material basis.

We will commence this work on (date) and prepare Daily Work tickets and include invoices for all materials and equipment used to complete this work. Copies of all Daily Work orders and delivery receipts will be presented to your on-site representative for his (or her) signature.

Enclosed is a copy of the labor rates that apply for this project. To all costs we will add our standard 10% overhead and 10% profit.

Your written confirmation to proceed with this work will be appreciated.

With best regards,

Eric Subcontractor

cc: Subs project manager and foreman

LETTER No. 3   Response to direction to accelerate your work

Dear Mr. General Contractor/Owner,   re: Project "X"

On (date), we received your verbal directive to accelerate our work. You wish to have our company complete our work in (building/area or place where work is to be accelerated) on (date) as reflected in the revised construction schedule issued to our firm dated (date).

Since we cannot estimate the cost of this work at this time, we will proceed on a Time and Materials basis. However, it appears that this work can be accomplished by directing our present ten (10) man crew to work an additional two (2) hours each day for the next four (4) weeks and have the entire crew to work eight hours each for the next three (3) Saturdays (insert actual dates). All such costs for the work are to be reimbursed upon receipt of our invoices that will include our standard markup of 10% overhead and 10% profit.

As you know the successful acceleration of our portion of the work is dependent upon other related trades completing their work in a timely fashion.

In addition to the premium time costs for all tradesmen assigned to this work, we will also be submitting costs incurred by our foreman and our project manager who are required to provide supervision during this period of acceleration.

Your written acceptance of our proposal will be appreciated so that we may direct our forces to proceed with this work.

Very truly yours,

Alice Subcontractor

(*Note:* Unless you can safely provide a lump sum cost to perform this work, proceed only on the basis of Time and Material. Also note that extended periods of overtime reduce crew production rates, and this must be taken into account when estimating the time to complete. But if you are proceeding on a Time and Material basis, the actual costs reflecting lower productivity will be included in those T&M tickets.)

LETTER No. 4   Response to General Contractor's Stop Work Order.

Dear Mr. General Contractor/Owner,   re: Project "X"

We have received your October 5, 1999 letter directing us to cease all work at the (project).

We have issued this order to our field supervisor and all work will cease effective (whatever time and date you state).

We have placed cancellation orders with our vendors and upon receipt of all such charges will submit our interim requisition to reflect all costs associated with this Stop Work Order.

Please provide instructions on the disposition of all materials and equipment currently stored on the site.

Very truly yours,

Larry Subcontractor

cc: To all subcontractors/vendors on project

LETTER No. 5 Response to General Contractor's request to stop work in one area but continue to proceed with work in other areas

Dear Mr. General Contractor/Owner,   re: Project "X"

We have received your (verbal/written) request to stop work on the northeast sector of the third floor of the Jackson Office Building (or whatever area where work is to cease) on (date and time), and we will continue working in all other areas of the building.

There may be additional costs associated with working out of sequence and we will advise your office within the next two (2) weeks if any added costs are to be forthcoming.

Very truly yours,

Jose Subcontractor

(*Note:* Don't commit to costs associated with this out-of-sequence work until you have thoroughly investigated its impact. Allow yourself sufficient time to thoroughly assess this situation because it may affect your cost to complete the contract work. The General Contractor/Owner will probably be expecting a claim for extra costs so don't be timid in requesting an extra charge—but you must be able to document the circumstances surrounding your request for this extra!)

LETTER No. 6   Request to General Contractor for interpretation of plans and/or specifications

For Drawing Interpretation

Dear Mr. General Contractor,   re: Project "X"

We refer you to Drawing A-4—Floor Plan—2d Floor dated April 21, 1998 and Detail 8, Drawing A-26 dated April 24, 1998 (or whatever specific drawings and details are at issue).

The detail on Drawing A-26 does not refer to the section of wall shown on Drawing A-4. It appears that Detail 4 is the applicable one.

We would appreciate your response within 10 days of receipt of this letter.

Very truly yours,

Malcolm Subcontractor

For Specification Interpretation

Dear Mr. General Contractor,   re: Project "X"

We refer you to Paragraph D.2.04 of Specification Section 09235 that stipulates that latex enamel paint is to be applied to all above ceiling pipes. However, Specification Section 16500, specifically Paragraph 6.05, states that no painting is to be applied to any pipes to be covered with insulation.

We have, therefore, excluded painting of all insulated pipes and wish to have your written confirmation that Specification Section 16500 prevails.

With best regards,

Malcolm Subcontractor

LETTER No. 7   Letter expressing disagreement over General Contractor's interpretation of the plans/specifications

Dear General Contractor,   re: Project "X

We are in receipt of your January 5, 1999 letter in which you direct us to comply with the foundation wall details indicated on Drawing S-100, May 1, 1998, although we are of the opinion that the wall sections shown on Drawing S-108, May 1, 1998 are the correct details.

According to the provisions of Article 4 of A.I.A. Document A201 (or whatever article applies) the architect is designated as the interpreter of the contract documents and we wish to have his or her ruling on this matter before proceeding with the work.

We will await his or her response before proceeding with this work.

With best regards,

Skip Subcontractor

(*Note:* The General Contractor's interpretation of the contract documents is not valid until [or if] the architect agrees with that ruling.)

LETTER No. 8   Letter to General Contractor requesting over-due payment

*When you don't know if the General Contractor
has received payment from the owner*

Dear Mr. General Contractor,   re: Project "X"

We submitted our Requisition No. 14 in the net amount of $235,550.00 on July 24, 1999 and Article 16 of our subcontract agreement stipulates that payment is due within 15 days of receipt of payment from the owner.

As of August 15, 1999 we have not received payment for this requisition and request that you advise us of the status of this payment.

Very truly yours,

Maria Subcontractor

*When you know that the General Contractor
has received payment from the owner*

Dear Mr. General Contractor,   re: Project "X"

We submitted our Requisition No. 14 in the net amount of $235,550.00 on July 24, 1999 and in accordance with Article 16 of our subcontract agreement we are to receive payment within 15 days of your receipt of payment from the owner. As of (date) this requisition remains unpaid.

It is our understanding that your company has been paid for the period in question and we wish to be advised when we can receive payment for our Requisition No. 14.

Very truly yours.

Maria Subcontractor

(What you've done with this letter is to let the General Contractor know that you have a source to obtain information about payment from the owner; General Contractors don't like subcontractors talking to owners about late payments.)

LETTER No. 9   Letter to General Contractor requesting reduction of retainage

When the subcontract agreement specifically includes reduction of retainage

Dear Mr.General Contractor,   re: Project "X"

We have completed 50% of our work as reflected in our Application for Payment No. 11, dated February 15, 1998. In accordance with Article 15 (or whatever article applies) in the General Conditions to the contract with the owner, we may receive one-half of our retainage after our submission of a written request for this payment. By a copy of this letter we are requesting this retainage reduction.

Enclosed is Application for Payment No. 12 which includes payment for one-half ($\frac{1}{2}$) of our retainage.

Very truly yours,

George Subcontractor

(This is another reason to request a copy of the General Contractor's contract with the owner to which a subcontractor is generally entitled to do. The owner/General Contractor contract may allow the General Contractor to request and receive 50% of his or her retainage when the project is 50% complete. However, there have been instances where the General Contractor did not pass any such funds onto the subcontractor until the end of the project.)

When there is no contract provision for reduction in retainage

Dear Mr. General Contractor,   re: Project "X"

With the submission and payment of Requisition No. 11, dated February 25, 1998, we will have completed 50% of our work and we request that our retainage be reduced from 10% to 5%.

Although the contract does not specifically include retainage reduction, we trust that our performance and quality of work to date may warrant such a consideration.

(Many owners who have observed a subcontractor's excellent performance and high quality levels will allow the General Contractor to apply for retainage reduction for that subcontractor. Hard work and good relations usually pay off!)

Very truly yours.

George Subcontractor

LETTER No. 10   Notification of delay to General Contractor in receiving shop drawings previously submitted

Dear Mr. General Contractor,   re: Project "X"

November 1, 1998

We submitted our shop drawing for the Cleaver-Brooks boilers on September 15, 1998. According to the contract specifications, we were to expect a three (3) week turn-around on all shop drawing reviews.

As of November 1, 1998 we have not received these drawings from your office. Delivery of the boilers is eight (8) to ten (10) weeks from receipt of approved shop drawings and this equipment will be required at the job site on or about January 15, 1999 in order to meet your current construction schedule.

Unless we receive authorization to release the boilers within three (3) working days from the date of this letter, we will not be responsible for any additional costs associated with the late delivery and installation of this equipment.

Very truly yours.

Pauline Subcontractor

(One question to be asked: Why did you wait until November 1st to write this letter when you should have written it on or about October 7th that is three weeks from the time of submission of the shop drawing. This is certainly a question the General Contractor will ask as he or she scrambles to obtain approval from the architect.)

LETTER No. 11   Notification of delay in receiving response to Request for Information (RFI) or Request for Clarification (RFC)

Dear Mr. General Contractor,   re: Project "X"

September 14, 1998

On September 7, 1999 we submitted RFI#23 to your office that pertained to clarification of the height of the acoustical ceilings in Corridor 105.

In this RFI we advised that the installation of the electrical conduit in this area cannot begin unless the ceiling height is lowered from 10'0" to 9'4".

As of this date (giving the General Contractor seven days to respond to the RFI), we have had no response to RFI#23 and have ceased work in this area. If we are unable to commence the installation of the electrical conduit system in Corridor 105 by Monday, September 16, we cannot be held responsible for any subsequent schedule delays and their associated costs.

(*Note:* dates are inserted to illustrate the need for prompt response to any delays in receiving answers to RFIs or RFCs. If your notification of delay is not prompt and additional costs are incurred due to a late response, the General Contractor will ask, "Why didn't you notify me sooner and I would have responded immediately." Of course, they say that after the fact!)

Very truly yours.

Alex Subcontractor

LETTER No. 12   Response to General Contractor's revised construction schedule

(If you are in agreement that the revised schedule represents *no additional costs* or related problems)

Dear Mr. General Contractor,   re: Project "X"

We are in receipt of your construction schedule for the above-referenced project, revised (date of revision) and will proceed with the work in accordance with this schedule.

(No need to mention *"at no* additional cost," in case you inadvertently find that there *are* additional costs as you proceed!)

Very truly yours,

Axel Subcontractor

(If you are of the opinion that there are to be additional costs or are *uncertain* whether additional costs are involved in complying with this revised schedule)

Dear Mr. General Contractor,   re: Project "X"

We are in receipt of your construction schedule for the above-referenced project revised (date of revision) and have determined that in order to comply with this new schedule, we may incur additional costs for the following reasons:

1. Overtime will be required for both our tradesmen, foremen, and project manager.
2. Loss of productivity may occur due to stacking of (name the trades) in (name and area of building where this may occur).
3. Additional costs to expedite (equipment or supplies).
4. (Any other costs that *may* be anticipated. Now is the time to alert the General Contractor rather than later.)

Within the next two weeks we will present our estimate of all such anticipated costs. If, however, you wish us to proceed with this work immediately, we request that your superintendent sign daily work tickets when presented by our on-site supervisor

                                        Very truly yours,

                                        Joe Subcontractor

(*Note:* It is prudent to obtain a clear understanding of how extra costs to accelerate will be paid, prior to commencing this work. Work out the details quickly, submit costs/estimate in writing and request approval *in writing*.)

LETTER No. 13   Request for punch list

(When the architect/engineer is lax in submitting a punch list and your work is complete, you need to jog the General Contractor; if not:

1. Your work may be damaged by other trades.
2. Your final payment or retainage will be delayed.

Dear Mr. General Contractor,   re: Project "X"

We have completed all work included in our subcontract agreement as of (date) and wish to receive a punch list promptly in order to commence all such work as may be necessary to receive our final payment (or retainage).

Any further delays in receipt of our punch list will ultimately delay our final payment and impose a serious financial hardship on our company.

Very truly yours,

Jane Subcontractor

(If no punch list is forthcoming, write another letter, but *this time* send a copy to the architect and owner—the General Contractor may be upset when you send a copy to the architect and owner, or may be grateful because they are also trying to obtain a punch list! If you send such a letter, call the General Contractor and let him or her know that you will be sending this letter with copies to the architect/engineer and owner.)

LETTER No. 14   Request to establish a cost for incomplete items in remaining punch list work

Dear Mr. General Contractor,   re: Project "X"

We have attempted on several occasions to complete all of the work contained in the architect's (engineer's) Punch List dated (date), but have been unable to do so for one or more of the following reasons:

Cannot gain access to the area.

Waiting for replacement parts or materials.

Can't get one of our subcontractors to respond promptly.

Any other reason.

So as not to delay payment of our entire retainage we wish to propose withholding the following sums for each incomplete item. Set forth below is our estimate of the cost to complete each incomplete item. We suggest withholding double this amount:

1. Replace light switch—Room 312

   Labor-$20.00, Materials—$18.00—Total: $38.00 × 2 = $76.00

2. Replace fixture Room 222

   Labor—$35.00, Fixture $85.00—Total: $120.00 × 2 = $240.00

   Total above: $316.00

Our total retainage is $3,500; therefore, we request release of $3,184.00 at this time. When the above two items are completed, we will request payment of the balance of our retainage.

Very truly yours,

Mario Subcontractor

LETTER No. 15   Request for General Contractor for "sign-off" on punch list

(There may be a time when the subcontractor's punch list is complete, the General Contractor recognizes it as such, but can't get the architect to sign off thereby making it official.)

Dear General Contractor,   re: Project "X"

As of (date) we completed all items in the architect's (engineer's) punch list dated [date(s)]. Although we requested an inspection(s) to verify completion on (date), no inspection has been scheduled. (Hopefully your previous requests were in writing!) Your superintendent has reviewed each item on our punch list on (date) and agrees that they have been completed. Although we recognize that the architect's sign-off is the official one, we request that you arrange release of our final payment (retainage) since any further delays will present a financial hardship for our firm.

(Send copies to the architect and owner, and if you don't get a response within a week or so, keep sending the same letter.)

Very truly yours,

Jose Subcontractor

LETTER No. 16   Request to General Contractor to review condition of work in an area to be occupied by owner when partial occupancy of the building is being considered

Dear Mr. General Contractor,   re: Project "X"

On (date) we completed (area—be specific by room number, location, etc.) which is to be occupied by (owner). Prior to turnover we request that the area be inspected by your superintendent and the architect (engineer) and that we receive written confirmation of acceptance.

We will not be responsible for damage for any of our work in this area after the owner accepts the space; however, we do not waive responsibility for any warranty/guarantee items.

(If you are a mechanical or electrical subcontractor, any equipment warranties will commence upon the owner's acceptance and should be so stated in this letter. Depending upon who is to perform routine maintenance, this should also be included in the letter, for example:

> Please be advised that the owner is to lubricate Fan EF-2 each week, and failure to do so may void the manufacturer's guarantee.)

LETTER No. 16(a)   Letter to General Contractor notifying them of damage to your work in areas that have been completed and turned over to owner. This usually occurs during the owner's move-in. It is a good idea to have one of your staff present when the movers arrive and partial occupancy takes place!

Dear Mr. General Contractor,   re: Project "X"

Our superintendent, John Brown, was present when Acme Moving Company moved furniture into the areas (be specific) we completed and turned over to the owner on (date). We observed that one employee of Acme damaged the east wall of Room 315, dented the metal door frame, and scratched the door leading into this room. (If an owner's representative was present, get them to sign an acknowledgment of the damage and who caused it.)

We bring this to your attention and will not be responsible to repair this damage.

Very truly yours.

Lee Park Subcontractor

LETTER No. 17 Notification to General Contractor that by their actions/inactions, subcontractor is being delayed in ability to start/perform his or her work

Dear Mr. General Contractor,   re: Project "X"

The delay in completing the excavation (or whatever work you are performing) in (area of building or site, if applicable) will not allow us to start (or continue with) our work.

Although the construction schedule dated (?) indicates that site (or applicable) work in this area was to have been completed by (date), as of the date of this letter, this portion of the (site/building) has not reached the level of completion that will allow our work to start.

Please provide us with a schedule update for our review. When we are permitted to continue/commence work, we will assess all costs associated with these delays and advise your office.

Very truly yours,

Andrew Subcontractor

(*Note:* Don't submit costs for delays/interruption in work with this letter unless you are absolutely certain they are all inclusive. You will need to thoroughly assess this situation before committing to requesting added costs, if the case may be. And you will be required to document and substantiate your request, in detail—so take your time when preparing any related costs!)

LETTER No. 18   Notification to General Contractor that other subcontractors are affecting their ability to perform work efficiently and according to the General Contractor's schedule

Dear Mr. General Contractor,   re: Project "X"

According to your construction schedule dated (?), we were to have commenced work in (insert specific area) on (date); however, we are being prevented from doing so because the metal studs have not been installed (or whatever is responsible for the delays).

Please advise when this area will be ready for us to begin our work. At such time we will advise your office of any costs associated with these delays.

Very truly yours,

Raymond Subcontractor

LETTER No. 19   Request for submission/acceptance of and "or equal" product or equipment

Dear Mr. General Contractor,   re: Project "X"

We are submitting seven (7) copies of shop drawings for (name product or equipment) as an "or equal" to (name product or equipment) set forth in (state specification section).

We are also submitting two (2) copies of a shop drawing for the specified product for comparison to our "or equal" submission.

(You should state the reason for this substitution. Most General Contractors and architect/engineers view the submission of "or equals" as an attempt by a General Contractor or subcontractor to provide a product that is less expensive and the alleged "savings" in cost between the "or equal" and the specified product will remain with the submitter. There may be many valid reasons for this request to substitute.

The "or equal" product may be similar in quality/performance to the specified product but offers a better delivery date. The "or equal" product may be more cost-effective for the owner to maintain. Replacement parts or factory service may be easier to obtain.)

Very truly yours,

Vito Subcontractor

LETTER No. 20   Confirmation of a verbal or telephone directive from a General Contractor or owner

Dear Mr. General Contractor/Owner,   re: Project "X"

We refer to your verbal (telephone) directive of (date) in which Mr. (Ms) *name* instructed our field supervisor, James Brown, to replace the damaged door to Room 217. We were requested to perform this work on a Time and Material basis and present all daily work tickets and material receipts to your office.

We will add our standard 10% overhead and 10% profit to all documented costs.

Very truly yours,

Authur Subcontractor

cc: James Brown

(*Note:* Always confirm verbal directives even though the General Contractor/owner may indicate that they will be forwarding their confirmation within a day or two. Include the following items in any confirmation letter:

1. Date directive received.
2. General Contractor's (owner's) representative (by name) authorizing work.
3. To whom the directive was received by your company.
4. The method by which the work will be invoiced—lump sum, T&M.
5. The percentage of overhead and profit to be applied to costs.
6. Request written confirmation, even though it has been promised.)

LETTER No. 21   Letter to General Contractor who has history of ignoring previous correspondence

Dear Mr. General Contractor,   re: Project "X"

June 1, 1999

On (date) we submitted a letter to your office requesting permission to substitute 25 gauge studs for the 20 gauge studs required by Detail 4, Drawing A-103, dated April 1, 1999. We indicated that we would withdraw our Proposed Change Order No. 12, if allowed to make this substitution.

To date, we have had no response to this request, and if we do not hear from your office to the contrary by June 7th, we will proceed to make the substitution of metal studs and cancel any credit due your office by withdrawing our PCO#12.

Very truly yours,

Bill Subcontractor

(*Note:* This is sort of a Reverse English letter. When a General Contractor fails to respond to requests and the subcontractor proceeds assuming that his or her proposal has been accepted, he or she could be mistaken. By providing the General Contractor with a date to respond, indicating that nonresponse is acceptance, a subcontractor is on a more firm footing, if the General Contractor at a later date recants his or her acceptance.)

LETTERS Nos. 22(a), (b), (c)   Claims letters

(**a.**) Notifying General Contractor of circumstances that could create a delay

(*Note:* Some subcontractors, when experiencing a delay beyond their control, want to appear optimistic and announce that the delay will not affect their performance. As a bit of insurance, write this kind of letter!)

Dear Mr. General Contractor,   re: Project "X"

The completion of the structural steel erection and placement of concrete slabs on metal deck in the northeast quadrant of the building will delay our core boring, waste and vent risers, and possibly other phases of rough-in. This work was to have been completed not later than (date) but we have been unable to do so.

When the slabs have been placed, we will assess the situation at that time to determine what effect, if any, these delays have impacted on our schedule.

Very truly yours,

Emil Subcontractor

LETTER No. 22(b)   Notifying the General Contractor that a delay has occurred

(*Note:* Although it is important to notify a General Contractor in writing when a delay has occurred, take your time in establishing the true *cost* of the delay. This letter should only alert the General Contractor that a delay has occurred giving your office time to fully assess the cost of the delay. Remember it is difficult to go back to the General Contractor and state, "Oh, I forgot to include the costs of "X" or "Y." Your first notification of *actual costs of the delay* must be complete.)

Dear Mr. General Contractor,   re: Project "X"

We refer to our letter of (date)(which should have been in the form of Letter No. 22(**a**) in which we referred to potential delays to our schedule pending completion of the concrete slab pours in the northeast quadrant of the building. These slabs were completed on (date) and, as a result, the start of our steel stud partition layout (or whichever operation has been delayed) has been delayed by four weeks.

We are currently assessing the costs to accelerate our work in order to compensate for this four (4)-week delay. If, however, you do not wish us to accelerate but to extend our completion date by the four (4)-week delay, please advise and we will prepare our costs based upon this revised completion date.

Very truly yours,

Abigail subcontractor

(*Note:* Although the General Contractor may not want to have you accelerate your work, the four (4)-week delay could still affect your operation and create added costs for:

1. Supervision required to remain on site for an additional month.

2. Other general conditions will be extended for another month.

3. May have to delay the start of that new project since personnel assigned to delayed project were scheduled to supervise that new project.)

LETTER No. 22(c)   Notifying the General Contractor of intent to file a delay claim

Dear Mr. General Contractor,   re: Project "X"

At the project meeting held at the Project "X" site today, we were advised by your project manager that certain delays have occurred in the completion of work necessary for our company to commence work (in a specific part of the building or on site or wherever).

Please be advised that delays in completing this work will impact our performance on the site.

When you have presented us with an updated schedule, we will determine what impact, if any, these delays will have to affect our work.

Very truly yours,

Rami Subcontractor

(*Note:* This letter is slightly different from Letter 22(**a**). Letter 22(**a**) would be sent because the subcontractor is notifying the General Contractor that a delay *has been* created, but this letter is in response to the General Contractor stating that there are delays in other work. You are now going on record that any delays will affect your work, implying that there will be extra costs involved.)

LETTER No. 23   Response to General Contractor's letter that the subcontractor does not have sufficient manpower on the job that may create delays

(*Note:* This is a tricky letter to respond to and needs a great deal of thought. If, in fact, there *is* sufficient manpower on the site, the General Contractor may be looking for a scapegoat and singling out your company as the culprit. Or maybe they are correct and more manpower is required as soon as possible to avoid further problems in maintaining the schedule.

Before responding, walk the site with your foreman and assess all facets of your work to determine whether the General Contractor is correct or incorrect. Then write the letter. Try to place the ball in their court and get them to explain why they are of the opinion that more manpower is required; this may give you some clue to their thinking and allow you more insight into properly responding to their charge. But one thing is certain, you must respond and respond quickly.)

Dear Mr. General Contractor,   re: Project "X"

We have received your (date) letter advising us that we have insufficient manpower to maintain your schedule requirements. After a careful review of our manpower requirements on (date) we find that "X" crews of workers, plus "Y" foreman are able to meet the schedule that was presented at the (date) job meeting.

We would appreciate your analysis of the current manpower and which operations are in question. Upon receipt of that information we will once again evaluate our on-site manpower commitments and report back to you.

Very truly yours,

Harry Subcontractor

LETTER No. 24   Request for payment of materials/equipment stored off site

(*Note:* First read your contract to determine whether payment for materials/equipment stored off-site is permissible. If it is, your letter will be rather simple; if it is *not* you may still be able to request payment, but the form of your letter must include a *compelling reason* why such payment should be honored.

If contract allows for payment

Dear Mr. General Contractor,   re: Project "X"

In accordance with Paragraph (article) of our subcontract agreement, we will be requesting payment for the off-site storage of (material/equipment) on our next Application for Payment. This equipment/material is currently stored at Santini Brothers warehouse, 555 Canal Street, Brooklyn, New York.

This Application for Payment will be accompanied by certification of storage in this bonded warehouse and the required insurance certificates. Each piece of equipment stored at (bonded warehouse) has been marked with the project name and address and other identifying marking required by Specification Section (??).

Very truly yours,

Sam Subcontractor

If contract does not allow for payment

Dear Mr. General Contractor,   re: Project "X"

Although the subcontract agreement does not permit payment for the off-site storage of materials and equipment, we are requesting that you consider payment for (equipment/material). Our ability to order and receive this (equipment/material) well in advance of the date when it is actually needed on-site will accelerate the installation of (whatever the work is) and should also assist (other trades) in completing their work more rapidly.

Since there is insufficient room for storage on-site of (materials/ equipment) and there is the potential for damage to the (equipment/material) if stored on-site, in the best interests of the job, we are requesting that you honor our request to requisition for this (material/equipment) stored off-site when the proper documentation accompanies our Application for Payment.

Very truly yours,

Alice Subcontractor

(*Note:* The phrase *in the best interests of the job* is important to add because in many cases, it *is* in the best interests of the project.)

LETTER No. 25   Request to have architect/engineer inspect work and accept same

(*Note:* Once again, refer to the appropriate section of the subcontract agreement and the contract specifications pertaining to inspections and sign-offs by the architect and engineer. These may occur at different times, depending upon the trades involved; but guarantees/warranties will generally commence with architect/engineer sign-offs and maintenance may shift from the subcontractor to the owner at that time.)

Dear Mr. General Contractor,   re: Project "X"

On (date) we completed the installation of (whatever). We wish to schedule an inspection by the architect (engineer) for the purpose of having them accept the installation in accordance with the provisions of Specification Section (X, Y).

Very truly yours,

Orlando Subcontractor

If there is no response, send another letter. If there is *still* no response refer back to Letter 21   The General Contractor No Response type letter and use that format—"If we don't have a response by (date) we will interpret that nonresponse as acceptance of our (installation)."

LETTER No. 26   Letter to General Contractor requesting copy of his or her bond and intent to notify bonding company of potential default on the bond

(*Note:* Merely requesting a copy of a General Contractor's bond when he or she has delayed payment for a considerable length of time and offer no legitimate reason for doing so may be sufficient to break this log jam. If late or nonpayment continues and the General Contractor offers no acceptable reason why this (these) payment(s) are being withheld, send a letter to the bonding company!)

Letter to General Contractor

Dear Mr. General Contractor,   re: Project "X"

In accordance with the provisions of (subcontract agreement or specification section ("X" or both—whichever applies), we are requesting a copy of your payment and performance bonds for the above referenced project.

Very truly yours,

Alex Subcontractor

Letter to bonding company

Dear Mr. Bonding Company,   re: Payment and Performance
Bond Nos.
Project: "X"

(Now you must state the facts relating to your request to "call the bond." Prepare a copy of the subcontract agreement that sets forth payment terms; include a history of when applications for payments were made and when they were received by the General Contractor. State facts regarding the current overdue payment and your company's efforts to collect this payment.)

All of this will be incorporated in the following letter to the bonding company:

"By copy of this letter we are requesting the terms and conditions of the Payment and Performance bond No. (insert number of bond, if known) be evoked so that we may receive payment for our Application for Payment

No. (?) submitted on (date), in the amount of ($_____). This payment is currently (X) days/weeks/months past due as of this date."

The following is included for your information and review:

1. Copy of subcontract agreement with (General Contractor).
2. Copies of previous and current requisitions.
3. Synopsis of application of payments submitted to (General Contractor) and dates when payments were received.
4. Copies of all correspondence and telephone calls made to (General Contractor) requesting payment on this past-due requisition.

We would appreciate your confirmation of receipt of this letter.

Very truly yours,

Anxious subcontractor

cc: Mr. General Contractor

(This will start a chain of events whereby the bonding company will contact the General Contractor to inquire whether there are legitimate reasons for the withholding of funds and they will attempt to resolve these payment issues. Don't expect an immediate response from the bonding company, but you can usually count on a call from the General Contractor who may be somewhat irate that you sent that letter to the bonding company: Of course, they will conveniently forget about *your repeated* telephone calls and letters to their accounting department requesting payment.)

LETTER No. 27   Letter to General Contractor advising him or her that subcontractor has encountered unforeseen conditions, uncovered work not indicated in the contract documents, or encountered "differing conditions"

(*Note:* These kinds of occurrences are generally associated with renovation or rehabilitation work, or site work—that is a subject all its own!)

Letter advising General Contractor of differing / concealed conditions uncovered during a Rehab / Renovation Project

Dear Mr. General Contractor,   re: Project "X"

During the demolition of (area in building) the conditions shown on the drawings (enumerate drawings and their date of issue); (indicate those conditions that were to have been anticipated—such as a masonry bearing wall) are at variance with the conditions actually uncovered. A terra-cotta wall was uncovered in this area and was determined by your project manager to be deteriorated to the point where it has no structural integrity. We have ceased work in this area until such time as you provide instructions on how to proceed.

(Once drawing/sketch/written instruction is received, submit a proposed change order, if additional costs are involved.)

Very truly yours,

Emil Subcontractor

Note: Many public agencies issuing contracts containing unit prices often allow a contractor to request a change in his or her unit prices if the actual quantities of work involved exceed 20–30%. This same interpretation is often used in the private sector as well. When "actual" conditions exceed "estimated" by a substantial amount—20–30%, the contractor may consider requesting an extra since *actual conditions* differ *substantially* from those estimated (assuming that the estimate has been prepared accurately. This may be true even when the contract stipulates that the site work is unclassified.)

Dear Mr. General Contractor,   re: Project "X"

During excavation at (location by grid line or other such designation) we uncovered soils unsuitable as defined by (geotechnical engineer) and were directed to remove them to elevation (X?) and replace all unsuitable soils with structural fill.

Test borings (include boring number) do not indicate the presence of unsuitable soils in the area where they were uncovered. We have engaged a licensed surveyor to prepare profiles of the area to substantiate our claim for additional costs and will submit our proposed change order when these documents have been received and reviewed.

(*Note:* If actual quantities exceed the estimate by a substantial percentage and:

1. Unit costs for this work, if included in the contract, may be cause to request an increase in the unit costs for this additional work.
2. If this is an unclassified site, these additional quantities may be the documentation required to substantiate a "differing conditions" contract change and support an extra cost for this work.)

LETTER No. 28   Letter to General Contractor stating that due to delay in obtaining architect/engineer certification of substantial completion, equipment, material warranties/guarantees will expire prematurely

(*Note:* Various manufacturers of equipment and materials allow time for product installation and start-up period before their warranties/guarantees become effective. Product/equipment warranties, per most construction contracts, commence upon acceptance by the architect/engineer or, in some cases, the owner. These acceptances should occur shortly before, during, or shortly after the architect issues his or her Certificate of Substantial Completion [refer to Article 9 of A.I.A. Document A210]. If a piece of equipment or product has been installed and is functioning properly for quite some time and the architect/engineer has been remiss in issuing his or her Certificate of Substantial Completion, the manufacturer's warranty/guarantee period may have already commenced—which means that the one (1) year standard guarantee has been activated and this particular warranty/guarantee will expire prior to the one-year period required by the contract. If that material/equipment fails, the subcontractor may be held responsible for repairs/replacement that are not reimbursable by the manufacturer.)

Dear Mr. General Contractor,   re: Project "X"

We wish to advise you that (product/material/equipment) has been installed in (project) and has been functioning properly since (date). This date can be substantiated by referring to Job Meeting Minutes No. (or whatever other documentation you can provide). To date we have not received formal acceptance of (product/material/equipment) even though we have repeatedly requested architect/engineer inspections and sign-offs.

We have been advised by (the manufacturer) that the one (1) year (or whatever period) of the warranty/guarantee had commenced effective (date) and this warranty/guarantee will expire on (date).

If you wish to extend the warranty/guarantee beyond that period please advise and we will submit these additional costs when received from the manufacturer.

Very truly yours,

Audrey Subcontractor

LETTER No. 29   Letter to General Contractor disputing back charges

(*Note:* Some back charges levied by General Contractors are legitimate and some are not. Whenever a back charge has been issued and your company is of the opinion that it is not justified, respond immediately. Remember the General Contractor has the power to withhold monies for back charges until convinced otherwise. One of the more common back charges involves cleaning and unless performed in accordance with the contract will produce back charges. But some General Contractors do not deal with this matter fairly and equitably!)

Dear Mr. General Contractor,   re: Project "X"

On (date) we received notification (or back charge change order) indicating that we would be charged for cleaning performed by your company.

We do not accept this back charge inasmuch as we have cleaned our debris on a weekly basis as required by the contract. We were never advised in advance of any such charges, and according to Article (X) in our subcontract agreement your office is to provide us with written notification (X) hours notice prior to proceeding with such action.

We would appreciate meeting with Mr. (Project Manager) at the job site as soon as possible to review the circumstances surrounding this back charge and resolve this issue promptly.

Very truly yours,

Leonard Subcontractor

(If the General Contractor has history of issuing cleaning back charges on a whim, bring a camera to the site and photograph the areas where it was your responsibility to clean. A camera with a time and date stamp is preferable. If other subcontractors have co-mingled their debris with yours, take closeups that could positively identify their debris.

If the back charge was for other reasons, review your subcontract agreement for any provisions that might have required the General Contractor to give advance notice prior to issuance of such a back charge. To refute any back charge you must have proof that it is unjustified. If not try to negotiate a settlement quickly and try not to make the same mistake any more—don't let these types of disputes linger!)

LETTER No. 30   Letter of Intent

(*Note:* A Letter of Intent should contain the following elements as a minimum:)

1. Specific work to be performed.
2. Cost of the work including provisions for fees.
3. Time frame in which work is to be performed—start and completion date.
4. Any events, if at all, that are to take place after the Letter of Intent expires, i.e., a contract for additional scope will be issued.
5. Written agreement signed by both parties.

(Upon receiving a Letter of Intent from the General Contractor and if it contains all of the above to the subcontractor's satisfaction, sign it and return—keeping one copy. But if it doesn't contain all acceptable conditions, respond accordingly.)

Dear Mr. General Contractor,   re: Project "X"

We have received your Letter of Intent, dated March 15, 1999 and we are in agreement with all provisions except the definition of "cost." As discussed, we are assigning Mr. Project Manager to this project and will be including $500.00 per week for project management costs until such time as the Letter of Intent expires. Please include this provision in an amendment to the Letter of Intent and we will execute both copies, returning one and keeping the other for our files.

Very truly yours,

Sidney M. Levy

A

OSHA REGULATIONS
(OSHA 2202-1995 Revised)
IN CONDENSED FORM

The OSHA regulations set forth below are in condensed form. The full version of each of these condensed topics are to be found in the references to the specific sections so noted alongside each topic and are to be found in Title 29 of the Code of Federal Regulations (CFR), Part 1926. The complete OSHA CFR Part 1926 should be referred to for a complete understanding of each topic listed below.

On February 6, 1995, OSHA enacted a new scaffolding safety rule. These new regulations became effective as of November 29, 1996 but were immediately challenged by the industry. OSHA agreed to revise them in the face of so much industry criticism, but as of this writing, no revisions have been forthcoming.

ABRASIVE GRINDING

All abrasive wheel bench and stand grinders shall be provided with safety guards that cover the spindle ends, nut and flange projections, and are strong enough to withstand the effects of a bursting wheel. 1926.303(b)(1) & (c)(1)

An adjustable work rest of rigid construction shall be used on floor and bench-mounted grinders, with the work rest kept adjusted to a clearance not to exceed ⅛ inch (o. 3175 cm) between the work rest and the surface of the wheel. 1926.303(c)(2)

All abrasive wheels shall be closely inspected and ring tested before mounted to ensure that they are free from cracks or other defects. 1926.303(c)(7)

ACCESS TO MEDICAL AND EXPOSURE RECORDS

Each employer shall permit employees, their designation representatives, and OSHA direct access to employer-maintained exposure and medical records. The standard limits access only to those employees who are, have been (including former employees), or will be exposed to toxic substances or harmful physical agents. 1910.26.33(a) & .33(b)(3)

Each employer must preserve and maintain accurate medical and exposure records for each employee. Exposure records and data analyses based on them are to be kept for 30 years. Medical records are to be kept for at least the duration of employment plus 30 years. Background data for exposure records such as laboratory reports and worksheets need to be kept for only 1 year. Records of employees who have worked for less than 1 year need not be retained after employment, but the employer must provide these records to the employee upon termination of employment. First-aid records of one-time treatment need not be retained for any specified period. 1926.33(d)(1)

ACCIDENT RECORD KEEPING AND REPORTING REQUIREMENTS

Each employer shall maintain in each establishment a log and summary (OSHA Form No. 200 or equivalent) of all recordable injuries and illnesses (resulting in a fatality, hospitalization, lost workdays, medical treatment, job transfer or termination, or loss of consciousness) for that establishment, and enter each recordable event no later than 6 working days after receiving the information. Where the complete log and summary records are maintained at a place other than the establishment, a copy of the log that reflects the injury and illnesses experience of the establishment complete and current to a date within 45 calendar days must be available at the original site. 1904.2(a) & (b)(2)

In addition to the log of occupational injuries and illnesses, each employer shall have available for inspection at each establishment within 6 working days after notification of a recordable case, a supplemental record (OSHA Form No. 101 or equivalent) for each occupational injury or illness for that establishment. 1904.4

Each employer shall post an annual summary of occupational injuries and illnesses for each establishment, compiled from the collected OSHA Form No. 200, which includes the year's totals, calendar year covered, company name, establishment name and address, certification signature, title, and date. An OSHA Form No. 200 shall be used in presenting the summary. The summary shall be posted by February 1 of each year and shall remain in place until March 1 of the same year. 1904.5(a) & (d)(1)

The log and summary, the supplementary record, and the annual summary shall be retained in each establishment for 5 years following the end of the year to which they relate. Records shall be made available, as authorized, upon request. 1904.6 & 7(a)&(b)

Within 8 hours after its occurrence, an employment accident that is fatal to one or more employees or that results in the hospitalization of 3 or more employees shall be reported by the employer, either orally or in writing, to the nearest OSHA Area Director. 1904.8

AIR TOOLS

Pneumatic power tools shall be secured to the hose in a positive manner to prevent disconnection. 1926.302(b)(1). Safety clips or retainers shall be securely installed and maintained on pneumatic impact tools to prevent attachments from being accidentally expelled. 1926.302(b)(2)

The manufacturer's safe operating pressure for all fittings shall not be exceeded. 1926.302(b)(5)

All hoses exceeding 1/2 inch (1.27 cm) inside diameter shall have a safety device at the source of supply or branch line to reduce pressure in case of hose failure. 1926.302(b)(7)

ASBESTOS

Each employer who has a workplace or work operation where exposure monitoring is required must perform monitoring to determine accurately the airborne concentrations of asbestos to which employees may be exposed. 1926.1101(f)(1)(i)

Employers also must ensure that no employee is exposed to an airborne concentration of asbestos in excess of 0.1f/cc as an 8-hours time-weighted average (TWA). 1926.1101(c)(1)

In addition, employers must ensure that no employee is exposed to an airborne concentration of asbestos in excess of 1 f/cc as averaged over a sampling period of 30 minutes. 1926.1101(c)(2)

Respirators must be used during (1) all Class 1 asbestos jobs; (2) all Class II work where an asbestos-containing material is not removed substantially intact; (3) all Class II and III work not using wet methods; (4) all Class II and III work without a negative exposure assessment; (5) all Class III jobs where thermal system insulation or surfacing asbestos-containing or presumed asbestos-containing material is cut, abraded, or broken; (6) all Class IV work within a regulated area where respirators are required; (7) all work where employees are exposed above the PEL or STEL; and (8) in emergencies. 1926.1101(h)(1)(i) through (viii)

The employer must provide and require the use of protective clothing—such as coveralls or similar whole-body clothing, head coverings, gloves, and foot coverings for:

- any employee exposed to airborne asbestos exceeding the PEL or STEL
- work without a negative exposure assessment, or
- any employee performing Class I work involving the removal of over 25 linear or 10 square feet (10 square meters) of thermal system insulation or surfacing asbestos-containing or presumed asbestos-containing materials. 1926.1101(i)(1)

The employer must provide a medical surveillance program for all employees who for a combined total of 30 or more days per year engage in Class I, II, or III work or are exposed at or above the PEL or STEL; or who wear negative-pressure repsirators. 1926.1101(m)(1)(i)

BELT SANDING MACHINES

Belt sanding machines shall be provided with guards at each nip point where the sanding belts run onto a pulley. 1926.304(f) The unused run of the sanding belt shall be guarded against accidental contact. 1926.304(f)

CHAINS   (See Wire Ropes, Chains, and Hooks)

COMPRESSED AIR, Use of

Compressed air used for cleaning purposes shall be reduced to less than 30 pounds per square inch (psi)(207 KPa) and then only with effective chip guarding and personal protective equipment. 1926.302(b)(4) This requirement does not apply to concrete form, mill scale, and similar cleaning operations. 1926.302(b)(4)

COMPRESSED GAS CYLINDERS

Valve protection caps shall be in place and secured when compressed gas cylinders are transported, moved, or stored. 1926.350(a)(1) Cylinder valves shall be closed when work is finished and when cylinders are empty or are moved. 1926.350(a)(8)

Compressed gas cylinders shall be secured in an upright position at all times, except if necessary for short periods of time when cylinders are actually being hoisted or carried. 1926.350(a)(9)

Cylinders shall be kept far enough away from the actual welding or cutting operations so that sparks, hot slag, or flame will not reach them. Cylinders shall be placed where they cannot become part of an electrical circuit. 1926.350(b)(1)&(2)

Oxygen and fuel gas regulators shall be in proper working order while in use. 1926.350(h)

For additional details not covered in the subpart, applicable, technical portions of American National Standards Institute (ANSI)Z49.1-1967, "Safety in Welding and Cutting," shall apply. 1926.350(j)

CONFINED SPACES

All employees required to enter into confined or enclosed spaces must be instructed as to the nature of the hazards involved, the necessary precautions to be taken, and in the use of required protective and emergency equipment. The employer shall comply with specific regulations that apply to work in dangerous or potentially dangerous areas. Confined or enclosed spaces include, but are not limited to, storage tanks, process vessels, binds, boilers, ventilation or exhaust ducts, sewers, underground utility vaults, tunnels, pipelines, and open top spaces more than 4 feet deep (1.2192 meters) such as pit tubs, vaults, and vessels. 1926.21(b)(i)and (ii)

CONCRETE AND MASONRY
CONSTRUCTION

No construction loads shall be placed on a concrete structure or portion of a concrete structure unless the employer determines, based on information received from a person who is qualified in structural design, that the structure or portion of the structure is capable of supporting the loads. 1926.701(a)

All protruding reinforced steel onto and into which employees could fall shall be guarded to eliminate the hazard of impalement. 1926.701(b)

No employee shall be permitted to work under concrete buckets while buckets are being elevated or lowered into position. 1926.701(e)(1)

To the extent practical, elevated concrete buckets shall be routed so that no employee or the fewest number of employees is exposed to the hazards associated with falling buckets. 1926.701(e)(2)

Formwork shall be designed, fabricated, erected, supported, braced, and maintained so that it is capable of supporting without failure all vertical and lateral loads that may reasonably be anticipated to be applied to that formwork. 1926.703(a)(1)

Forms and shores (except those used for slabs on grade and slip forms) shall not be removed until the employer determines that the concrete has gained sufficient strength to support its weight and superimposed loads. Such determination shall be based on compliance with one of the following:

- The plans and specifications stipulate conditions for removal of forms and shores, and such conditions have been followed, or:

- The concrete has been properly tested with an appropriate ASTM standard test method designed to indicate that the concrete has gained sufficient strength to support its weight and superimposed loads. (ASTM, 1916 Race St., Phila., PA 19103 (215)299-5400. 1926.703(e)(1)(i)&(ii)

A limited access zone shall be established whenever a masonry wall is being constructed. The limited access zone shall conform to the following:

- The limited access zone shall be established prior to the start of construction of the wall.

- The limited access zone shall be equal to the height of the wall to be constructed plus 4 feet (1.2192 meters) and shall run the entire length of the wall.

- The limited access zone shall be established on the side of the wall that will be unscaffolded.

- The limited access zone shall be established to entry by employees actively engaged in constructing the wall. No other employees shall be permitted to enter the zone.

- The limited access zone shall remain in place until the wall is adequately supported to prevent overturning and to prevent collapse; where the height of a wall is more that 8 feet (2.4384 meters), the limited access zone shall remain in place until the requirements of paragraph(b) of this section have been met. 1926.706(a)(1)thru(5)

All masonry walls more than 8 feet (2.4384 meters) in height shall be adequately braced to prevent overturning and to prevent collapse unless the wall is adequately supported so that it will not overturn or collapse. The bracing shall remain in place until permanent supporting elements of the structure are in place. 1926.706(b)

Lift-slab operations shall be designed and planned by a registered professional engineer who has experience in lift-slab construction. Such plans and designs shall be implemented by the employer and shall include detailed instructions and sketches indicating the pre-scribed method of erection. 1926.705(a)

Jacking equipment shall be capable of supporting at least $2\frac{1}{2}$ times the load being lifted during jacking operations and the equipment shall not be overloaded. 1926.705(d)

No employee, except those essential to the jacking operation, shall be permitted in the building/structure while any jacking operation is taking place unless the building/structure has been reinforced suffi-ciently to ensure its integrity during erection. 1926.705(k)(1)

Equipment shall be designed and installed so that the lifting rods can-not slip out of position or the employer shall institute other measures, such as the use of locking or blocking devices, which will provide positive connection between the lifting rods and attachments and will prevent components from disengaging during lifting operations. 1926, 705(p)

CRANES AND DERRICKS

The employer shall comply with the manufacturer's specifications and limitations. 1926.550(a)(1)

Rated load capacities, recommended operating speeds, and special hazard warnings or instructions shall be conspicuously posted on all equipment. Instructions or warnings shall be visible from the opera-tor's station. 1926.550(a)(2)

Equipment shall be inspected by a competent person before each use and during use, and all deficiencies corrected before further use. 1926.550(a)(5)

Accessible areas within the swing radius of the rear of the rotating superstructure shall be properly barricaded to prevent employees from being struck or crushed by the crane. 1926.550(a)(9)

Except where electrical distribution and transmission lines have been de-energized and visibly grounded at point of work, or where insulating barriers not a part of an attachment to the equipment or machinery have been erected to prevent physical contact with the lines, no part of a crane or its load shall be operated within 10 feet (3.048 meters) of a line rated 50 kilovolts (kV) or below; 10 feet (3.048 meters) plus 0.4 inches (1.016 cm) for each kV over 50 kV for lines rated over 50kV, or twice the length of the line insulator, but never less than 10 feet (3.048 meters). 1926.550(a)(19)

An annual inspection of the hoisting equipment shall be made by a competent person. Records shall be kept of the dates and results of each inspection. 1926.550(a)(6)

All crawler, truck, or locomotive cranes in use shall meet the requirements as prescribed in the ANSI B30.5-1968, Safety Code for

Crawler, Locomotive and Truck Cranes. ANSI, 11 West 42d Street, N.Y. , N.Y. 10036; (212)642-4900. 1926.550(b)(2)

The use of a crane or derrick to hoist employees on a personnel platform is prohibited, except when the erection, use, and dismantling of a conventional means of reaching the worksite—such as a personnel hoist, ladder, stairway, aerial lift, elevating work platform or scaffold—would be more hazardous or is not possible because of structural design or worksite conditions. Where a decision is reached that this is the case, then 29 CRF 1926.550(g) shall be reviewed and complied with. 1926.550(g)(2)

DISPOSAL CHUTES

Whenever materials are dropped more than 20 feet (6.096 meters) to any exterior point of a building, an enclosed chute shall be used. 1926.252(a)

When debris is dropped through holes in the floor without the use of chutes, that area where the material is dropped shall be enclosed with barricades not less than 42 inches high (106.68 cm) and not less than 6 feet (1.8288 meters) back from the projected edges of the opening above. Warning signs of the hazard of falling material shall be posted at each level. 1926.252(b)

DRINKING WATER

An adequate supply of potable water shall be provided in all places of employment. 1926.51(a)(1)

Portable drinking water containers shall be capable of being tightly closed and equipped with a tap. 1926.51(a)(2)

Using a common drinking cup is prohibited. 1926.51(a)(4)

Where single service cups (to be used but once) are supplied, both a sanitary container for unused cups and a receptacle for used cups shall be provided. 1926.51(a)(5)

ELECTRICAL INSTALLATIONS

Sections 1926.402 through 1926.408 contain installation safety requirements for electrical equipment and installations used to provide electric power and light at the job site. These sections apply to installations, both temporary and permanent, used on the job site; but these sections do not apply to existing permanent installations that were in place before the construction activity commenced. 1926.402(a)

Employers must provide either ground-fault circuit interrupters (GFCIs) or an assured equipment grounding conductor program to protect employees from ground-fault hazards at construction sites. The two options are detailed below.

(1) All 120 volt, single-phase, 15- and 20-ampere receptacles that are not part of the permanent wiring must be protected by GFCIs. Receptacles on smaller generators are exempt under certain conditions.

(2) An assured equipment grounding conductor program covering extension cords, receptacles, and cord-and plug connected equipment must be implemented. The program must include the following:

- A written description of the program.
- At least one competent person to implement the program.
- Daily visual inspections of extension cords and cord-and-plug connected equipment for defects. Equipment found damaged or defective shall not be used until repaired.
- Continuity tests of the equipment grounding conductors or receptacles, extension cords, and cord-and-plug connected equipment. These tests must generally be made every three months.
- Paragraphs (f)(1) through (f)(11) of this standard contain grounding requirements for systems, circuits, and equipment. 1926.404(b)(1)(i) thru (iii)(E)

Lamps for general illumination must be protected from breakage and metal shell sockets must be grounded. 1926.405(a)(2)(ii)(E)

Temporary lights must not be suspended by their cords unless they are so designed. 1926.405(a)(2)(ii)(F)

Portable lighting used in wet or conductive locations such as tanks or boilers must be operated at no more than 12 volts or must be protected by GFCIs. 1926.405(a)(2)(ii)(G)

Extension cords must be of the 3-wire type. Extension cords and flexible cords used with temporary and portable lights must be designed for hard or extra hard usage (for example, types S, ST, and SO). 1926.405(a)(2)(ii)(j)

Listed, labeled, or certified equipment shall be installed and used in accordance with instructions included in the listing, labeling, or certification. 1926.403(b)(2)

ELECTRIC WORK PRACTICES

Employers must not allow employees to work near live parts of electrical circuits, unless the employees are protected by one of the following means:

- De-energizing and grounding the parts.

- Guarding the part by insulation.
- Any other effective means. 1926.416(a)(1)

In work areas where the exact location of underground electrical power lines are unknown, employees using jack hammers, bars, or other hand tools that may contact the lines must be protected by insulating gloves, aprons, or other protective clothing that will provide equivalent electrical protection. 1926.416(a)(2) & .95(a)

Barriers or other means of guarding must be used to ensure that work space for electrical equipment will not be used as a passageway during periods when energized parts of equipment are exposed. 1926.416(b)(1)

Worn or frayed electrical cords or cables must not be used. Extension cords must not be fastened with staples, hung from nails, or suspended by wire. 1926.416(e)(1)&(2)

Flexible cords must be connected to devices and fittings so the strain relief is provided that will prevent pull from being directly transmitted to joints or terminal screws. 1926.405(g)(2)(iv)

Equipment or circuits that are de-energized must be rendered inoperative and must have tags attached at all points where the equipment or circuits could be energized. 1926.417(b)

EXCAVATING AND TRENCHING

The estimated location of utility installations—such as sewer, telephone, fuel, electric, water lines, or any other underground installations that reasonably may be expected to be encountered during excavation work—shall be determined prior to opening an excavation. 1926.651(b)(1)

Utility companies or owners shall be contacted within established or customary local response times, advised of the proposed work, and asked to establish the location of the utility underground utility installations within 24 hours (unless a longer period is required by state or local law), or if the exact location of these installations cannot be established, the employer may proceed, provided the employer does so with caution, and provided detection equipment or other acceptable means to locate utility installations are used. 1926.651(b)(2)

When excavation operations approach the estimated location of underground installations, the exact location of the installations shall be determined by safe and acceptable means. While the excavation is open, underground installations shall be protected, supported, or removed, as necessary, to safeguard employees. 1926.651(b)(3)&(4)

Each employee in an excavation shall be protected from cave-ins by an adequate protective system except when:

- Excavations are made entirely in stable rock, or excavations are less than 5 feet (1.524 meters) in depth and examination of the ground by a competent person provides no indication of a potential cave-in. 1926.652(a)(1)(i)&(ii)

- Protective systems shall have the capacity to resist, without failure, all loads that are intended or could reasonably be expected to be applied or transmitted to the system. 1926.652(a)(2)

Employees shall be protected from excavated or other materials or equipment that could pose a hazard by falling or rolling into excavations. Protection shall be provided by placing and keeping such materials or equipment at least 2 feet (0.6096 meters) from the edge of excavations, or by the use of retaining devices that are sufficient to prevent materials or equipment from falling or rolling into excavations, or by a combination of both, if necessary. 1926.651(j)(2)

Daily inspections of excavation, the adjacent areas, and protective systems shall be made by a competent person for evidence of a situation that could result in possible cave-ins, indication of failure of protective systems, hazardous atmospheres, or other hazardous conditions. An inspection shall be conducted by the competent person prior to the start of work and as needed throughout the shift. Inspections shall also be made after every rainstorm or other hazard-increasing occurrence. These inspections are only required when employee exposure can be reasonably anticipated. 1926.651(k)(1)

Where a competent person finds evidence of a situation that could result in a possible cave-in, indications of failure of protective systems, hazardous atmospheres, or other hazardous conditions, exposed employees shall be removed from the hazardous area until the necessary precautions have been taken to ensure their safety. 1926.651(k)(2)

A stairway, ladder, ramp, or other safe means of egress shall be located in trench excavations that are 4 feet (1.2192 meters) or more in depth so as to require no more that 25 feet (7.62 meters) of lateral travel for employees. 1926.651(c)(2)

EXPLOSIVES AND BLASTING

Only authorized and qualified persons shall be permitted to handle and use explosives. 1926.900(a)

Explosives and related materials shall be stored in approved facilities required under the applicable provisions of the Bureau of Alcohol,

Tobacco, and Firearms regulations contained in 27 CFR part 55, Commerce in Explosives. 1926.904(a)

Smoking and open flames shall not be permitted within 50 feet (15.24 meters) of explosives and detonator storage magazines. 1926.904(c)

Procedures that permit safe and efficient loading shall be established before loading is started. 1926.905(a)

EYE AND FACE PROTECTION

Eye and face protection shall be provided when machines or operations present potential eye or face injury. 1926.102(a)(1)

Eye and face protective equipment shall meet the requirements of ANSI Z87.1-1968—Practice for Occupational and Educational Eye and Face Protection. 1926.102(a)(2)

Employees involved in welding operations shall be furnished with filter lenses or plates of at least proper shade number. 1926.102(b)(1)

Employees exposed to laser beams shall be furnished with suitable laser safety goggles that will protect for the specific wavelength of the laser and the optical density adequate for the energy involved. 1926.102(b)(2)

FALL PROTECTION   (See Floor Openings, Open Sides and Hatchways)

FIRE PROTECTION

A fire fighting program is to be followed throughout all phases of the construction and demolition work involved. It shall provide for effective fire fighting equipment to be available without delay, and designed to effectively meet all fire hazards as they occur. 1926.150(a)(1)

Fire fighting equipment shall be conspicuously located and readily accessible at all times, shall be periodically inspected and maintained in operation condition. 1926.150(a)(2)(3)&(4)

Carbon tetrachloride and other toxic vaporizing liquid fire extinguishers are prohibited. 1926.150(c)(1)(vii)

If the building includes the installation of automatic sprinkler protection, the installation shall closely follow the construction and be placed in service as soon as applicable laws permit, following completion of each story. 1926.150(d)(1)

A fire extinguisher, rated not less that 2A, shall be provided for each 3,000 square feet (278 square meters) of the protected building area, or major fraction thereof. Travel distance from any point of the protected area to the nearest fire extinguisher shall not exceed 100 feet (30.48 meter). 1926.150(c)(1)(i)

One or more fire extinguishers, rated not less than 2A, shall be provided on each floor. In multistory buildings, at least one fire extinguisher shall be located adjacent to stairway. 1926.150(c)(1)(iv)

The employer shall establish an alarm system at the work site so that employees and the local fire department can be alerted for an emergency. 1926.150(e)(1)

FLAGMEN

When signs, signals, and barricades do not provide necessary protection on or adjacent to a highway or street, flagmen or other appropriate traffic controls shall be provided. 1926.210(a)(1)

Flagmen shall be provided with and wear a red or orange warning garment while flagging. Warning garments worn at night shall be of reflectorized material. 1926.210(a)(4)

FLAMMABLE AND COMBUSTIBLE LIQUIDS

Only approved containers and portable tanks shall be used for storing and handling flammable and combustible liquids. 1926.152.(a)(1)

No more that 25 gallons (94.75 liters) of flammable or combustible liquids shall be stored in a room outside of an approved storage cabinet. No more than three storage cabinets may be located in a single storage area. 1926.152(b)(1),(2)&(3)

Inside storage rooms for flammable and combustible liquids shall be of fire-resistive construction, have self-closing fire doors at all openings, 4-inch (10.16-cm.) sills or depressed floors, a ventilation system that provides at least 6 air changes within the room each hour, and electrical wiring and equipment approved for Class 1, Division 1 locations. 1926.152(b)(4)

Storage in containers outside buildings shall not exceed 1,100 gallons (4,169 liters) in any one pile or area. The storage area shall be graded to divert possible spills away from buildings or other exposures, or shall be surrounded by a curb or dike. Storage areas shall be located at least 20 feet (6.096 meters) from any building and shall be free from weeds, debris, and other combustible materials not necessary to the storage. 1926.152(c)(1), (3), (4)&(5)

Flammable liquids shall be kept in closed containers when not actually in use. 1926.152(f)(1)

Conspicuous and legible signs prohibiting smoking shall be posted in service and refueling areas. 1926.152(g)(9)

FLOOR OPENINGS, OPEN SIDES, AND HATCHWAYS

Floor openings shall be guarded by a standard railing, toe boards, or cover. In general, the railing shall be provided on all exposed sides, except at entrances to stairways. 1926.501(b)(4)

Every open sides floor or platform, 6 feet (1.8288 meters) or more above adjacent floor or ground level, shall be guarded by a standard railing, or the equivalent, on all open sides except where there is entrance to a ramp, stairway, or fixed ladder. 1026.501(b)(1) and 1926.502(b) and (b)(13)

Each employee on ramps, runways, and other walkways shall be protected from falling 6 feet (1.8288) or more to lower levels by a guardrail system. 1926.501(b)(6)

When guardrail systems are used around holes that are used as points of access (such as ladderways), they shall be provided with a gate, or be so offset that a person cannot walk directly into the hole. 1926.502(b)(13)

Each employee on walking/working surfaces shall be protected from falling through holes (including skylights) more than 6 feet (1.8288 meters) above lower levels, by personnel fall arrest systems, covers, or guardrail systems erected around such holes. 1926.501(b)(4)

GASES, VAPORS, FUMES, DUSTS, and MISTS

Exposure to toxic gases, vapors, fumes, dusts, and mists at a concentration above those specifications in the Threshold Limit Values of Airborne Contaminants for 1970 of the American Conference of Government Industrial Hygienists (ACGIH), shall be avoided. ACGIH, 6500 Glemway Avenue, Bldg. D7, Cincinnati, OH 45211; (513)661-7881. 1926.55(a)

Administrative or engineering controls must be implemented whenever feasible to comply with TLVs. 1926.55(b)

When engineering and administrative controls are not feasible to achieve full compliance, protective equipment or other protective measures shall be used to keep the exposure of employees to air contaminants within the limits prescribed. Any equipment and technical measures used for this purpose must first be approved for each particular use by a competent industrial hygienist or other technically qualified person. Whenever respirators are used, their use shall comply with Paragraph 1926.103. 1926.55(b)

GENERAL DUTY CLAUSE

Hazardous conditions or practices not covered in an OSHA standard may be covered under Section 5(a)(1) of the Occupational Safety and Health Act of 1970 that states: "Each employer shall furnish to each of his employees employment and a place of employment which are free from recognized hazards that are causing or are likely to cause death or serious physical harm to his employees."

GENERAL SAFETY AND HEALTH REQUIREMENTS

The employer shall initiate and maintain such programs as may be necessary to provide for frequent and regular inspections of the job site, materials, and equipment by designated competent persons. 1926.20(b)(1)&(2)

The employer should avail himself of the safety and health training programs the Secretary provides. 1926.21(b)(1)

The employer shall instruct each employee in the recognition and avoidance of unsafe conditions and in the regulations applicable to his work environment to control or eliminate any hazards or other exposure to illness or injury. 1926.21(b)(2)

The use of any machinery, tool, material, or equipment that is not in compliance with any applicable requirement of Part 1926 is prohibited. 1926.20(b)(3)

The employer shall permit only those employees qualified by training or experience to operate equipment and machinery. 1926.20(b)(4)

The standards contained in this part shall apply with respect to employment performed in a workplace in a State, the District of Columbia, the Commonwealth of Puerto Rico, the Guam, Trust Territory of the Pacific Continental Shelf Lands Act, Johnson Island, and the Canal Zone. 1926.(c)

HAND TOOLS

Employers shall not issue or permit the use of unsafe hand tools. 1926.301(a)

Wrenches shall not be used when jaws are sprung to the point where slippage occurs. Impact tools shall be kept free of mushroomed heads. The wooden handles of tools shall be kept free of splinters or cracks and shall be kept tight in the tool. 1926.301(b)(c)&(d)

Electric power-operated tools shall either be approved double-insulated, or be properly grounded in accordance with subpart K of the standard. 1926.302(a)(1)

HAZARD COMMUNICATION

The purpose of this standard is to ensure that the hazards of all chemicals produced or imported are evaluated, and that information concerning their hazards is transmitted to employers and employees. This transmittal of information is to be accomplished by means of comprehensive hazard communication programs, which are to include container labeling and other forms of warning, material safety data sheets, and employee training. 1926.59(a)(1)

Employers shall develop, implement, and maintain at the workplace a written hazard communication program for their workplaces. Employers must inform their employees of the availability of the program, including the required list(s) of hazardous chemicals and material safety data sheets required. 1926.59(e)(1)(i)&(ii)

The employer shall ensure that each container of hazardous chemicals in the workplace is labeled, tagged, or marked with the identity of the hazardous chemical(s) contained therein; and must show hazard warnings appropriate for employee protection. 1926.59(f)(5)(i)&(ii)

Chemical manufacturers and importers shall obtain or develop a material safety data sheet for each hazardous chemical they produce or import. Employers shall have a material safety data sheet for each hazardous chemical they use. 1926.59(g)(1)

Employers shall provide employees with information and training on hazardous chemicals in their work area at the time of their initial assignment, and whenever a new hazard is introduced into their work area. Employers shall also provide employees with information on any operations in their work area where hazardous chemicals are present, and the location and availability of the written hazard communication program, including the required list(s) of hazardous chemicals and material safety data sheets required by the standard. 1926.59(h)(1)(i)thru(iii)

Employers who produce, use, or store hazardous chemicals at multiemployer workplaces shall additionally ensure that their hazard communication program includes the methods the employer will use to provide other employer(s) with a copy of the material safety data sheet for hazardous chemicals other employer(s)' employees may be exposed to while working; the methods the employer will use to inform other employer(s) of any precautionary measures for the protection of employees; and the methods the employer will use to inform the other employer(s) of the labeling system used in the workplace. 1926.59(e)(2)

HAZARDOUS WASTE OPERATIONS AND EMERGENCY RESPONSES

Unless the employer can demonstrate that the operation does not involve employee exposure or the reasonable possibility for employee exposure to safety or health hazards, he or she must do the following:

- Clean-up operations required by a governmental body, whether federal, state, local or other involving hazardous substances that are conducted at uncontrolled hazardous waste sites;

- Correct actions involving clean-up operations at sites covered by the Resource Conservation and Recovery Act of 1976 (RCRA) as amended (42U.S.C. 6901 et seq.);

- Voluntary clean-up operations at sites recognized by federal, state, local, or other governmental bodies as uncontrolled hazardous waste sites;

- Clean-up operations involving hazardous wastes that are conducted at treatment, storage, and disposal (TSD) facilities regulated by 40CFR parts 264 and 265 pursuant to RCRA; or by agencies under agreement with U.S.E.P.A. to implement RCRA regulations; and

- Ensure that emergency response operations are conducted for releases of, or substantial threats of releases of, hazardous substances without regard to the location of the hazard. 1926.65(a)(1)(i)thru(v)

HEAD PROTECTION

Head protective equipment (helmets) shall be worn in areas where there is a possible danger of head injuries from impact, flying or falling objects, electrical shock, and burns. 1926.100(a)

Helmets for protection against impact and penetration of falling and flying objects shall meet the requirements of ANSI Z89.1-1969. 1926.100(b)

Helmets for protection against electrical shock and burns shall meet the requirements of ANSI Z89.2-1971. 1926.100(c)

HEARING PROTECTION

Feasible engineering or administrative controls shall be utilized to protect employees against sound levels in excess of those shown in Table D-2. 1926.52(b)

When engineering or administrative controls fail to reduce sound levels within the limits of Table D-2, ear protective devices shall be provided and used. 1926.52(b)&.101(a)

In all cases where the sound levels exceed the values shown in Table D-2, a continuing, effective hearing conservation program shall be administered. 1926.52(d)(1)

Table D-2   Permissible Noise Exposures

Duration per day, hours:	Sound Level/dBA slow response
8	90
6	92
4	95
3	97
2	100
1 $\frac{1}{2}$	102
1	105
$\frac{1}{2}$	110
$\frac{1}{4}$ or less	115

1926.52(d)(1)

Exposure to impulsive or impact noise should not exceed 140dB peak sound pressure level. 1926.52(e)

Plain cotton is not an acceptable protective device. 1926.101(c)

HEATING DEVICES, TEMPORARY

Fresh air shall be supplied in sufficient quantities to maintain the health and safety of workers. 1926.154(a)(1)

Solid fuel salamanders are prohibited in buildings and on scaffolds. 1926.154(d)

HOISTS, MATERIALS, AND PERSONNEL

The employer shall comply with the manufacturer's specifications and limitations. 1926.552(a)(1)

Rated load capacities, recommended operating speeds, and special hazard warnings or instructions shall be posted on cars and platforms. 1926.552(a)(2)

Hoistway entrances of material hoists shall be protected by substantial full width gates or bars. 1926.552(b)(2)

Hoistway doors or gates of personnel hoist shall be no less than 6 feet 6 inches (1.812 meters) high and shall be protected with mechanical locks that cannot be operated from the landing side and that are accessible only to persons on the car. 1926.552(c)(4)

Overhead protective coverings shall be provided on the top of the hoist cage or platform. 1926.552(b)(3)&(c)(7)

All material hoists shall conform to the requirements of ANSI A10.5-1969 Safety Requirements for Material Hoists. 1926.552(b)(8)

HOOKS   (See Wire Ropes, Chains and Hooks)

HOUSEKEEPING

Form and scrap lumber with protruding nails and other debris shall be kept clear from all work areas. 1926.25(a)

Combustible scrap and debris shall be removed at regular intervals. 1926.25(b)

Containers shall be provided for collection and separation of all refuse. Covers shall be provided on containers used for flammable or harmful substances. 1926.25(c)

Wastes shall be disposed of at frequent intervals. 1926.25(c)

ILLUMINATION

Construction areas, ramps, runways, corridors, offices, shops, and storage areas shall be lighted to not less than the minimum illumination intensities listed in Table D-3 while any work is in progress.

Table D-3   Minimum Illumination Intensities in Footcandles.

Footcandles: Area of Operation
5. . . . . General construction area lighting.
3. . . . . General construction areas, concrete placement, excavation, waste areas, accessways, active storage areas, loading platforms, refueling, and field maintenance areas.
5. . . . . Indoor warehouses, corridors, hallways, and exitways.
5. . . . . Tunnels, shafts, and general underground work areas (Exception: minimum of 10 footcandles is required at tunnel and shaft heading during drilling, mucking, and scaling. Bureau of Mines approved light caps shall be acceptable for use in the tunnel heading.)
10. . . . . General construction plant and shops (e.g., batch plants, screening plants, mechanical and electrical equipment rooms, carpenter shops, rigging lofts and active store rooms, barracks or living quarters, locker or dressing rooms, mess halls, indoor toilets, and workrooms.
30. . . . . First-aid stations, infirmaries, and offices.
1926.56(a)

JOINTERS

Each hand-fed planner and jointed with a horizontal head shall be equipped with a cylindrical cutting head. The opening in the table shall be kept as small as possible. 1926.304(f)

Each hand-fed jointer with a horizontal cutting head shall have an automatic guard to cover the section of the head on the working side of the fence or cage. 1926.304(f)

A jointer guard shall automatically adjust itself to cover the unused portion of the head and shall remain in contact with the material at all times. 1926.304(f)

Each hand-fed jointer with horizontal cutting head shall have a guard to cover the section of the head back of the cage or fence. 1926.304(f)

LADDERS

Portable and fixed ladders with structural defects—such as broken or missing rungs, cleats or steps, broken or split rails, or corroded components—shall be withdrawn from service immediately tagging "DO NOT USE" or marking in a manner that identifies them as defective, or shall be blocked, such as with a plywood attachment that spans several rungs. Repairs must restore ladder to its original design criteria. 1926.1053(b)(16), (17)(i)thru(iii)&(8)

Portable nonself supporting ladders shall be placed on a substantial base, have clear access at top and bottom, and be placed at an angle so the horizontal distance from the top support to the foot of the ladder is approximately one-quarter of the working height of the ladder. Portable ladders used for access to an upper landing surface must extend a minimum of 3 feet (0.9144 meters) above the landing surface, or where not practical, be provided with grab rails and be secured against movement while in use. 1926.1053(b)(1)&(b)(5)(i)

Ladders must have nonconductive side rails if they are used where the worker or the ladder could contact energized electrical conductors or equipment. 1926.1053(b)(12)

Job-made ladders shall be constructed for their intended use. Cleats shall be uniformly spaced not less than 10 inches (25.4 cm) apart, nor more than 14 inches (35.56 cm) apart. 1926.1053(a)(3)(i)

A ladder (or stairway) must be provided at all work points of access where there is a break in elevation of 19 inches (48.26 cm) or more except if a suitable ramp, runway, embankment, or personnel hoist is provided to give safe access to all elevations. 1926.1051(a)

Wood job-made ladders with spliced side rails must be used at an angle where the horizontal distance is one-eighth the working length of the ladder.

- Fixed ladders must be used at a pitch no greater than 90 degrees from the horizontal, measured from the back side of the ladder.

- Ladders must be used only on stable and level surfaces unless secured to prevent accidental movement.

- Ladders must not be used on slippery surfaces unless secured or provided with slip-resistant feet to prevent accidental movement. Slip-resistant feet must not be used as a substitute for care in placing, lashing, or holding a ladder upon a slippery surface. 1926.1053(b)(5)(ii) thru (b)(7)

Employers must provide a training program for each employee using ladders and stairways. The program must enable each employee to recognize hazards related to ladders and stairways and to use proper procedures to minimize these hazards. For example, employers must ensure that each employee is trained by a competent person in the following areas, as applicable.

- The nature of fall hazards in the work area.

- The correct procedures for erecting, maintaining, and disassembling the fall protection systems to be used.

- The proper construction, use, placement, and care in handling of all stairways and ladders, and;

- The maximum intended load-carrying capacities of ladders used.

- In addition, retraining must be provided for each employee, as necessary, so that the employee maintains the understanding and knowledge acquired through compliance with the standard. 1926.1060(a)&(b)

LASERS

Only qualified and trained employees shall be assigned to install, adjust, and operate laser equipment. 1926.54(a)

Employees shall wear proper (antilaser) eye protection when working in areas where there is a potential exposure to direct or reflected laser light greater than 0.005 watts (5 milliwatts) 1926.54(c)

Beam shutters or caps shall be utilized, or the laser turned off, when laser transmission is not actually required. When the laser is left unattended for a substantial period of time—such as during lunch hour, overnight, or at a change of shifts—the laser shall be turned off. 1926.54(e)

Employees shall not be exposed to light intensities in excess of the following: direct starting—1 microwatt per square centimeter, incidental

observing—1 milliwatt per square centimeter diffused reflected light—
2 $\frac{1}{2}$ per square centimeter. 1926.54(j)(1), (2)&(3)

Employees shall not be exposed to microwave power densities in excess of 10 milliwatts per square centimeter. 1926.54(1)

LIQUIFIED PETROLEUM GAS

Each system shall have containers, valves, connectors, manifold valve assemblies, and regulators of an approved type. 1926.153(a)(1)

All cylinders shall meet DOT specifications. 1926.153(a)(2)

Every container and vaporizer shall be provided with one or more approved safety relief valves or devices. 1926.153(d)(1)

Containers shall be placed upright on firm foundations or otherwise firmly secured. 1926.153(g)&(h)(11)

Portable heaters shall be equipped with an approved automatic device to shut off the flow of gas in the event of flame failure. 1926.153(h)(8)

All cylinders shall be equipped with an excess flow valve to minimize the flow of gas in the event the fuel line becomes ruptured. 1926.153(i)(2)

Storage of liquefied petroleum gas within buildings is prohibited. 1926.153(i)

Storage locations shall have at least one approved portable fire extinguisher rated not less than 20-B. C. 1926.153(L)

MEDICAL SERVICES AND FIRST AID

The employer shall ensure the availability of medical personnel for advice and consultation on matters of occupational health. 1926.50(a)

When a medical facility is not reasonably accessible for the treatment of injured employees, a person trained to render first aid shall be available at the worksite. 1926.50(c)

First-aid supplies approved by the consulting physician shall be readily available. 1926.50(d)(1)

The telephone numbers of the physicians, hospitals, or ambulances shall be conspicuously posted. 1926. 50(f)

MOTOR VEHICLES AND MECHANIZED EQUIPMENT

All vehicles in use shall be checked at the beginning of each shift to ensure that all parts, equipment, and accessories that affect safe operation are in proper operating conditions and free from defects. All defects shall be corrected before the vehicle is placed in service. 1926.01(b)(14)

No employers shall use any vehicle, earthmoving, or compacting equipment having an obstructed view to the rear unless:

- The vehicle has a reverse signal alarm distinguishable from the surrounding noise level, or

- The vehicle is backed up only when an observer signals that it is safe to do so. 1926.601(b)(4)(i)&(ii) & 602(a)(9)(i)&(ii)

Heavy machinery, equipment, or parts thereof that are suspended or held aloft shall be substantially blocked to prevent falling or shifting before employees are permitted to work under or between them. 1926.600(a)(3)(i)

NOISE   (See Hearing Protection)

PERSONNEL PROTECTIVE EQUIPMENT

The employer is responsible for requiring the wearing of appropriate personnel protective equipment in all operations where there is an exposure to hazardous conditions or where the need is indicated for using such equipment to reduce the hazard to the employees. 1926.38(a) and 1926.95(a)thru(c)

Lifelines, safety belts, and lanyards shall be used only for employee safeguarding. 1926.502(d)(18)

Employees working over or near water, where the danger of drowning exists, shall be provided with U. S. Coast Guard-approved life jackets or buoyant work vests. 1926.106(a)

POWER-ACTUATED TOOLS

Only trained employees shall be allowed to operate power-actuated tools. 1926.302(e)(1)

All power-actuated tools shall be tested daily before use and all defects discovered before or during use shall be corrected. 1926.302(e)(2)&(3)

Tools shall not be loaded until immediately before use. Loaded tools shall not be left unattended. 1926.302(e)(5)&(6)

POWER TRANSMISSION AND DISTRIBUTION

Existing conditions shall be determined before starting work, by an inspection or a test. Such conditions shall include, but not be limited to, energized lines and equipment, condition of poles, and the location of circuits and equipment including power and communications, cable television, and fire alarm circuits. 1926.950(b)(1)

Electric equipment and lines shall be considered energized until determined otherwise by testing or until grounding. 1926.950(b)(2)&.954(a)

Operating voltage of equipment and lines shall be determined before working on or near energized parts. 1926.950(b)(3)

Rubber protective equipment shall comply with the provisions of the ANSI J6 series, and shall be visually inspected before use. 1926.951(a)(1)(i)&(ii)

POWER TRANSMISSION, MECHANICAL

Belts, gears, shafts, pulleys, sprockets, spindles, drums, flywheels, chains, and other reciprocating, rotating, or moving parts of equipment shall be guarded if such parts are exposed to contact by employees or otherwise constitute a hazard. 1926.307(a)(b)(c)(d)(e)(f)(h)(i) and (k)

Guarding shall meet the requirements of ANSI B15, 1-1953 (R 1958), Safety Code for Mechanical Power Transmission Apparatus. 1926.300(b)(2)

PROCESS SAFETY MANAGEMENT OF HIGHLY HAZARDOUS CHEMICALS

Employers shall develop a written plan of action regarding employee participation and consult with employees and their representatives on the conduct and development of process hazard analyses and on the development of the other elements of process safety management. 1926.64(c)(1)&(2)

The employer shall complete a compilation of written process safety information prior to conducting a process hazard analysis (PHA) 1926.64(d)

The employer shall perform a process hazard analysis appropriate to the complexity of the company's processes and shall identify, evaluate, and control the hazards involved in the process. 1926.64(e)(1)

The employer shall develop and implement written operating procedures that provide clear instructions for safely conducting activities involved in each covered process consistent with process safety information. 1926.64(f)(1)

Each employee presently involved in operating a process, and each employee before being involved in operating a newly assigned process, shall be trained in an overview of the process and in the operating procedures specified in paragraph (f) 1926.64(g)(1)

The employer, when selecting a contractor, shall obtain and evaluate information regarding the contract employer's safety performance and programs. 1926. (h)(2)(i)

The contract employer shall assure that each contract employee is trained in the work practices necessary to safely perform his/her job. 1926.64(h)(3)(i)

The employer shall perform a pre-start-up safety review for the new facilities and for modified facilities when the modification is significant enough to require a change in the process safety information. 1926.64(i)(1)

The employer shall establish and implement written procedures to maintain the ongoing integrity of process equipment. 1926.64(j)(2)

The employer shall establish and implement written procedures to manage changes to process chemicals, technology, equipment, and procedures, and changes to facilities that affect a covered process. 1926.64(L)(1)

RADIATION, IONIZING

Pertinent provisions of the Atomic Energy Commission's Standards for Protection Against Radiation (10 CFR Part 20) relating to protection against occupational radiation exposure shall apply. 1926.53(a)

Any activity that involves the use of radioactive materials or X-rays, whether or not under license from the Atomic Energy Commission, shall be performed by competent persons specially trained in the proper and safe operation of such equipment. 1926.53(b)

RAILINGS

A standard rail shall consist of a top rail, intermediate rail, toe board, and posts and shall have a vertical height of approximately 42 inches (106.68 cm) from the upper surfaces of the top rail to the floor or platform. 1926.502(b)(1)

The top rail of a railing shall be smooth-surfaced, with a strength to withstand at least 200 pounds (90 kilograms), the minimum requirement applied in any direction at any point on the top rail, with a minimum of deflection. The intermediate rail shall be approximately halfway between the top rail and the floor. 1926.50(b)(3)&(6)

A stair railing shall be of construction similar to a standard railing with a vertical height of 36 inches (76 cm) from the upper surface of the top rail to the surface of tread in line with the face of riser at forward edge of tread. 1926.1052(c)(3)(i)

RESPIRATORY PROTECTION

In emergencies, or when feasible engineering or administrative controls are not effective in controlling toxic substances, appropriate respiratory protective equipment shall be provided by the employer and shall be used. 1926.103(a)(1)

Respiratory protective devices shall be approved by the U.S. Bureau of Mines/National Institute for Occupational Safety and Health or acceptable to the U.S. Department of Labor for the specific contaminant to which the employee is exposed. 1926.103(a)(2)

Respiratory protective devices shall be appropriate for the hazardous material involved and the extent and nature of the work requirements and conditions. 1926.103(b)(2)

Employees required to use respiratory protective devices shall be thoroughly trained in their use. 1926.103(c)(1)

Respiratory protective equipment shall be inspected regularly and maintained in good condition. 1926.103(c)(2)

ROLLOVER PROTECTIVE STRUCTURES (ROPS)

Rollover protective structures (ROPS) apply to the following types of materials handling equipment: All rubber tired, self-propelled scrapers, rubber-tire front-end loaders, rubber-tired dozers, wheel-type agricultural and industrial tractors, crawler tractors, crawler type loaders, and motor graders, with or without attachments that are used in construction work. This requirement does not apply to side boom pipelaying tractors. 1926.1000(a)(1)

SAFETY NETS

Safety nets must be installed as close as practicable under the walking/working surface on which employees are working, but in no case more than 30 feet (9.1 meters) below such level. When nets are used on bridges, the potential fall area from the walking/working surface to the net shall be unobstructed. 1926.502(c)(1)

Safety nets and their installations must be capable of absorbing an impact force equal to that produced by the drop test. 1926.502(c)(4)

SAWS, BAND

All portions of band saw blades shall be enclosed or guarded, except for the working portion of the blade between the bottom of the guide rolls and the table. 1926.304(f)

Band saw wheels shall be fully encased. 1926.304(f)

SAWS, PORTABLE CIRCULAR

Portable, power-driven circular saws shall be equipped with guards above and below the base plate or shoe. The lower guard shall cover the saw to the depth of the teeth, except for the minimum arc required to allow proper retraction and contact with the work, and shall automatically return to the covering position when the blade is removed from the work. 1926.304(d)

SAWS, RADIAL

Radial saws shall have an upper guard that completely encloses the upper half of the saw blade. The sides of the lower exposed portion of the blade shall be guarded by a device that will automatically adjust to the thickness of and remain in contact with the material being cut. 1926.304(g)(1)

Radial saws used for ripping shall have nonkickback fingers or dogs. 1926.304(f)

Radial saws shall be installed so that the cutting head will return to the starting position when released by the operator. 1926.304(f)

SAWS, SWING OR SLIDING CUTOFF

All swing or sliding cutoff saws shall be provided with a hood that will completely enclose the upper half of the saw. 1926.304(f)

Limit stops shall be provided to prevent swing or sliding type cutoff saws from extending beyond the front or back edges of the table. 1926.304(f)

Each swing or sliding cutoff saw shall be provided with an effective device to return the saw automatically to the back of the table when released at any point of its travel. 1926.304(f)

Inverted sawing of sliding cutoff saws shall be provided with a hood that will cover the part of the saw that protrudes above the top of the table or material being cut. 1926.304(f)

SAWS, TABLE

Circular table saws shall have a hood over the portion of the saw above the table, so mounted that the hood will automatically adjust itself to the thickness of and remain in contact with the material being cut. 1926.304(h)(1)

Circular table saws shall have a spreader aligned with the blade, spaced no more than $\frac{1}{2}$ inch (1.27 cm) behind the largest blade mounted in the saw. This provision does not apply when grooving, dadoing, or rabbiting. 1926.304(f)

Circular table saws used for ripping shall have nonkickback fingers or dogs. 1926.304(f)

Feeder attachments shall have the feed rolls or other moving parts covered or guarded so as to protect the operator from hazardous points. 1926.304(c)

SCAFFOLDS (General)

Scaffolds shall be erected on sound, rigid footing, capable of carrying the maximum intended load without settling or displacement. 1926.451(a)(2)

Scaffolds and their components shall be capable of supporting, without failure, at least 4 times the maximum intended load. 1926.451(a)(7)

Guardrails and toe boards shall be installed on all open sides and ends of platforms more than 10 feet (3.048 meters) above the ground or floor, except needle beam scaffolds and floats where other means of fall protection is provided. Scaffolds 4 feet (1.2192 meters) to 10 feet (3.048 meters) in height, having a minimum dimension in either direction of less that 45 inches (114.30 cm), shall have standard guardrails installed on all open sides and ends of the platform. 1926.451(a)(4)

There shall be a screen with maximum $\frac{1}{2}$ inch (1.27 cm) openings between the toe board and the guardrail, where persons are required to work or pass under the scaffold. 1926.451(a)(6)

All planking shall be Scaffold Grade or equivalent as recognized by approved rules for the species of wood used. 1926.451(a)(10)

The maximum permissible spans for a 2 × 10 inch (5.08 × 25.4 cm) or wide planks are shown in the following table:

	Full thickness undressed lumber			Normal thickness lumber	
Working load (pounds per square foot)	25	50	75	25	50
Permissible span	10	8	6	8	6

The maximum permissible span for the 1 $\frac{1}{4}$ × 9 inch (66.04 × 22.86 cm) or wider plank of full thickness is 4 feet (1.2192 meters), with medium loading of 50 pounds per square feet (4.5 kilograms per square meter) 1926.451(a)(11)

Scaffold planking shall be overlapped a minimum of 12 inches (30.48 cm) or secured from movement. 1926.451(a)(12)

Scaffold planks shall extend over their end supports not less than 6 inches (15.24 cm) nor more than 12 inches (30.48 cm) 1926.451(a)(14)

All scaffolding and accessories shall have any defective parts immediately replaced or repaired. 1926.451(a)(8)

An access ladder or equivalent safe access shall be provided. 1926.451(a)(13)

SCAFFOLDS (MOBILE)

Platforms shall be tightly planked for the full width of the scaffold except for necessary entrance openings. Platforms shall be secured in place. 1926.451(e)(4)

Guardrails made of lumber—not less than 2 × 4inches (5.08 × 10.16 cm)(or other material providing equivalent protection), approximately 42 inches high (106.68 cm), with a midrails of 1 × 6-inch (2.54 × 15.24-cm) lumber (or other material providing equivalent protection), and toe boards—shall be installed at all open sides and ends of all scaffolds more than 10 feet (3.048 meters) above the ground or floor. Toe boards shall be a minimum of 4 inches (10.16 cm) in height. Where persons are required to work or pass under the scaffold, wire mesh shall be installed between the toe board and the guardrails, extending along the entire opening, consisting of No. 18 gauge U.S. Standard wire 1/2-inch (1.27-cm) mesh, or the equivalent. 1926.451(e)(10)&(a)(6)

SCAFFOLDS (SWINGING)

On suspension scaffolds designed for a working load of 500 pounds (225 kilograms), no more than 2 men shall be permitted to work at one time. On suspension scaffolds with a working load of 750 pounds (337.5 kilograms), no more than 3 men shall be permitted to work at one time. Each employee shall be protected by an approved safety belt attached to a lifeline. The lifeline shall be securely attached to substantial members of the structure (not scaffold), or to securely rigged lines, which will safely suspend the employee in case of a fall. To keep the lifeline continuously attached with minimum slack to a fixed structure, the attachment point of the lifeline shall be appropriately changed as the work progresses. 1926.451(i)(8)

SCAFFOLDS (TUBULAR WELDED FRAME)

Scaffolds shall be properly braced by cross or diagonal braces or both for securing vertical members together laterally. The cross braces shall be of such length as will automatically square and align vertical members so that the erected scaffolds are always plumb, square, and rigid. All brace connections shall be made secure. 1926.451(d)(3)

Guardrails and toe boards shall be installed on all open sides and ends of platforms more than 10 feet (3.048 meters) above the ground or floor. 1926.451(d)(10)

STAIRS

A stairway or ladder must be provided at all worker points of access where there is a break in elevation of 19 inches (48.26 cm) or more and no ramp, runway, sloped embankment, or personnel hoist is provided. 1926.1051(a)

Except during construction of the actual stairway, skeleton metal frame structures and steps must not be used (where treads and/or landings are to be installed at a later date), unless the stairs are fitted with secured temporary treads and landings. 1926.1052(b)(2)

Where there is only one point of access between levels, it must be kept clear to permit free passage by workers. If free passage becomes restricted, a second point of access must be provided and used. 1926.1051(a)(3)

When there are more than 2 points of access between levels, at least one point of access must be kept clear. 1926.1051(a)(4)

All stairway and ladder fall protection systems must be provided and installed as required by the stairway and ladder rules before employees begin work that requires them to use stairways or ladders and their respective fall protection systems. 1926.1051(b)

Stairways that will not be a permanent part of the structure on which construction work is performed must have landings at least 30 inches deep and 22 inches wide (76.2 x 55.8 cm) at every 12 feet (3.6576 meters) or less of vertical rise. 1926.1052(a)(1)

Stairways must be installed at least 30 degrees, and no more than 50 degrees, from the horizontal. 1926.1052(a)(2)

Variations in riser height, or stair tread, or landing depth, must not exceed $\frac{1}{4}$ inch (.6425 cm) in any stairway system, including any foundation structure used as one or more treads of the stairs. 1926.1052(a)(3)

When doors or gates open directly onto a stairway, a platform must be provided, and the swing of the door shall not reduce the effective width of the platform to less than 20 inches (50.80 cm). 1926.1052(a)(4)

Except during construction of the actual stairway, stairways with metal pan landings and treads must not be used where the treads or landings have not been filled with concrete or other material, unless the pans of the stairs and/or landings are temporarily filled in with wood or other material. All treads and landings must be replaced when worn below the top edge of the pan. 1926.1052(b)(1)

Stairways having 4 or more risers, or rising more than 30 inches in height (76.2 cm), whichever is less, must have at least one handrail. A stair rail also must be installed along each unprotected side or edge. When the top edge of a stair rail system also serves as a handrail, the height of the top edge must be no more than 37 inches (93.98 cm) nor less than 36 inches (91.44 cm) from the upper surface of the stair rail to the surface of the tread in line with the face of riser at forward edge of tread. 1926.1052(c)(1)(i)&(ii)

Winding and spiral stairways must be equipped with a handrail offset sufficiently to prevent walking on those portions of the stairways where the tread width is less than 6 inches (15.24 cm) 1926.1052(c)(2)

Midrails, screens, mesh, intermediate vertical members, or equivalent intermediate structural members must be provided between the top rail and stairway steps of the stair rail system. 1926.0152(c)(4)

Midrails, when used, must be located midway between the top of the stair rail system and the stairway steps. 1926.1052(c)(4)(i)

The height of handrails must not be more than 37 inches (93.98 cm) nor less than 30 inches (76.2 cm) from the upper surface of the handrail to the surface of the tread in line with face of riser at forward edge of tread. 1926.1052(c)(6)

The height of the top edge of a stair rail system used as a handrail must not be more than 37 inches (93.98 cm) nor less than 36 inches (91.44 cm) from the upper surface of the stair rail system to the surface of the tread in line with face of riser at forward edge of tread. 1926.1052(c)(7)

Temporary handrails must have a minimum clearance of 3 inches (7.62 cm) between the handrail and walls, stair rail systems, and other objects. 1926.1052(c)(11)

Unprotected sides and edges of stairway landings must be provided with a standard 42-inch (106.68-cm) guardrail system. 1926.1052(c)(12)

STEEL ERECTION

Permanent floors shall be installed so there is not more than 8 stories between the erection floor and the uppermost permanent floor, except when structural integrity is maintained by the design. 1926.750(a)(1)

During skeleton steel erection, a tightly planked temporary floor shall be maintained within 2 stories or 30 feet (9.144 meters), whichever is less, below and directly under that portion of each tier of beams on which any work is being performed. 1926.750(b)(2)(i)

During skeleton steel erection of buildings and structures not adaptable to temporary floors, and where scaffolds are not used, safety nets shall be installed and maintained whenever the potential fall distance exceeds 2 stories or 25 feet (7.62 meters). 1926.750(b)(1)(ii)

A safety railing of ½-inch (1.27 cm) wire rope or equivalent shall be installed around the perimeter of all temporarily floored buildings, approximately 42 inches high (106.68 cm), during structural steel assembly. 1926.750(b)(1)(iii)When placing structural members, the load shall not be released from the hoisting line until the member is secured by at least two bolts, or the equivalent, at each connection, and drawn up wrench tight. 1926.751(a)

STORAGE

All materials stored in tiers shall be secured to prevent sliding, falling, or collapsing. 1926.250(a)(1)

Aisles and passageways shall be kept clear and in good repair. 1926.250(a)(3).

Storage of materials shall not obstruct exits. 1926.151(d)(1)

Materials shall be stored with due regard to their fire characteristics. 1926.151(d)(2)

TIRE CAGES

A safety tire rack, cage, or equivalent protection shall be provided and used when inflating, mounting, or dismounting tires installed on split rims, or rims equipped with locking rings or similar devices. 1926.600(a)(2)

TOE BOARDS (FLOOR AND WALL OPENINGS AND STAIRWAYS)

Railings protecting floor openings, platforms, and scaffolds shall be equipped with toe boards wherever beneath the open side, persons can pass, there is moving machinery, or there is equipment with which falling materials could cause a hazard. 1926.501(c)(1)

A standard toe board shall be at least 3 ½ inches (9 cm) in height and may be of any substantial material either solid or open, with openings not to exceed 1 inch (2.54 cm) in greatest dimension. 1926.502(j)(3)

TOILETS

Toilets shall be provided according to the following: 20 or fewer persons—one facility; 20 or more persons—one toilet seat and one urinal per 40 persons; 200 or more persons—one toilet seat and one urinal per 50 workers. 1926.51(c)(1)

This requirement does not apply to mobile crews having transportation readily available to nearby toilet facilities. 1926.51(c)(4)

UNDERGROUND CONSTRUCTION

The employer shall provide and maintain safe means of access and egress to all work stations. 1926.800(b)

The employer shall control access to all openings to prevent unauthorized entry underground. Unused chutes, manways, or other openings shall be tightly covered, bulkheaded, or fenced off, and shall be posted with signs indicating "Keep Out" or similar language. Complete or unused sections of the underground facility shall be barricaded. 1926.800(b)(3)

Unless underground facilities are sufficiently completed so that the permanent environmental controls are effective and the remaining construction activity will not cause any environmental hazard or structural failure within the facilities, the employer shall maintain a check-in/check-out procedure that will ensure that above-ground designated personnel can determine an accurate count of the number of persons underground in the event of an emergency. 1926.800(c)

All employees shall be instructed to recognize and avoid hazards associated with underground construction activities. 1926.800(d)

Hazardous classifications are potentially gassy and gassy operations. 1926.800(h)

The employer shall assign a competent person to perform all air monitoring to determine proper ventilation and quantitative measurements of potentially hazardous gases. 1926.800(j)(1)(i)(A)

Fresh air shall be supplied to all underground work areas in sufficient quantities to prevent dangerous or harmful accumulation of dust, fumes, mist, vapors, or gases. 1926.800(k)(1)(i)

WALL OPENINGS

Wall openings, from which there is a drop of more than 6 feet (1.8288 meters) and the bottom of the opening egress than 39 inches (99.06 cm) above the working surface, shall be guarded. 1926.501(b)(14)

When an employee is exposed to falling objects, the employer must ensure that each employee wear a hard hat and erect toe board, screens, or guardrail systems; or erect a canopy structure and keep potential fall objects far enough from the edge of the high level; or barricade area to which objects could fall. 1926.501(c)

WASHING FACILITIES

The employers shall provide adequate washing facilities for employees engaged in operations involving harmful substances. 1926.51(f)

Washing facilities shall be near the work site and shall be so equipped as to enable employees to remove all harmful substances. 1926.51(f)

WELDING, CUTTING, AND HEATING

Employers shall instruct employees in the safe use of welding equipment. 1926.350(d) & 1926.351(d)

Proper precautions (isolating welding and cutting, removing fire hazards from the vicinity, providing a fire watch) for fire prevention shall be taken in areas where welding or other "hot work" is being done. No welding, cutting, or heating shall be done where the application of flammable paints, or the presence of other flammable compounds or heavy dust concentrations creates a fire hazard. 1926.352(a)(b)(c)&(f)

Arc welding and cutting operations shall be shielded by noncombustible or flameproof screens to protect employees and other persons in the vicinity from direct arc rays. 1926.351(e)

When electrode holders are to be left unattended, the electrodes shall be removed and the holder shall be placed or protected so that they cannot make electrical contact with employees or conducting objects. 1926.351(d)(1)

All arc welding and cutting cables shall be completely insulated and be capable of handling the maximum current requirements for the job. There shall be no repairs or splices within 10 feet (3.048 meters) of the electrode holder except where splices are insulated equal to the insulation of the cable. Defective cable shall be repaired or replaced. 1926.351(b)(1), (2)&(4)

Fuel gas and oxygen hose shall be easily distinguishable and shall not be interchangeable. Hoses shall be inspected at the beginning of each shift and shall be repaired or replaced if defective. 1926.350(f)(1)&(3)

General mechanical ventilation, local exhaust ventilation, air line respirators, and other protection shall be provided, as required, when welding, cutting, or heating:

- Zinc, lead, cadmium, chromium, mercury, or materials bearing based or coated with beryllium in enclosed spaces.

- Stainless steel with inert-gas equipment.

- In confined spaces; and

- Where an unusual condition can cause an unsafe accumulation of contaminants. 1926.353(b)(1); (c)(1)(i)thru(iv); (c)(2)(i)thru(iv); (d)(1)(iv)&(e)(1)

Proper eye protective equipment to prevent exposure of personnel shall be provided. 1926.353(e)(2)

WIRE ROPES, CHAINS, AND ROPES

Wire ropes, chains, ropes, and other rigging equipment shall be inspected prior to use and as necessary during use to ensure their safety. Defective gear shall be removed from service. 1926.251(a)(1)

Job or shop hooks and links or makeshift fasteners formed from bolts, rods, or other attachments shall not be used. 1926.251(b)(3)

When U-bolts are used for eye splices, the U-bolt shall be applied so that the "U" section is in contact with the dead-end of the rope. 1926.251(c)(5)(i)

When U-bolt wire rope clips are used to form eyes, the following table shall be used to determine the number and spacing of clips. 1926.251(c)(5)

Number and Spacing of U-Bolt Wire Rope Clips

Improved plow steel, rope diameter (inches)	Number of clips Drop Forged	Other Mat'l	Min. Spacing(inches)
$\frac{1}{2}$ (1.27 cm)	3	4	3 (7.62 cm)
$\frac{5}{8}$ (.625 cm)	3	4	3 $\frac{3}{4}$ (8.37 cm)
$\frac{3}{4}$ (.75 cm)	4	5	4 $\frac{1}{2}$ (11.43 cm)
$\frac{7}{8}$ (.875 cm)	4	5	5 $\frac{1}{4}$ (12.95 cm)
1 (2.4 cm)	5	6	6 (15.24 cm)
1 $\frac{1}{8}$ (2.665 cm)	6	6	6 $\frac{3}{4}$ (15.99 cm)
1 $\frac{1}{4}$ (2.79 cm)	6	7	7 $\frac{1}{2}$ (19.05 cm)
1 $\frac{3}{8}$ (2.915 cm)	7	7	8 $\frac{1}{4}$ (20.57 cm)
1 $\frac{1}{2}$ (3.81 cm)	7	8	9 (22.86 cm)

WOODWORKING MACHINERY

All fixed power-driven woodworking tools shall be provided with a disconnect switch that can be either locked or tagged in the off position. 1926.304(a)

All woodworking tools and machinery shall meet applicable requirements of ANSI 01.1-1961, Safety Code for Woodworking Machinery. 1926.304(f)

Index

ABOUT THE AUTHOR

Sidney M. Levy for many years was senior vice president of Frank Mercede & Sons, a widely respected general contractor in Connecticut. Now owner of his own construction consulting business in Maryland, he has worked harmoniously with subcontractors for more than 40 years. I\n this book, based on his experience, he shares the tools subcontractors need to succeed.

CD-ROM WARRANTY

This software is protected by both United States copyright law and international copyright treaty provision. You must treat this software just like a book. By saying "just like a book," McGraw-Hill means, for example, that this software may be used by any number of people and may be freely moved from one computer location to another, so long as there is no possibility of its being used at one location or on one computer while it also is being used at another. Just as a book cannot be read by two different people in two different places at the same time, neither can the software be used by two different people in two different places at the same time (unless, of course, McGraw-Hill's copyright is being violated).

LIMITED WARRANTY

McGraw-Hill takes great care to provide you with top-quality software, thoroughly checked to prevent virus infections. McGraw-Hill warrants the physical CD-ROM contained herein to be free of defects in materials and workmanship for a period of sixty days from the purchase date. If McGraw-Hill receives written notification within the warranty period of defects in materials or workmanship, and such notification is determined by McGraw-Hill to be correct, McGraw-Hill will replace the defective CD-ROM. Send requests to:

McGraw-Hill
Customer Services
P.O. Box 545
Blacklick, OH 43004-0545

The entire and exclusive liability and remedy for breach of this Limited Warranty shall be limited to replacement of a defective CD-ROM and shall not include or extend to any claim for or right to cover any other damages, including but not limited to, loss of profit, data, or use of the software, or special, incidental, or consequential damages or other similar claims, even if McGraw-Hill has been specifically advised of the possibility of such damages. In no event will McGraw-Hill's liability for any damages to you or any other person ever exceed the lower of suggested list price or actual price paid for the license to use the software, regardless of any form of the claim.

McGRAW-HILL, SPECIFICALLY DISCLAIMS ALL OTHER WARRANTIES, EXPRESS OR IMPLIED, INCLUDING, BUT NOT LIMITED TO, ANY IMPLIED WARRANTY OF MERCHANTABILITY OR FITNESS FOR A PARTICULAR PURPOSE.

Specifically, McGraw-Hill makes no representation or warranty that the software is fit for any particular purpose and any implied warranty of merchantability is limited to the sixty-day duration of the Limited Warranty covering the physical CD-ROM only (and not the software) and is otherwise expressly and specifically disclaimed.

This limited warranty gives you specific legal rights; you may have others which may vary from state to state. Some states do not allow the exclusion of incidental or consequential damages, or the limitation on how long an implied warranty lasts, so some of the above may not apply to you.